HISTORIC LANDMARKS *of* PHILADELPHIA

IN MEMORY OF
THE MEN AND WOMEN
OF THE
PENNSYLVANIA
RAILROAD

HISTORIC LANDMARKS *of* PHILADELPHIA

ROGER W. MOSS

photographs by TOM CRANE

A Barra Foundation Book

UNIVERSITY OF PENNSYLVANIA PRESS
PHILADELPHIA

Published by
University of Pennsylvania Press
Philadelphia, Pennsylvania 19104-4112

Printed in Canada on acid-free paper
10 9 8 7 6 5 4 3 2 1

Library of Congress Cataloging-in-Publication Data

Moss, Roger W., 1940–
Historic landmarks of Philadelphia / Roger W. Moss ; photographs by Tom Crane.
p. cm.
"A Barra Foundation Book."
Includes bibliographical references and index.
ISBN 978-0-8122-4106-8 (alk. paper)
1. Architecture—Pennsylvania—Philadelphia. 2. Historic buildings—Pennsylvania—Philadelphia. 3. Philadelphia (Pa.)—Buildings, structures, etc. I. Crane, Tom. II. Title.
NA735.P5M66 2008
974.8′11—dc22 2008025564

End papers: The Academy of Music on South Broad Street opened in 1855. This is the main auditorium as seen from the stage.

Page ii: The World War II Memorial in Thirtieth Street Station (1952) was sculpted by Walker Hancock (1901–1998) in memory of the men and women of the Pennsylvania Railroad who died serving their country.

Page iii: Alexander Stirling Calder sculpted three allegorical figures for the Swann Memorial Fountain—also known as the Fountain of the Three Rivers—designed by Wilson Eyre, Jr., for Logan Circle (1924). In the distance is the Philadelphia Museum of Art.

Page iv: The First Bank of the United States (1795–1797) is based on the Royal Exchange in Dublin, now the Dublin City Hall. It may be the earliest classical revival building in America with a "giant order" marble portico.

Page viii: Free Library of Philadelphia grand stair. The seated figure of Dr. William Pepper is by the Austrian-born sculptor Karl Ritter (1867–1915).

for Robert L. McNeil Jr.

Patron and Friend

WILLIAM PEPPER
1843-1898
FOUNDER

CONTENTS

COLONIAL AND FEDERAL PHILADELPHIA

1. Fort Mifflin
2. Independence Hall
3. Congress Hall
4. Old City Hall
5. Carpenters' Hall
6. Philosophical Hall
7. Pennsylvania Hospital
8. First Bank of the United States
9. New Market

CLASSICAL PHILADELPHIA

10. Fairmount Water Works
11. Second Bank of the United States
12. Eastern State Penitentiary
13. Dorrance Hamilton Hall, University of the Arts
14. Walnut Street Theatre
15. United States Naval Home
16. Merchants' Exchange
17. Founder's Hall, Girard College
18. Atwater Kent Museum
19. Philadelphia Contributionship for the Insurance of Houses from Loss by Fire
20. Philadelphia Club

VICTORIAN PHILADELPHIA

21. Athenæum of Philadelphia
22. Laurel Hill Cemetery
23. Freedom Theatre
24. Institute of the Pennsylvania Hospital
25. Academy of Music
26. Wagner Free Institute of Science of Philadelphia
27. Union League of Philadelphia
28. Masonic Temple
29. Philadelphia City Hall
30. Pennsylvania Academy of Fine Arts
31. Philadelphia High School for Creative and Performing Arts
32. Victory Building
33. Memorial Hall
34. Boathouse Row
35. Philadelphia Zoological Gardens Gatehouses
36. Anne and Jerome Fisher Fine Arts Library, University of Pennsylvania
37. Philadelphia and Reading Railroad Terminal Head House and Shed

TWENTIETH-CENTURY PHILADELPHIA

38. The Bellevue
39. John Wanamaker Department Store
40. Historical Society of Pennsylvania
41. Racquet Club of Philadelphia
42. Benjamin Franklin Bridge
43. Thirtieth Street Station
44. United States Custom House
45. Philadelphia Savings Fund Society Building

Benjamin Franklin Parkway

46. Philadelphia Museum of Art
47. Insurance Company of North America Building
48. Free Library of Philadelphia
49. Rodin Museum

50/51. Board of Education Administration Building and Fidelity Mutual Life Insurance Building

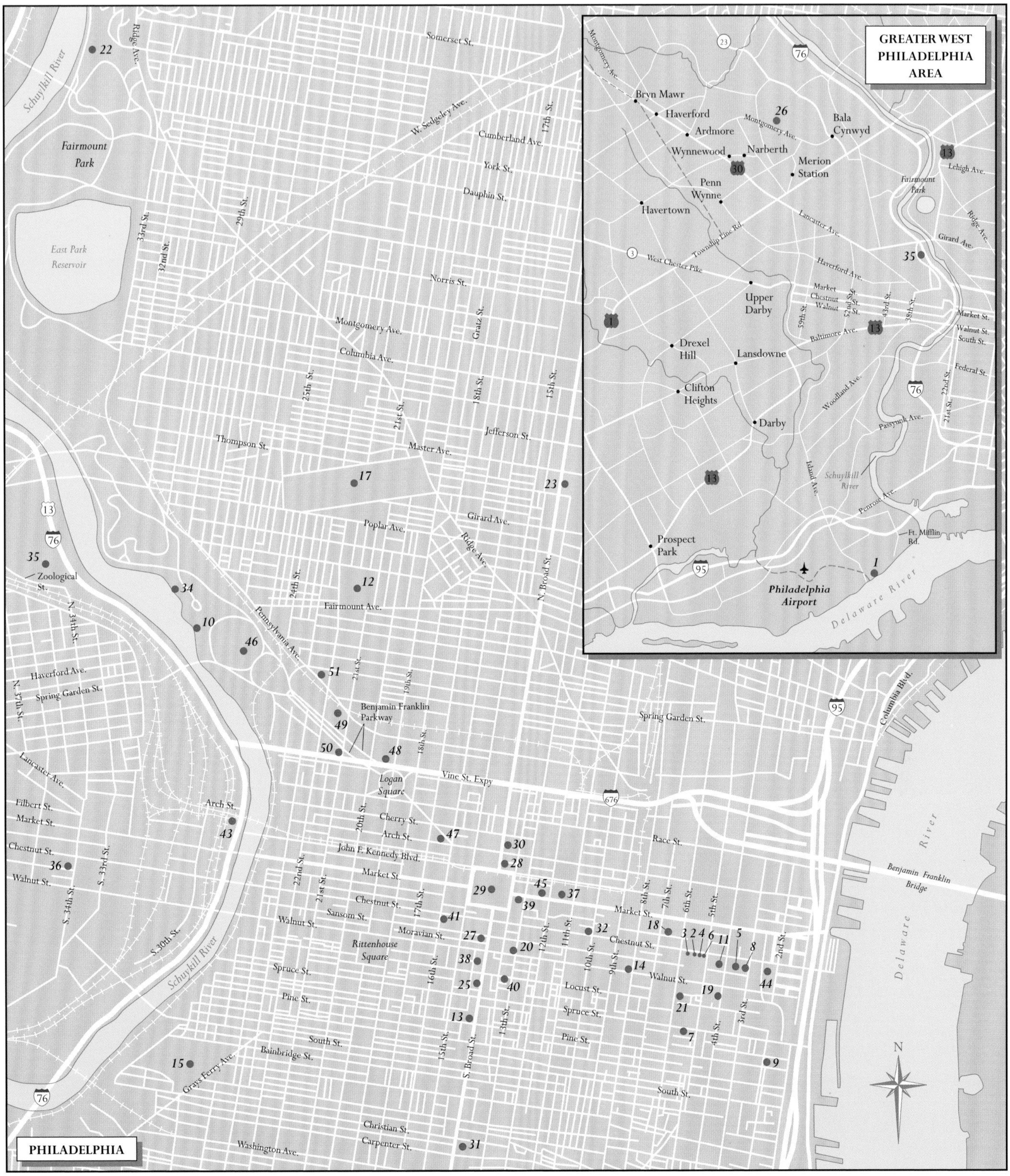
PHILADELPHIA
GREATER WEST PHILADELPHIA AREA
Schuylkill River
Fairmount Park
East Park Reservoir
Ridge Ave.
Somerset St.
W. Sedgeley Ave.
Cumberland Ave.
York St.
Dauphin St.
Norris St.
Montgomery Ave.
Columbia Ave.
Thompson St.
Master Ave.
Jefferson St.
Girard Ave.
Poplar Ave.
Fairmount Ave.
Pennsylvania Ave.
Zoological St.
N. 34th St.
Haverford Ave.
Spring Garden St.
N. 37th St.
Lancaster Ave.
Benjamin Franklin Parkway
Logan Square
Vine St. Expy
Arch St.
Cherry St.
John F. Kennedy Blvd.
Market St.
Filbert St.
Chestnut St.
Walnut St.
Sansom St.
Moravian St.
Rittenhouse Square
Spruce St.
Locust St.
Pine St.
South St.
Bainbridge St.
Grays Ferry Ave.
Christian St.
Carpenter St.
Washington Ave.
Race St.
Columbia Blvd.
Benjamin Franklin Bridge
Delaware River
N. Broad St.
S. Broad St.
33rd St.
32nd St.
29th St.
25th St.
24th St.
21st St.
20th St.
22nd St.
19th St.
18th St.
17th St.
16th St.
15th St.
13th St.
12th St.
11th St.
10th St.
9th St.
8th St.
7th St.
6th St.
5th St.
4th St.
3rd St.
2nd St.
Gratz St.
S. 34th St.
S. 33rd St.
S. 30th St.
13
76
95
676
N
1 2 3 4 5 6 7 8 9 10 11 12 13 14 15 17 18 19 20 21 22 23 25 27 28 29 30 31 32 34 35 36 37 38 39 40 41 43 44 45 46 47 48 49 50 51
Montgomery Ave.
Bryn Mawr
Haverford
Ardmore
Wynnewood
Narberth
Bala Cynwyd
Merion Station
Penn Wynne
Havertown
Township Line Rd.
West Chester Pike
Lancaster Ave.
Haverford Ave.
Upper Darby
Market
Chestnut
Walnut
59th St.
52nd St.
43rd St.
38th St.
Baltimore Ave.
Drexel Hill
Lansdowne
Clifton Heights
Darby
Woodland Ave.
Passyunk Ave.
Island Ave.
Penrose Ave.
Ft. Mifflin Rd.
Prospect Park
Philadelphia Airport
Lehigh Ave.
Ridge Ave.
Girard Ave.
Market St.
Walnut St.
South St.
Federal St.
22nd St.
21st St.
23
3
26
35

INTRODUCTION

"I pray you, let us satisfy our eyes
With the memorials and the things of fame
That do renown this city."

—TWELFTH NIGHT, ACT III, SCENE 3

It is my fate as a cultural historian to suffer from sensory overload, a condition traceable to a decision made many years ago to live and work in the City of Philadelphia. The symptoms are daily aggravated by the unavoidable presence of historic buildings which, regardless of the American tendency to sweep aside the past in favor of a transient present, have been accumulating for over three hundred years.

A decade ago I set out with master photographer Tom Crane to celebrate the surviving and accessible historic architecture of Philadelphia. But I wanted to do more than give a passing glance at hundreds (perhaps thousands) of buildings, each accompanied by a black and white snapshot. Acceptable guidebooks of that type already existed. Instead, I wanted to select fifty of the historic houses open to the public, fifty historic sacred places, and fifty institutional landmark buildings—and devote an entire book to each group. Such an expansive format would allow me to explain why the building was erected in the first place, who created it, and how it had changed over time—illustrated with several high quality photographs. In addition, I wanted to liberally reproduce historic images and provide a detailed bibliography for each building to document what I had written and provide additional sources for readers who wanted to learn more. The books covering the historic houses and historic sacred places have already been published, and now the third and final volume is complete.

This book differs from the previous volumes in two notable ways. First, the building types are more diverse, institutional, and monumental, ranging from concert halls to prisons, train stations to museums, banks to libraries. Second, the buildings are arranged chronologically rather than geographically. This places a useful emphasis on Philadelphia's evolution from modest mercantile outpost of a colonial power, to capital of a proud new nation, to a robust world-renowned manufacturing center, to a twenty-first-century center of medicine, education, and culture.

This, then, is a book about existing historic landmark buildings, prominent or memorable structures symbolizing stages in the progress of Philadelphia. To be included here the subject must be within the city limits and have been erected more than fifty years ago. Thirty of the fifty structures selected to be discussed are officially designated National Historic Landmarks by the secretary of the interior "because they possess exceptional value or quality in illustrating

"Back of the State House, Philadelphia" by William Birch & Son, 1799, shows Independence Hall after the steeple had been removed from the tower in 1781 and before the present steeple was erected in 1828. Athenæum of Philadelphia Collection.

or interpreting the heritage of the United States." These were automatically included.

There are fewer than 2,500 designated Landmarks in the United States, structures that have been identified as being "nationally significant" and having "meaning to all Americans."[1] As of this writing, there are sixty-five National Historic Landmarks in Philadelphia, half of them historic houses or sacred places, most of which I discuss in *Historic Houses of Philadelphia* (University of Pennsylvania Press, 1998) or *Historic Sacred Places of Philadelphia* (University of Pennsylvania Press, 2004). In addition to the official National Historic Landmarks included in the following pages, I have selected another twenty structures predating World War II that might arguably be so designated and most certainly

FIGURE 1. The towers and steeples of the State House (Independence Hall) and several churches dominate the eighteenth-century Philadelphia skyline as illustrated in "An East Prospective of the City of Philadelphia" (London: Carington Bowles, 1778). Historical Society of Pennsylvania.

are of landmark significance to the history of Philadelphia, if not to the nation. Most likely it will become a sport of architectural historians to compile long lists of buildings I "should have included," particularly because I give so much space to buildings associated with the Benjamin Franklin Parkway, which in its entirety should be a National Historic Landmark. I can only plead that the format of the books in this series (fifty buildings per volume) forces me to select only a few candidates from what was originally a much longer list.

FIGURE 2. Benjamin Henry Latrobe's famous Bank of Pennsylvania (erected 1798–1800, demolished 1867) occupied a site on the west side of Second Street between Chestnut and Walnut Streets. The building shown to the left is City Tavern by master builder Thomas Procter (erected 1773; demolished 1854; subsequently reconstructed by the National Park Service). William Birch and Son, 1800. Athenæum of Philadelphia Collection.

What follows is an architectural history—albeit more lavishly illustrated than the typical work of its type—yet I am deeply conscious of following in the well-worn footsteps of several view-book authors who used significant architecture as a metaphor for the progress of Philadelphia. At the end of the eighteenth century, when our city was the cultural and political capital of the new nation and many of the founding fathers might be encountered sauntering down High or Chestnut Street, William Birch (1755–1834) assembled a book of his own engravings that identified and illustrated what he considered to be the most notable civic monuments. His *City of Philadelphia*—popularly known as *Birch's Views*—was the first widely available Philadelphia "coffee table" book, engagingly illustrated with hand-colored engravings and, like modern books of this genre, thin on text.[2] The scale of Birch's city was intimate; the population, including the outlying liberties, numbered fewer than 65,000 souls.[3] Yet all this was about to change. Within a few years, Birch's modest Federal city would be replaced by a robust Victorian commercial and industrial colossus. With forgivable hyperbole, Birch writes that the ground on which Philadelphia stood at the eve of the nineteenth century

> was less than a century ago, in a state of wild nature; covered with wood, and inhabited by Indians. It has in this short time, been raised, as it were, by magic power, to the eminence of an opulent city, famous for its trade and commerce,

FIGURE 3. Master builder Robert Smith's Walnut Street Prison at the southeast corner of Sixth and Walnut Streets faced the State House yard. The prison was erected in 1774 and demolished in 1836. William Birch and Son, 1800. Athenæum of Philadelphia Collection.

crowded in its port, with vessels of its own producing, and visited by others from all parts of the world. . . . This Work will stand as a memorial of its progress for the first century; the buildings, of any consequence, are generally included.[4]

In Birch's day the major architectural landmarks—certainly the largest and most visible buildings of consequence—were sacred places, especially the large churches of the Episcopalians, Presbyterians, and Lutherans (Figure 1). Birch also illustrates a few noteworthy Federal houses of recent vintage, the wharves and markets traditionally associated with a mercantile city, and, of course, the already venerated Pennsylvania State House, now known as Independence Hall— which in 1800 had already for half a century been the signature structure of Philadelphia. Birch also includes two banks—a building type that had not existed in Philadelphia until after the Revolution—and a group of structures that civic-minded Victorians of future generations would consider most indicative of a maturing metropolis: a library, a theater, an almshouse, a hospital, and a substantial stone prison (Figures 2–3).

A quarter century later Cephas G. Childs (1793–1871) produced his own *Views of Philadelphia* (1827), confessing "the hope, that his 'Views' will not be without interest to those who, at a future period, may desire to review the history of our rapidly improving city, and that they may serve to illustrate, not unfavorably, the state of the Arts at the present period." In his original proposal for the *Views*, Childs remarks that Philadelphia "contains finer specimens of Architectural taste than any city on the American continent. Her edifices for the promotion of domestic comfort, of art and science, charity and religion, are no where surpassed."[5]

Like Birch, Childs begins with places of worship, including Old Swedes, Christ Church, the Friends meeting house, Saint Stephen's, and the First Unitarian Church.[6] By this time the Pennsylvania State House had been purchased by the City of Philadelphia and declared a shrine to Independence.[7] Charitable responsibility for the less fortunate had found tangible expression in the Pennsylvania Hospital, the Widows' and Orphans' Asylum, and the Pennsylvania Institute for the Deaf and Dumb (Figure 4). Three banks are also thought to be worthy of notice: the First Bank of the United States (by then known as Girard's Bank), the Second Bank of the United States, and Benjamin Henry Latrobe's Bank of Pennsylvania. Master builder Robert Smith's Walnut Street Prison of Birch's day has been replaced by John Haviland's revolutionary Eastern State Penitentiary. The Fairmount Water Works—the first North American municipal water system—has appeared on the banks of the Schuylkill River, the United States Mint occupies a neoclassical pile by William Strickland, and the University of

Pennsylvania has moved into the house described by Birch as intended for the President of the United States (Figure 5). Childs is clearly pleased by the addition of two landmarks of arts and culture: the Pennsylvania Academy of the Fine Arts and the Academy of Natural Sciences.

The third early Philadelphia view book is the product of the Swiss-born artist John Casper Wild (c. 1804–1846), whose *Panorama and Views of Philadelphia* appeared in 1838.[8] The buildings he selected for lithographic illustration are strikingly different from those illustrated by Birch and Childs. There are no residential structures and only two churches: Christ Church (Second Street above Market, 1727), included for its antiquity, and Saint John's Church (Thirteenth Street below Market, 1831), the first Gothic-style Catholic church in Philadelphia.[9] The city's icons such as Independence Hall (illustrated with its reconstructed tower by William Strickland), the Pennsylvania Institution for the Deaf and Dumb, the University of Pennsylvania, the First and Second Banks of the United States (but not Latrobe's Bank of Pennsylvania), the United States Mint and the Fairmount Water Works are included (Figure 6). John Haviland's Eastern State Prison has been joined by Thomas Ustick Walter's Moyamensing Prison and his monumental Girard College (Figure 7). William Strickland has

FIGURE 4. A society for the relief of "Indigent Widows and Single Women" (founded 1817) and the "Philadelphia Orphans' Asylum" (founded in 1814) were housed in two buildings at Eighteenth and Race Streets. William Strickland designed the Orphans' Asylum (left) in 1823 after a tragic fire destroyed an earlier structure. Both were demolished in the later nineteenth century. Cephas G. Childs, 1827. Athenæum of Philadelphia Collection.

added his Merchants' Exchange and the United States Naval Asylum, both future National Historic Landmarks, and Laurel Hill Cemetery, Philadelphia's first entry into the rural cemetery movement, by the immigrant Scot John Notman, appears as a new building type. Prophetically there is also a view from the Inclined Plane (where, in 1836, an American steam locomotive had first ascended a steep grade under its own power), a hint of the new age of steam that will soon thrust up smokestacks to rival the church steeples of Birch's day.

Even a cursory examination of these early nineteenth-century view books reveals how landmark structures become tangible indications of change over time, although all three books were published too early to include examples from the great industrial engine of Philadelphia's wealth in the later nineteenth and early twentieth centuries: no yards for building steel ships or factories producing Baldwin locomotives or Stetson hats. Nonetheless, it is remarkable how many of the buildings singled out by Birch, Childs, and Wild remain standing after a century and a half and are included in this gathering of *historic* landmarks, albeit not always serving their intended purposes. Since all of these buildings were once new, one cannot escape wondering which among the late twentieth- and early twenty-first-century Philadelphia structures would be included here if I were to follow these three authors and include such recent "landmarks" as the Kimmel Center, Liberty Place, and sports stadia named for various banks? Fortunately the enduring merits of such recent creations can be left to the judgment of future historians.

From Wild's *Views* in 1838 until the appearance of Moses King's *Philadelphia and Notable Philadelphians* in 1902, most books containing more than a passing reference to the city's architecture followed in the footsteps of John Fanning Watson (1779–1860), who illustrated his *Annals of Philadelphia* (1830 and later editions) with buildings (many of which were no longer standing) associated primarily with notable persons of early Philadelphia.[10] Most significant of the books following Watson were Willis P. Hazard's expansion of Watson's *Annals* to three volumes (1891) and the monumental three-volume history of the city by J. Thomas Scharf (1820–1888) and Thompson Westcott (1843–1898), which appeared in 1884. Both these multivolume histories are illustrated with numerous engravings of both historic structures and recently erected buildings of prominence, although the images are incidental to the extensive narratives.

By the dawn of the twentieth century, given the advent of photography, continuous-roll wood-pulp paper, and high-speed printing presses, Moses King (1853–1909) could easily produce a prodigiously illustrated book entitled *Philadelphia and Notable Philadelphians* (New York, 1902) with 2,152 images—592 of them buildings and city views. The 1,560 portraits of hirsute leading citizens guaranteed sales, of course, especially since they appeared together with "notable Philadelphians of the Past," including the likes of William Penn, William White, Robert Morris, and Benjamin Franklin. What self-made Victorian industrialist or politician could resist such compelling marketing?

When Moses King turns his attention to Philadelphia's buildings, he freely plunders historic images drawn from Birch, Childs, and Wild, supplementing these with John Lewis Krimmel's (Figure 8) evocative early nineteenth-century genre paintings of street scenes and commercial chromolithographs—all reproduced photographically.[11] He even slips in current events with historic buildings in the background, such as Prince Henry, brother of Emperor William of Germany, visiting Independence Hall in 1902 ("after the launching of the Emperor's yacht *Meteor*") and the Land Title Building on Broad Street erected the same year. Finally, King's photo-illustrated section of Philadelphia—"the most American of all cities"—includes virtually every landmark erected prior to 1902 that I included in this book. King's *Philadelphia and Notable Philadelphians* is probably the largest and most comprehensive view book on Philadelphia ever published.

None of these books could be called *architectural* histories in the modern sense of the term; they lack documentation and critical essays placing the buildings in historic and cultural context; neither are the buildings dated nor their architects and builders identified. The first modern book to examine the entire sweep of Philadelphia's architecture, combining historic images and critical text, is George B. Tatum's *Penn's Great Town: 250 Years of Philadelphia Architecture Illustrated in Prints and Drawings* (University of Pennsylvania Press, 1961), which reproduces a wide variety of images identified as to source and accompanied by thoughtful and carefully researched brief essays of genuine merit, albeit now dated by the discoveries of two generations of architectural historians, many of whom Tatum trained or influenced at the University of Pennsylvania and the University of Delaware. Prepared to accompany an exhibition of prints and drawings at the Art Alliance on Rittenhouse Square, *Penn's Great Town* includes both surviving buildings and notable landmarks that are no longer standing. No new photographs were commissioned.[12]

Which brings me to the current project, which is a companion to *Historic Houses of Philadelphia* (University of Pennsylvania Press, 1998) and *Historic Sacred Places of Philadelphia* (University of Pennsylvania Press, 2004). It completes the projected trilogy focused on one hundred fifty of the most important and accessible historic structures of the city, and includes nearly 600 historic images and newly commissioned color photographs and 150,000+ words of supporting text and documentation. Such a survey aimed at a general audience has never before been attempted, and it is unlikely to be duplicated any time soon.

For the past decade, master photographer Tom Crane and I have worked together on these books, and I cannot decide at this point whether to be relieved that we have completed what we set out to do, or to regret that there are no more buildings to visit and photograph with this supremely talented and unflappable professional who has become a treasured friend during the course of our long collaboration. Unfortunately, one of the original partners of this project, designer Adrianne Onderdonk Dudden, died before she could undertake the layout for this final volume, leaving it to Neil West, who, taking inspiration from Dudden's designs for *Historic Houses* and *Historic Sacred Places*, has produced the handsome book you now hold. Each of the three books is subtly different yet clearly intended to form a whole when shelved together.

Figure 5. The University of Pennsylvania acquired this handsome Late Georgian house in 1802. Erected by the Commonwealth of Pennsylvania in the 1790s on Ninth Street between Chestnut and Market Streets as a residence for the President of the United States, it was never occupied by Washington or Adams. In 1807 the house was enlarged to the form shown here. Cephas G. Childs, 1827. Athenæum of Philadelphia Collection.

Early in the preparation for this book, I had the essential assistance of Jean Wolf, preservationist, historian, and long-time colleague, who performed much of the tedious leg work of compiling the bibliography for each entry according to my specifications. I'm grateful for her skilled help during the busy months when *Historic Sacred Places* was passing through the editorial process and being published. Everything was ready when Tom Crane and I could finally turn our attention to *Landmarks*. I'm also fortunate to have such sympathetic yet demanding editors in Jo M. Joslyn and Alison Anderson at the University of Pennsylvania Press and Gail Caskey Winkler, Ph.D., FASID at home. These three helped me stay the course, corrected punctuation, and detected several other slips; but those errors that must inevitably remain are my fault alone. I also want to acknowledge the enthusiastic interest of Lea Carson Sherk, President, and the directors of The Athenæum of Philadelphia. On virtually every page of all three volumes there is evidence of the debt I owe to the Athenæum's collections and staff, especially

FIGURE 6. William Strickland's United States Mint (1829–1833; demolished 1907) was erected on a large lot of ground located on the west side of Juniper Street at Chestnut Street. J. C. Wild, 1838. Athenæum of Philadelphia Collection

Bruce Laverty, the Gladys Brooks Curator of Architecture, and Michael J. Seneca, director of the Regional Digital Imagining Center at the Athenæum.

None of these books would have been possible had it not been for the generous support of Robert L. McNeil, Jr., founder, former president and board chair of The Barra Foundation, Inc. He assembled the team and provided unwavering encouragement through all the years of planning, writing, photography, designing and printing three volumes on accessible Philadelphia historic architecture. His foresight, confidence, and financial support were critical to the success of the project. More than forty years ago, when I was a graduate student, Robert McNeil's foundation created a research fellowship that permitted me to write a doctoral dissertation on the Carpenters' Company of Philadelphia. He has remained both patron and friend though the subsequent decades, and I hope he sees *Houses*, *Sacred Places*, and now, *Landmarks,* as partial repayment of an irredeemable debt of gratitude.

A Note on Philadelphia Builders and Architects

In the pages that follow, we will meet some of Philadelphia's most important architects and builders. In many cases they are represented by their best surviving buildings. For more than 200 years, Philadelphia has been a notable center of architecture. From our colonial master builders, Robert Smith and Thomas Nevell, through Benjamin Henry Latrobe, William Strickland, Robert Mills, John Haviland and Thomas Ustick Walter, to John Notman, Samuel Sloan, Frank Furness, and T. P. Chandler, Jr., in the nineteenth century, to Horace Trumbauer, Paul Philippe Cret, George Howe, Louis I. Kahn, and Robert Venturi in the twentieth century, Philadelphia architects have been acknowledged leaders in their profession. Their buildings and the force of their educational institutions, societies, and writings have influenced the course of American architecture.

By the early eighteenth century, Philadelphia was amply supplied with a diverse cadre of carpenters, joiners, bricklayers, glaziers, painters, plasterers, and tool makers capable of building a worthy town. In a sense, all the building trades began on an equal footing in the first decades after the founding of Philadelphia. No craft guilds or strong government regulations set the style or materials of construction. Providing shelter was a personal matter dependent upon the skill of the settler or his ability to provide or acquire workmen and materials. That these early residents—perhaps with the great fire of London being a fairly recent memory—clearly favored brick over wood in construction might suggest the master mason or bricklayer would play the dominant role in planning and erecting buildings. In fact, this was not the case throughout most of the colonial period. The master house carpenter was usually responsible for the entire fabric and subcontracted the brickwork, joinery, glazing, plastering, and painting. The reasons for this are to be found in English craft tradition, where the master carpenter maintained his domination even after buildings of wood became rare in London, Bristol, and other urban centers in the British Empire. Fortunately we have an excellent authority to explain how the system worked in the English scholarly printer Joseph Moxon (1627–1691), who began publishing parts of his *Mechanick Exercises, Or, the Doctrine of Handy-works* (London, 1677) on the eve of the founding of Pennsylvania.[13]

Intended to delineate the basic tools and techniques employed in several manual crafts, Moxon's *Mechanick Exercises* provides a close, practical look over the shoulder of the men in joinery, carpentry, and bricklaying, and gives insight into the working relationships of the various building crafts. By tracing the step-by-step method for building a house or other types of structures, he shows clearly the dominant role of the Master Builder ("Master Workman"), whom he

FIGURE 7. Thomas Ustick Walter launched his career with the Gothic and Egyptianesque style Moyamensing Prison at Tenth and Reed streets (erected 1832–1835, demolished 1968). J. C. Wild, 1838. Athenæum of Philadelphia Collection.

assumes to be a house carpenter. Moxon also assumes that the individual commissioning a building would be conversant with books of architecture or have a clear idea of what type of house he wanted. General demands of size and site would be conveyed to the Master Workman who would lay out the ground plan, interior partitions, major structural members, trim and ornaments on a draft rendered to scale from every side. "Unless we shall suppose our Master-Workman to understand *Perspective*; for then he may, on a single piece of Paper, describe the whole Building, as it shall appear to the Eye at any assigned Station."[14] How common such "drafts" were in colonial Philadelphia is difficult to say. The few examples that survive certainly do not suggest the kind of detailing that Moxon assumes. Yet we do know that several master builders owned drawing instruments and were capable of executing fairly skilled plans and elevations, even if few understood perspective. According to the rules of the Carpenters' Company of the City and County of Philadelphia, "drawing designs are to be charged by the Carpenter in proportion to the trouble." These probably varied depending on the importance of the structure and the demands of the patron.[15]

The appearance of large public buildings in Philadelphia after 1700 introduced an additional figure who has become a popular myth of colonial architecture. This person represented the commissioning organization. A large vestry or government body could not deal practically with the builders; therefore, a supervisor or overseer was delegated to represent them. Thus the construction of the State House (Independence Hall) was left in the hands of Andrew Hamilton, Christ Church to John Kearsley, and Library Hall and the President's House to Richard Wells—even though it is unlikely that any of these worthies had ever put pen to paper to create an architectural design.[16]

When the great hunt for the authors of Philadelphia's colonial buildings began in the late nineteenth century, it was the supervisor whose name was discovered in the archives and vestry minutes as receiving and distributing funds. Consequently, these men were listed as "architect" in countless popular accounts, attributions regularly repeated by guide book authors who rely on secondary accounts. We now know that the gentleman amateur architect of the Thomas Jefferson type, armed with a library of builders' guides and architectural pattern books from which he pieced together his dream house, was less common than previously thought. If we look at the subscribers to Abraham Swan's *The British Architect*—the first book of architecture printed in America (Philadelphia, 1774)—of the 187 persons who paid for the book in advance and thus became "encouragers" of the project, 62 were master builders, 111 house carpenters, 2 painters, 2 plasterers, 2 cabinetmakers, and only 2 merchants and

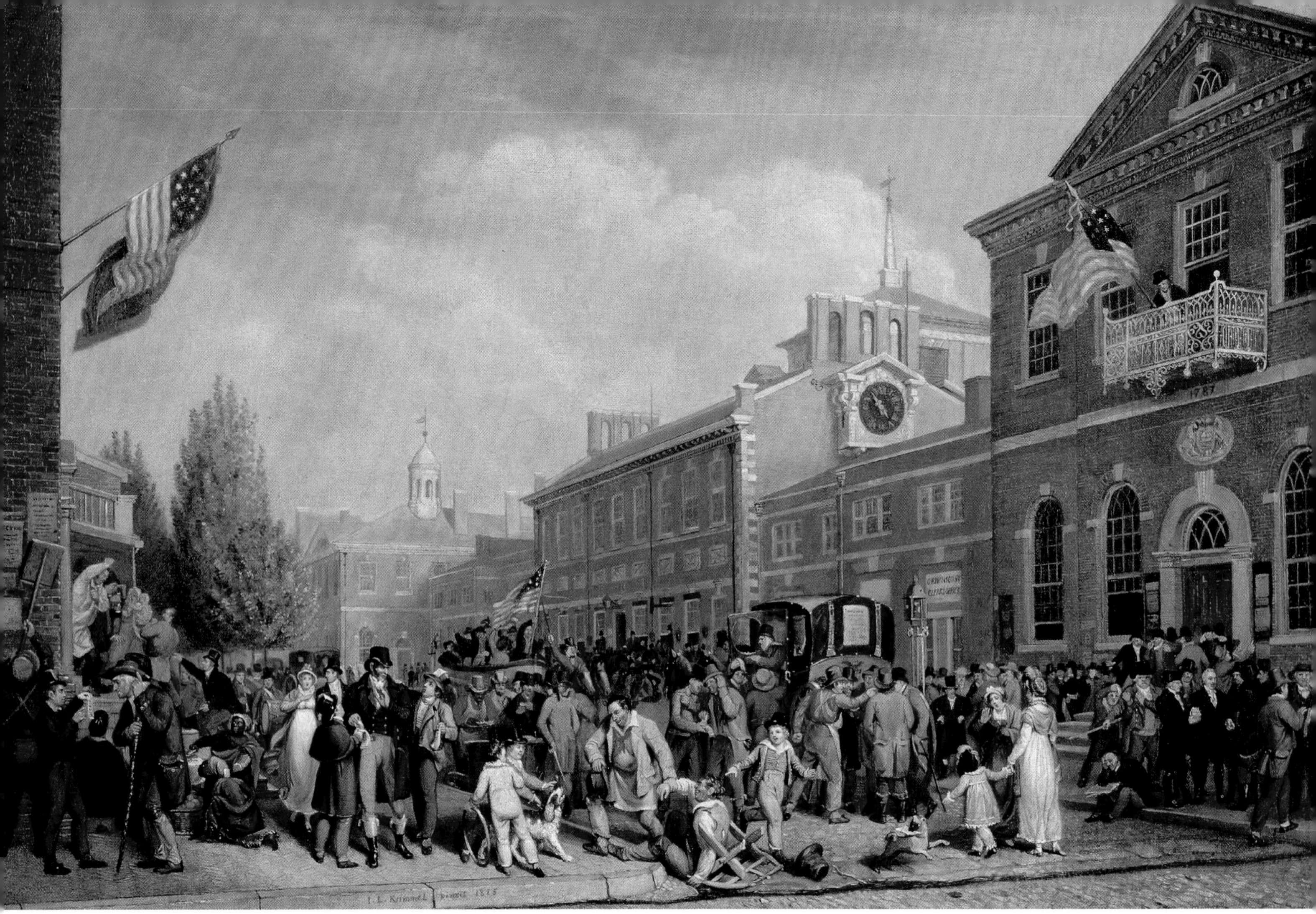

FIGURE 8. John Lewis Krimmel, *Election Day 1815*. Oil on canvas. Illustrated are three National Historic Landmarks: Independence Hall, Congress Hall, and Old City Hall. William Strickland's recreation of the Independence Hall steeple was several years in the future. Courtesy, Winterthur Museum.

2 gentlemen (one of whom lived in Maryland). In addition there were a ship joiner, a tanner, a sea captain, and a tallow chandler. In Philadelphia it was the *practical builders* who supported the first architectural publication venture, not the likely client.[17] Working up plans—as Edmund Woolley did for the State House—was a regular part of the master builder's responsibility. The supervisor was doubtless consulted and he probably carried the plans back to his principals for discussion and approval. But the ultimate form and, especially, the final details, were the result of the knowledge and manual skills of the master builder and his crew of workmen.

Many of the colonial master builders of Philadelphia—most notably Robert Smith, Thomas Nevell, and Benjamin Loxley—were capable of sophisticated Georgian designs based on European pattern books that would have been agreeably acceptable, albeit a few decades out of date, in any provincial English city.[18] We need only look at Mount Pleasant and Christ Church for proof of their skills. But none of these men, trained from youth to the wood chisel and molding plane, successfully escaped to the professional architect's protractor, compass, and watercolor brush, however often their grateful clients might flatter them with the title of architect.

European-trained architects, that is, individuals who expected to make their living by *designing and supervising* the construction of buildings, rather than building them, began to appear in America in the late eighteenth century. Several French and British architects and engineers worked briefly here during and following the Revolution, but it was Benjamin Henry Latrobe (1764–1820), who arrived from England in 1796, who is generally credited with training the first group of American architects. Unlike many of the historic houses and sacred places discussed in the previous volumes of this series, the larger-scale landmark buildings discussed in the pages that follow—Independence Hall and Carpenters' Hall being notable exceptions—are the work of our earliest professional architects: Latrobe's apprentice, native-born William Strickland, and *his* apprentice, Thomas Ustick Walter, the later English immigrant, John Haviland, and Scottish immigrants, most notably John Notman and John McArthur, Jr. These and others will be introduced at the appropriate place in the pages that follow.

Notes to Introduction

1. The National Historic Landmarks website is http:www.cr.nps.gov/landmarks.htm

2. The best account of Birch's views is Martin P. Snyder, "William Birch: His Philadelphia Views," *PMHB* 73 (1949): 271ff, and Martin P. Snyder, "Birch's Philadelphia Views: New Discoveries," *PMHB* 88 (1964): 164ff. When I first moved to Philadelphia in the 1960s, well-thumbed original copies of the Birch views could still be found prominently displayed in the libraries of Main Line and Chestnut Hill homes, and virtually every private club in the city had copies of the plates framed on its walls.

3. The U.S. Census of 1800 counted 41,220 persons in Philadelphia proper, and an additional 20,000+ in the liberties. http:www.census.gov/population

4. William Birch, *The City of Philadelphia* (Philadelphia, 1800), Introduction. A decade later, James Mease used similar language in his *Picture of Philadelphia*, giving an account of its origin, increase, and improvements in arts, sciences, manufactures, commerce, and revenue (Philadelphia, 1811 and subsequent editions). Mease included a list of notable public buildings, but his work contains few illustrations.

5. See Martin P. Snyder, *Mirror of America* (Gladwyne, Pa., privately printed, 1996), 41–77. A collation of Childs's *Views* appears on pp. 70–77.

6. Moss, *Historic Sacred Places*, 34–39, 40–45, 4–5, 46–49, 130–35, 202.

7. Moss, "Historic Preservation in Philadelphia," *Historic Houses*, 3–19.

8. The tireless Philadelphia lawyer and scholar Martin P. Snyder, whose work on Birch and Childs has already been cited above, also sorted out the Wild views in his "J. C. Wild and His Philadelphia Views," *PMHB* 77 (January 1953): 32–53.

9. See the discussion of Saint John the Evangelist Church in Moss, *Historic Sacred Places*, 136–39.

10. The antiquarian John Fanning Watson is considered by many to be Philadelphia's first historian. "The history of [Philadelphia's] Rise & Progress is *curious & instructive*," he exclaimed, "*no other City* has arisen to equal greatness in so short a time, by the *industry & resources* of its *population*!" Watson was interested in a broader definition of progress than Birch, Childs, and

Wild. But he clearly thought buildings were an important aspect of the story. To that end he engaged the English artist William L. Breton to prepare watercolors of "ancient houses & places in Philadelphia, as they were in the beginning, or 70 & 80 years ago!" For the first edition of his *Annals of Philadelphia* (1830), 26 plates were lithographed or engraved from Breton's watercolors. Of the buildings illustrated by Watson, most were houses, taverns, and sacred places memorialized for their association with founders or former worthies of the city. Watson's work is the tap root that continues to provide rich nourishment to Philadelphia antiquarians and historic preservationists. The standard biography of Watson is Deborah Dependahl Waters, "Philadelphia's Boswell: John Fanning Watson," *PMHB* 98 (January 1974): 3–52. On William L. Breton see Martin P. Snyder, "William L. Breton, Nineteenth-Century Philadelphia Artist," *PMHB* 86 (April 1961): 178–209.

11. On John Lewis Krimmel (1786–1821), see Anneliese Harding, *John Lewis Krimmel, Genre Artist of the Early Republic* (Winterthur, Del.: Winterthur Museum, 1994). Krimmel's sketch books are at Winterthur.

12. Prior to the publication of George B. Tatum's *Penn's Great Town*, most Philadelphians thought of architectural history in terms of the many books by the antiquarian Harold Donaldson Eberlein, who dwelt more on families and personalities than on buildings. Eberlein rarely footnoted his sources and uncritically repeated ancient myths and scandals whispered to him over tea by "Old Philadelphians." The most valuable part of his books—particularly later titles such as *Portrait of a Colonial City* (Philadelphia: J.B. Lippincott, 1939)—are the photographs by Cortlandt Van Dyke Hubbard. The standard bibliography is Jacquelyn Gwyn, *Harold Donaldson Eberlein, 1875–1965: A Bibliography* (Philadelphia: The Athenæum of Philadelphia, 1964). See also Bradley C. Brooks, "The Would-Be Philadelphian: Harold Donaldson Eberlein, Author and Antiquarian," *PMHB* 125, 4 (October 2001): 351–71. A less well-known pre-Tatum publication is a still useful series of essays on key Philadelphia landmarks published in 1953 as a volume of the Transactions of the American Philosophical Society under the title *Historic Philadelphia from the Founding Until the Early Nineteenth Century: Papers Dealing with Its People and Buildings*, ed. Luther P. Eisenhart (TAPS n.s. 43, pt. 1), which for its time was a model of scholarship.

13. The best biographical sketch of Joseph Moxon is by Eileen Harris and Nicholas Savage, *British Architectural Books and Writers* (Cambridge: Cambridge University Press, 1990), 324–25. See also H. Davis and H. Carter, eds., *Mechanick Exercises or The Whole Art of Printing* (London, 1962) which provides a bibliography of Moxon's publications.

14. For an excellent introduction to early architectural drawing, see James F. O'Gorman, *The Perspective of Anglo-American Architecture* (Philadelphia: The Athenæum of Philadelphia, 1995), 6–7. According to O'Gorman, "Perspective sketches or presentation drawings were rare in the English-speaking world before the nineteenth century. The usual eighteenth-century architectural drawing was orthographic, as demonstrated by the paper remains of English and North American architects, and by books such as James Gibbs's *Rules for Drawing the Several Parts of Architecture* of 1732." On the evolution of architectural drawing from the early eighteenth to the late twentieth century with particular reference to Philadelphia, see James F. O'Gorman, Jeffrey A. Cohen, George E. Thomas, and G. Holmes Perkins, *Drawing Toward Building: Philadelphia Architectural Graphics, 1732–1986* (Philadelphia: University of Pennsylvania Press, 1986).

15. Carpenters' Company of the City and County of Philadelphia, *Articles of the Carpenters Company of Philadelphia: and their Rules for measuring and valuing house-carpenters work* (Philadelphia, 1786). A reprint of the *Articles* of 1786 is available from the Company.

16. Nonetheless, this tradition has been given new credence by Jeffrey A. Cohen in his 1986 essay which attributes an Independence Hall drawing to Andrew Hamilton because it lacks "a carpenter's practical knowledge" and seems "to reinforce the theory that the drawing was done by an amateur designer relatively new to both building and making plans." Unfortunately he is referring to a simple elevation in the Historical Society of Pennsylvania collection which may or may not be the one displayed by Hamilton. At the same time he ignores a skilled

set of surviving drawings (also at the Historical Society) which fits the description of the drawings submitted to Governor Penn by Woolley. O'Gorman et al., *Drawing Toward Building*, 33–35.

17. Although Captain John Macpherson, owner of Mount Pleasant, sold a copy of Abraham Swan's *A Collection of Designs in Architecture* (London, 1757) to Thomas Nevell, the builder of this grandest of Middle Georgian Philadelphia houses. See Moss, *Historic Houses*, 95–96. For a discussion of the "encouragers" to Swan, see Roger W. Moss, "Master Builders: A History of the Colonial Philadelphia Building Trades," Ph.D. dissertation, University of Delaware (Ann Arbor, Mich.: University Microfilms, 1972), 70–71.

18. On Robert Smith, see Charles E. Peterson, Constance M. Greiff, and Maria M. Thompson, *Robert Smith: Architect, Builder, Patriot, 1722–1777* (Philadelphia: The Athenæum of Philadelphia, 2000). On Nevell, see Hannah B. Roach, "Thomas Nevell (1721–1797): Carpenter, Educator, Patriot," *Journal of the Society of Architectural Historians* 24 (1965): 153–64. On Loxley, see Charles E. Peterson, "Benjamin Loxley and Carpenters' Hall," *JSAH* 15 (1956): 23–26.

COLONIAL AND FEDERAL PHILADELPHIA

Fort Mifflin

Independence Hall

Congress Hall

Old City Hall

Carpenters' Hall

Philosophical Hall

Pennsylvania Hospital

First Bank of the United States

New Market

Carpenters' Hall (1770–1773) was designed by Robert Smith, the leading master builder of Colonial Philadelphia, who died in 1777 while supervising the fortification of the Delaware River against attack by the British Navy.

FORT MIFFLIN

1 Fort Mifflin Road
Philadelphia, PA 19153

John Montrésor, engineer,
1772–1775
Pierre Charles L'Enfant,
Anne-Louis Tousard, and others,
1794–1904
National Historic Landmark,
1970

Telephone for visitor
information: 215.685.4167
www.fortmifflin.us

IN THE BEGINNING WAS THE RIVER. The Delaware determined the site of Penn's great town, and its sheltered waters—draining a vast and promising hinterland—would nurture Philadelphia's commercial success. And it was to control the Delaware that a fort was built on Mud Island below the mouth of Philadelphia's other river, the Schuylkill.

Following the defeat of France and Spain in the French and Indian War (1754–1763), the British government found its American colonies increasingly fractious over trade and taxation. George III's ministers also decided to shift most of the financial burden of erecting forts—the better to regulate and defend such trading centers as Boston and Philadelphia—to the colonial governments. Thus was the British engineer Captain John Montrésor (1736–1799) dispatched

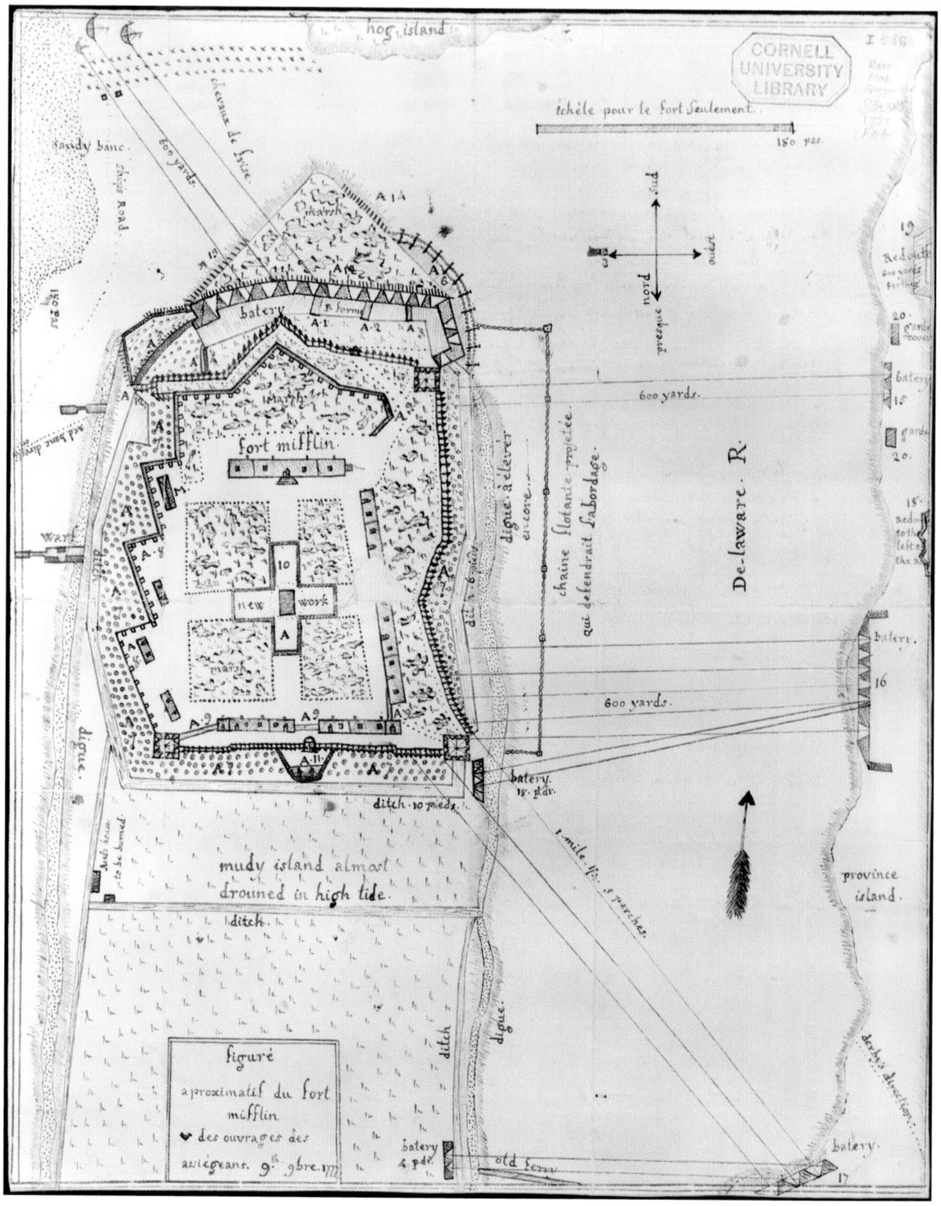

Map of Fort Mifflin drawn by the French engineer François Louis de Fleury on November 9, 1777, just before the battle began. Carl A. Kroch Library, Cornell University.

to Philadelphia in 1771 to design what was to be a massive stone fort on the Delaware below colonial America's largest city. The Pennsylvania Assembly, however, balked at the projected cost. Over the next two years, Governor John Penn struggled to convince the increasingly skeptical Americans to provide funds for "an Object of the greatest Importance for the Defense and Protection of this flourishing and populous City against His Majesty's Enemies in Time of War." The Assembly grudgingly provided for only a modest beginning to the Mud Island fort.

By 1774 it looked as though a fort really would be needed, but the enemy would most likely be George III's army and navy. The following year work began anew to complete Montrésor's design, now informally named for General Thomas Mifflin (1744–1800). It was here that the rebellious Americans came in the fall of 1777 to stop the British fleet.

Ironically, the city Fort Mifflin was designed to protect had already fallen to General Sir William Howe's legions. The British had outflanked General George Washington by landing at the Head of Elk on the Chesapeake Bay in August. Then they outfought the Continentals at Chadds Ford in the bloody Battle of the Brandywine. Eventually Washington had no choice but to abandon Philadelphia. So General Howe had the city, but the Americans still controlled the countryside and the banks of the Delaware along which desperately needed supplies for Howe's 18,000 soldiers had to pass. A large British fleet lurked in Delaware Bay.

The main gate portal dates from the early nineteenth century and was probably part of the L'Enfant plan of 1794. The flag is a replica of the one flown over Fort Mifflin during the British attack in 1777.

The stage had been set for a major engagement. For the British no less a figure than Fort Mifflin's original designer, Captain John Montrésor, planned the attack and fortified the Pennsylvania shore opposite Mud Island. The final assault began on November 10, 1777, and Montrésor recorded in his journal that it was already "cold as in the depth of winter" with "a white frost and the ice one half inch thick." Throughout the following five days the two sides exchanged fire until the American defenders were forced to evacuate under the cover of darkness, "leaving their colors standing." According to the account of Joseph Martin, an American private defending the fort, after being under attack without interruption for several days, "Our men were cut up like cornstalks. . . . When the firing had in some measure subsided and I could look about me, I found the Fort exhibited a picture of desolation. The whole area of the Fort was as completely ploughed as a field. The buildings of every kind hanging in broken fragments, and the guns were all dismounted, and how many of the garrison were sent to the world of spirits, I knew not."

Fort Mifflin fell to overwhelming force, but the defenders had delayed the British and thwarted their plan to subdue Pennsylvania. Sir James Murray thought it a costly victory. "Mud Island," he wrote, "was a most unfortunate obstacle, and cost us two of the most precious months of the war." Short of supplies, the British army remained cooped up in Philadelphia for the bitter winter

View over the east ramparts to the Delaware River that Fort Mifflin was built to control. At high tide part of Mud Island is actually below water level, making dikes and ditches necessary to keep the island dry.

of 1777–1778. On June 18, 1778, Sir Henry Clinton ordered the British forces out of the city and into New Jersey and on to New York.

The modest fortifications erected by Captain John Montrésor and the American defenders, which the British destroyed in 1777, were gradually repaired and greatly expanded in the subsequent decades as alarms both foreign and domestic called attention to Philadelphia's vulnerability to attack by sea, particularly in the periods 1794–1802, 1813–1820, 1835–1839, and during the American Civil War, when the fort was used primarily as a prison for captured Confederates. In 1904 Fort Mifflin was deactivated as a military post and the armaments dismantled and sold. Within a few decades, however, the site became the focus of restoration, particularly after it was transferred to the City of Philadelphia in 1956, although Fort Mifflin was not opened to the public until 1968. Since then an ongoing campaign has restored and stabilized such major features as the barracks, officers' quarters, commandant's house, main gate, and the north sally port. "The fort that saved America," as it has come to be known, is once again manned, but now by well-trained guides who explain one of the most evocative historic sites in Philadelphia.

View from the east ramparts to the parade ground shows (left to right) the artillery shed (c. 1837), the commandant's house (1796), the soldiers' barracks (c. 1798), and the quartermaster's store (1843). The iron semicircles are the bases for gun emplacements. The USAir flight in the process of landing demonstrates the proximity of the fort to Philadelphia International Airport.

INDEPENDENCE HALL

(Pennsylvania State House)

Independence Square
Chestnut Street between Fifth and Sixth Streets
Philadelphia, PA 19106

Edmund Woolley, Master Builder, 1732–1753
William Strickland, reconstructed steeple, 1828
World Heritage Site, 1979

Telephone for visitor information: 215.965.2305
www.nps.gov/inde/

With the exception of the Capitol in Washington, Independence Hall is the most recognizable building in the United States. Yet the very familiarity of this iconic image—so redolent of our eighteenth-century revolution and nation forming—tends to obscure its rightful place as an outstanding example of early American Georgian architecture, proudly erected as a symbol of a rapidly maturing provincial colony loyal to the British Crown. So let's look first, not at the momentous events associated with Independence Hall, but at the origins of the building erected as the Pennsylvania State House.

When William Penn granted Philadelphia its city charter in 1701, it was little more than a village on the edge of a heavily forested wilderness with modest population and limited trade. Nor were there any public buildings of consequence. All this would rapidly change in the coming decades. Soon the skyline would boast lofty steeples above commodious sacred places erected to serve the multitude of immigrants—professing divergent beliefs—who were drawn from Great Britain and Europe by Penn's pledge of liberality. The Pennsylvania Assembly would anticipate the architectural maturity that would soon be demonstrated by churches when, in 1729, funds were appropriated for a State House. A building committee—consisting of Andrew Hamilton (Speaker of the Assembly),

"Back of the State House, Philadelphia" by William Birch & Son, 1799, shows the tower of the State House after Edmund Woolley's steeple had been removed in 1781. The soapstone "tall case clock" on the west gable was added in 1752, removed when Robert Mills demolished the arcades in 1815, and then replicated by the architects of Independence National Historical Park. Athenæum of Philadelphia Collection.

Dr. John Kearsley, and Thomas Lawrence—selected an undeveloped site at the western edge of town and began purchasing individual building lots to assemble the frontage on the south side of Chestnut Street between Fifth and Sixth Streets. By 1732 they were ready to build and Speaker Hamilton presented the Assembly with "a Draught [drawing] of the State-house, containing the Plan and Elevation of that Building." On the basis of that reference it has until recently been assumed that the politician and the architect were one and the same. In fact, we have no way of knowing what Hamilton showed the Assembly; we do know he represented the Assembly for the project, but it is unlikely he had much to do with the actual design.

Thanks to careful research by the historians of Independence National Historical Park, we are now fairly certain the State House was designed and constructed by master builder Edmund Woolley (c. 1695–1771), who submitted an invoice to Governor Penn for "drawing the elevation and the front, one end, the roof balcony, chimneys, and turret of the State House with the fronts and plans of the two offices and piazzas, also the plans of the first and second floors of the State House" (spelling and punctuation have been modernized). Woolley was a British-trained master builder and one of the founders or an early member of the Carpenters' Company (pages 42–47). He doubtless served a rigorous apprenticeship in the shop of a skilled master builder and throughout his career accumulated a library of architectural pattern books of the type widely used by

The Chestnut Street façade of Independence Hall faces north; the steeple is a reconstruction by William Strickland (1828). The original steeple, which did not have clock faces, was designed and built by Edmund Woolley (1749–1753) to hold the great bell now popularly known as the "Liberty Bell."

the leading builder-architects of the eighteenth century, one of which—his copy of William Halfpenny's *Practical Architecture* (London, 1730)—survives. It provided modular proportions of the classical orders according to Palladio and illustrations of doors and windows designed by Colen Campbell and Inigo Jones. Woolley, together with his partner Ebenezer Tomlinson (fl. 1720–1765), spent eight years erecting the new State House. During this period he accepted Thomas Nevell (1721–1797) as an apprentice; Nevell would, like his master, become one of the leading master builders in Philadelphia, responsible for designing and building Mount Pleasant (see *Historic Houses*, pages 94–97).

In 1749 the Pennsylvania Assembly authorized the construction of "a Building on the South Side of the said [State] House to contain the staircase, with a suitable Place thereon for hanging a Bell." Master builder Woolley, as was typical in the eighteenth century, again served as both architect and contractor; he was paid for providing drawings for the stair tower and steeple ("drawing drafts"), purchasing the building materials, hiring and paying the other craftsmen, and hanging the great bell we now call the Liberty Bell, which cracked and twice had to be recast and rehung. (Woolley billed for "getting the Bell up & down & up again & twice hanging Bells.") The stair tower and steeple were completed in 1753.

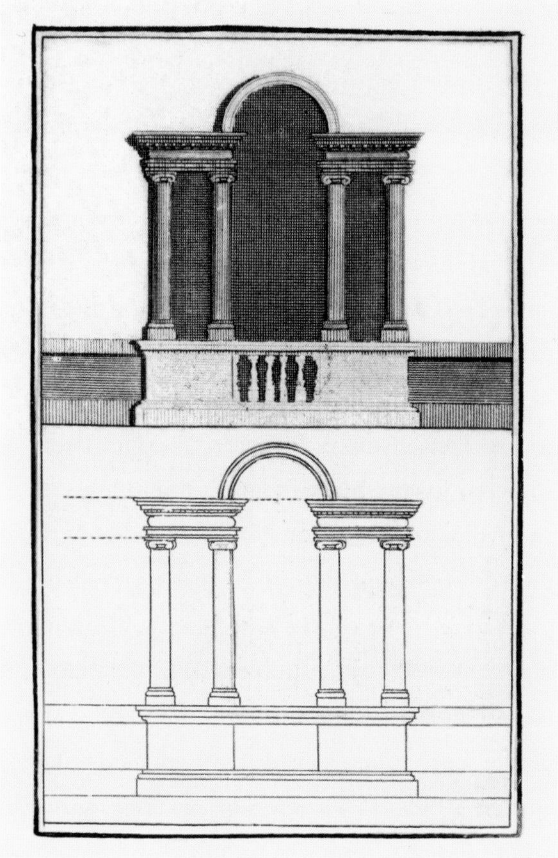

This plate from William Halfpenny's *Practical Architecture, or a Sure Guide to the true working according to the Rules of that science* (London, 1724 and later editions) provided master builders such as Edmund Woolley with the correct proportions for complex compositions, including the Venetian window in the tower of Independence Hall. Woolley owned a copy of this and other architectural pattern books that were sold to settle his estate. Athenæum of Philadelphia Collection, Robert L. Raley Collection of The Carpenters' Company.

The State House was a substantial structure for its time and place. In addition to its new tower and steeple, the two-story brick central block, trimmed with marble keystones and soapstone quoins, measured approximately 100 by 45 feet with a decked-gable roof and balustrade. The nine-bay Chestnut Street façade appeared even more imposing because the open arcades ("piazzas") linked the State House to a pair of office buildings, each approximately 50 feet long. The ground floor of the State House, divided into two large rooms separated by a wide passage, provided a room for the Assembly and another for the Supreme Court of the Province. Woolley's original design placed the staircase at the south end of the passage within the main block of the building, but this was demolished when the stair tower and steeple were erected, 1749–1753. On the second floor a chamber was provided for meetings of the Provincial Council while another accommodated Assembly committees. Stretching across the Chestnut Street front of the second floor was the "gallery" or "long room" used for public entertainment.

Intended for the Pennsylvania Assembly, this room was used by the Second Continental Congress beginning in May 1775. Here the Declaration of Independence was signed and five years later the captured colors of General Lord Cornwallis's defeated army were presented to Congress, symbolically marking the successful conclusion of the war for independence. The Constitution of the United States was also drafted and submitted to the states for ratification from this room in 1787.

Fate propelled the Pennsylvania State House to international prominence when delegates of the protesting American colonies selected it in May 1775 as the site of the Second Continental Congress. (The First Continental Congress met at Carpenters' Hall.) Armed conflict in Massachusetts led to the appointment of George Washington to head the Continental Army, and in July 1776 came Richard Henry Lee's fateful resolution, "That these United Colonies are, and of right ought to be, free and independent States." Except during the British occupation of Philadelphia, Congress continued to meet in the State House until 1783.

Architecturally there was one major alteration to the State House during the Revolution. Edmund Woolley's wooden steeple was found to be dangerously deteriorated in 1781. The steeple was removed and the brick tower capped with a low hip roof as shown in the famous Birch view of the State House yard (page 25).

Following the departure of Congress in 1783, the Pennsylvania Assembly returned to its room on the ground floor until the Constitutional Convention convened to draft the Constitution in May 1787. The new federal government met briefly in New York until relocating to Philadelphia in 1790. By this time

The chief executives of the Province of Pennsylvania, the Governor's Council, met in this second floor chamber from 1741 to 1775. It has been furnished by the Park Service with important examples of Pennsylvania decorative arts, including chairs made by Thomas Affleck for Governor John Penn, the Morris family desk and bookcase, c. 1740, and a musical tall case clock made by Peter Stretch, c. 1740.

State House Square had acquired two new buildings, City Hall to the east (pages 38–41) and the County Court House on the west (pages 32–37). When the national government arrived, Congress occupied the Court House (now Congress Hall) and the United States Supreme Court occupied City Hall. After the federal government moved to Washington, and the state government moved to Lancaster and later Harrisburg, the old State House stood empty. In 1815 the City of Philadelphia leased the building and, to make it attractive to potential tenants, stripped out the Assembly Room woodwork. Woolley's arcades and flanking office wings were also removed in favor of fireproof offices designed by Robert Mills (1781–1855). Three years later the city purchased State House Square and all the buildings for $70,000 from the Commonwealth of Pennsylvania (see *Historic Houses*, pages 3–4).

Appreciation of the State House as a shrine to the stirring events of the Revolutionary era began to emerge in the 1820s as the United States approached the fiftieth anniversary of the Declaration of Independence. The Marquis de Lafayette was entertained in the "Hall of Independence" in 1824, and in 1828

↑ On the west side of the main passage is the Supreme Court.

the City Councils of Philadelphia engaged William Strickland (pages 80–83) to recreate Woolley's spire to the stair tower as it appeared on July 4, 1776. Three years later, Strickland's chief competitor, the architect John Haviland (pages 116–117), was engaged to return the Assembly Room "to its ancient Form." (The Haviland woodwork, which bore little resemblance to the eighteenth-century original, was removed by the National Park Service during the 1960s restoration of Independence Hall and is now installed in the Lit Brothers building on Market Street.)

Throughout the nineteenth century, particularly at the time of the Centennial in 1876, there were various efforts to restore the Assembly Room. In the

Above the Assembly Room is a space provided for committee meetings but now interpreted as it might have appeared during the Revolution.

1890s, the Common and Select Councils of Philadelphia authorized the Philadelphia Chapter of the Daughters of the American Revolution to supervise a restoration of Independence Square, including the demolition of Robert Mills's office buildings and recreation of the arcades and wings between Independence Hall, Old City Hall, and Congress Hall.

Following World War II, Independence National Historical Park was established, and in 1951 the City of Philadelphia agreed to grant the National Park Service custody and permission to operate Independence Square and the Independence Hall group of buildings, while retaining legal title. The Park Service assembled a team of architects and historians to prepare historic structure reports and conduct an extensive program of conservation and rehabilitation. Today the Independence Hall complex is the most carefully documented and restored group of buildings in Philadelphia.

The Long Gallery was intended for public entertainment. This space was occupied by various organizations in the nineteenth century, most notably Charles Willson Peale's museum.

CONGRESS HALL

(Philadelphia County Court House)
Independence Square
Sixth and Chestnut Streets, Philadelphia, PA 19106

Unidentified builder, possibly William Williams, 1787–1789
Extended by William Williams, master builder, 1793–1795

Telephone for visitor information: 215.965.2305
www.nps.gov/inde/

On identical lots of ground flanking Independence Hall—at the corners of Fifth and Chestnut and Sixth and Chestnut Streets—are two handsome Late Georgian, two-and-one-half-story brick buildings with tall cupolas. The land had been purchased in 1736 while the State House was under construction. Even at that early date the intent was to erect "two publick Buildings . . . of the like outward Form, Structure and Dimensions, the one for the Use of the County, and the other for the Use of the City of Philadelphia, and are to be for the Holding of Courts, or Common Halls, and not for Private Dwellings." Half a century would pass before this grand scheme was realized.

In 1785 the Assembly of Pennsylvania appropriated funds to erect the long contemplated building to house the courts of Philadelphia County on the lot at Sixth and Chestnut Streets. Work began in 1787 and was completed in the spring of 1789. The following September, Robert Morris of Pennsylvania invited the United States Congress, then meeting in New York City, to relocate to Philadelphia. To encourage the move he offered "any or all the public buildings in Philadelphia, the property of the State, in case Congress should, at any time, incline to make use of that city for the temporary residence of the Federal Government." Over the protests of New York, it was agreed to accept Morris's offer, and in late 1790 the Congress occupied the new County Court House. The House of Representatives and Senate would remain on Chestnut Street until 1800, while the new "Federal City" in the District of Columbia was being prepared.

↓ The House of Representatives occupied the ground floor. To accommodate the new representatives after the admission of Vermont and Kentucky to the Union, Congress Hall was extended so this room could be enlarged.

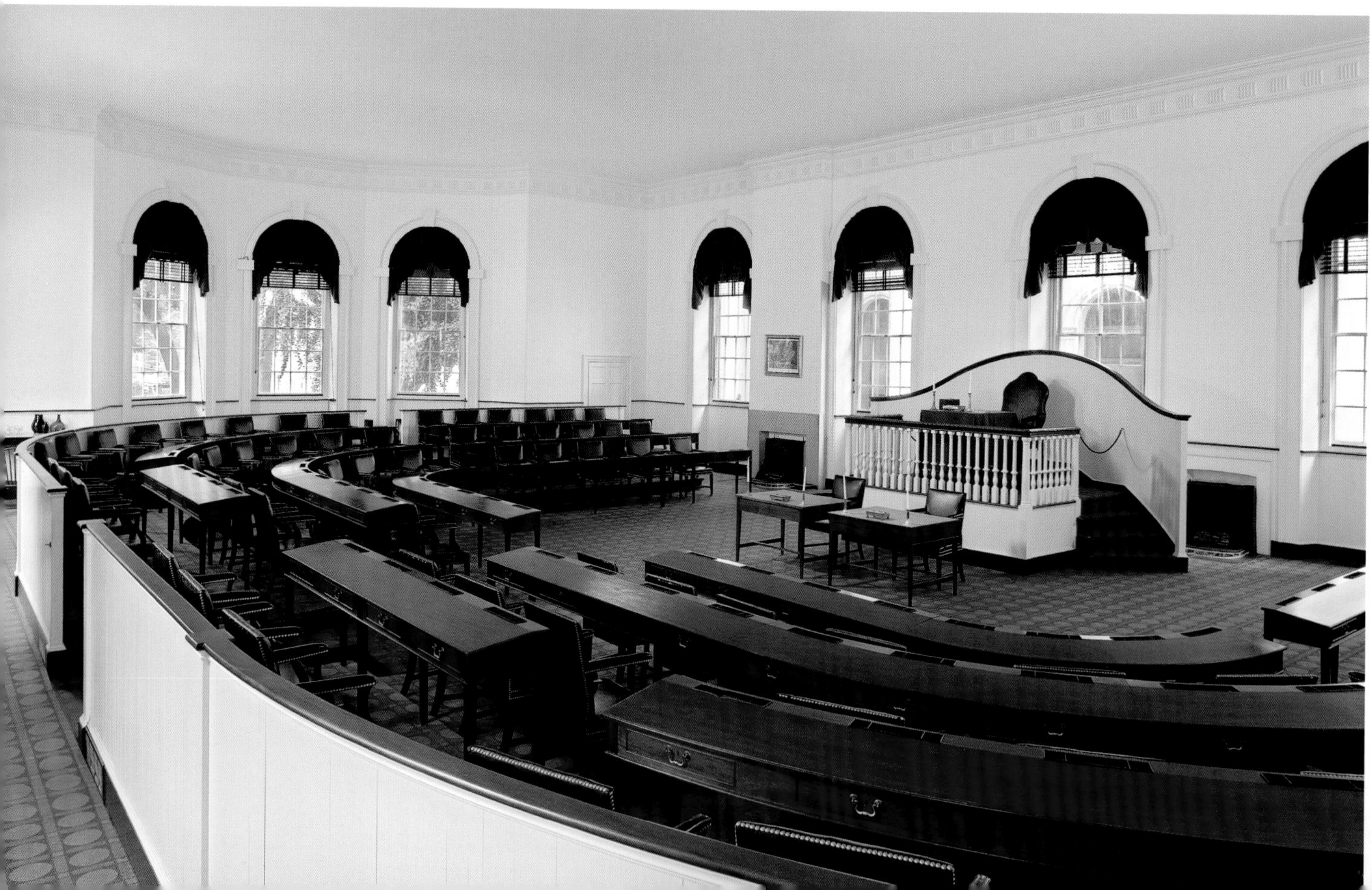

NO STOPPING ANY TIME
NO TURN ON RED
CHESTNUT ST
JUDGE EDWARD R. BECKER WAY
NO TURN ON RED

Congress Hall was erected in 1787–1789 as the Philadelphia County Court House. When Philadelphia became the capital of the United States in 1790, the United States Senate and the House of Representatives occupied the building.

The United States Senate occupied the chamber above the House of Representatives. According to one visitor, "it is furnished and fitted up in a much superior style" to the hall of the House.

Adapting simple court rooms for the use of Congress required considerable modification. On the ground floor, where the House of Representatives would meet, a public gallery was created and the chamber outfitted with mahogany tables and chairs upholstered in black leather by master Philadelphia cabinet-maker Thomas Affleck. The floor was covered with ingrain carpeting, and the windows were fitted with venetian blinds. At the west side of the room, a dais for the speaker was provided. On the second floor, where the smaller Senate would meet, individual desks and chairs with red leather upholstery, also from Affleck's shop, were provided. The Senate chamber floor was nearly covered wall to wall with a hand-knotted Axminster carpet of neoclassical design featuring a large American eagle grasping an olive branch and a bundle of thirteen arrows. The British traveler Isaac Weld, Jr., who visited Philadelphia in 1795, was not impressed by the federal city, calling the public buildings "heavy tasteless

Animosities between Federalists and Republicans sometimes erupted in physical violence in Congress Hall, as on February 15, 1798, between Republican Representative Matthew Lyon of Vermont and Federalist Representative Roger Griswold of Connecticut. This cartoon entitled "Congressional Pugilists" is accompanied by the doggerel: "He in a trice struck Lyon thrice / Upon his head, enrag'd Sir, / Who seized the tongs to ease his wrongs, / And Griswold thus engag'd, Sir." Athenæum of Philadelphia Collection.

piles of red brick" ornamented with blue marble. Nonetheless, he toured Congress Hall. "The room allotted to the representatives of the lower house," he records, "is about sixty feet in length, and fitted up in the plainest manner. At one end of it is a gallery, open to every person that chuses to enter it; the staircase leading to which runs directly from the public street. The senate chamber is in the story above this, and it is furnished and fitted up in a much superior style to that of the lower house."

As the size of Congress—particularly the House—increased after the Census of 1790 and the admission of Vermont (1791), Kentucky (1792), and probably in anticipation of Tennessee (1796), Congress Hall had to be extended by 26 feet to the south, adding two window bays to both stories plus two additional chimneys. As a result of this extension, the House chamber was enlarged and, on the second floor, the Senate moved south into the new extension, which increased the number of second-floor offices from two to four. A new gallery in the Senate chamber erected in 1795 provided for about fifty spectators.

The commission to extend Congress Hall had been given to William Williams (1749?–1794), one of the leading master builders of federal Philadelphia, who might well have become a full-fledged architect had not his life been tragically cut short, probably by the yellow fever that ravaged the city in 1794. A native Philadelphian, Williams claimed to have studied architecture in London and returned in 1772, advertising that he was prepared to design buildings in "a new, bold, light and elegant taste, which has been lately introduced by the great architect of the Adelphi Buildings at Durham Yard [Robert and James Adam]." Williams's advertisement is one of the earliest Philadelphia references to Adamesque neoclassicism. He also owned English architectural pattern books that were new in the 1770s, such as N. Wallis's *Book of Ornaments in the Palmyrene Taste* (London, 1771).

During the Revolution William Williams married the daughter of master builder Robert Smith and served as a lieutenant colonel in the Continental Army. Captured by the British at the Battle of Germantown, he later escaped, rejoined his regiment, and served throughout the war. After the Revolution, Williams is known to have designed the "Grand Federal Edifice" float that led the parade on July 4, 1788, to celebrate the ratification of the U.S. Constitution. It took the form of a dome resting on thirteen columns in the Corinthian order, rich in the adopted symbolism of the new nation. According to one account,

> The frieze decorated with thirteen stars; ten of the columns complete and three left unfinished [for those states that had not yet ratified the Constitution]. On the pedestals of the columns were inscribed, in ornamented ciphers, the initials of the thirteen American states. On the top of the dome a handsome cupola, surmounted by a figure of Plenty bearing cornucopias and other emblems of her character. Round the pedestal of the edifice were these words: "In Union the fabric stands firm."

Williams also worked on Library Hall (1789–1790) designed by the amateur architect William Thornton, consulted on Thornton's design for the United States Capitol (where he crossed swords with another gentleman architect, Thomas Jefferson), and probably designed and erected the substantial Federal style residence at Ninth and Market Streets begun in 1792 for the President of the United States (completed by others 1797; demolished c. 1829, page 9).

During its decade on Chestnut Street, Congress authorized the Bank of the United States (pages 60–65), began to enlarge the Union by admitting new states, and recognized the adoption of the Bill of Rights. Here, too, George Washington was inaugurated president for his second term, delivered his famous farewell address in 1797, and oversaw the peaceful transition from his presidency to that of John Adams.

After Congress moved to Washington in 1800, Congress Hall reverted to its intended use as a court house. By the end of the nineteenth century, virtually all vestiges of the 1790–1800 interior configuration had been lost. In 1895 the Pennsylvania Society of the Colonial Dames restored the Senate chamber with

George C. Mason, Jr. (1849–1924) as architect. By 1900 the Philadelphia Chapter of the American Institute of Architects began conducting both research and a physical examination of the structure, leading in 1911–1912 to additional restoration and rehabilitation under the direction of Frank Miles Day (1861–1918). Once Independence Square came under Park Service management after World War II, detailed historic structure reports were prepared and Congress Hall was reinterpreted to the 1790–1800 period.

The east committee room adjoins the Senate on the second floor of Congress Hall.

OLD CITY HALL

(United States Supreme Court)
Independence Square
Fifth and Chestnut Streets
Philadelphia, PA 19106

David Evans, master builder, 1790–1791

Telephone for visitor information: 215.965.2305
www.nps.gov/ind/.

The Federal Style building now known as Old City Hall was the last eighteenth-century structure erected on Independence Square. The land had been purchased for this purpose in 1736, but half a century passed before actual construction began. In 1789, the Philadelphia City Council appointed a committee, including master builder David Evans, "to prepare a plan and estimate the Expense of erecting a City Hall." The committee reported that the City should proceed "with all possible expedition because if the Congress of the United States should reside here the public Buildings will be so much occupied that there will probably be no place for holding the Mayor's Court, or the Sittings of the Corporation, except in the old Court House in High [Market] Street, which is extremely inconvenient and unfit for the purpose." The funds to erect the new hall came from a public lottery authorized by the Pennsylvania Assembly. As anticipated, Congress did come to town and occupied the new Philadelphia County Court House (pages 32–37) at the other end of the block.

Under the supervision of David Evans, work on the new City Hall commenced in 1790 and the building was ready for occupancy by August 1791. As intended from the beginning, City Hall was patterned on the building now known as Congress Hall at the corner of Sixth and Chestnut Streets. The two-and-one-half-story brick structure trimmed with marble measures fifty feet by seventy feet. The five-bay Chestnut Street façade is relieved by a projecting three-bay pedimented pavilion with an arched entrance and fanlight. The roof is hipped and surmounted by an octagonal cupola. As at Congress Hall, there is a semi-octagonal bay projecting from the south wall. As soon as City Hall was completed, the Supreme Court of the United States promptly settled into the first floor room originally intended for the Mayor's Court. City Council and city courts contented themselves with rooms on the second floor.

David Evans (1733–1817) had become a successful master builder by the 1760s, and was a member of the Carpenters' Company (pages 42–47). Literate and familiar with architectural pattern books, he also became a member of Franklin's Library Company—to which he presented a valuable set of Abraham Swan's *Collection of Designs in Architecture* in 1764. He also subscribed to the Philadelphia edition of Swan's *The British Architect* (1774), the first book on architecture published in America. Following the Revolution, Evans becomes one of the leading figures responsible for introducing the Late Georgian or Federal Style that was coming into favor in America. He designed and built Philosophical Hall (pages 48–53) directly behind the site of City Hall. He also entered the competition to design Library Hall across Fifth Street from Philosophical Hall in 1789, although William Thornton won the design commission. That same year Evans became a member of the Common Council of Philadelphia, a position

⇜ Old City Hall was erected in 1790–1791 to house the Select and Common Councils of Philadelphia. Upon its completion, the building housed the Supreme Court of the United States until the federal government moved to the District of Columbia.

PennMutual
CHESTNUT ST
JUDGE EDWARD R. BECKER WAY
ONE WAY

he held until 1791 and during which he served on the City Hall committee. Even as his health began to decline, David Evans and his son of the same name worked together to complete the Pennsylvania Hospital from 1794 to 1804 (pages 54–59).

The original ground floor plan of Evans's City Hall contained an open stair hall, an office for the treasurer, and the Mayor's Court Room, which occupied the entire southern half of the first floor, including the projecting bay that contained the judges' rostrum. The second floor provided rooms for the Select Council and Common Council and related offices. The Common Council occupied the chamber directly above the Mayor's Court Room, including the projecting bay. As at Congress Hall, these bays, often referred to as "octagons," were actually half-octagons. They provided a focal point for rooms of public assembly,

↑ The ground floor courtroom was restored by the Park Service as it might have appeared when used as the Mayor's Court.

much as the apse of a religious structure provides direction in a space, here focusing attention on the presiding judge or other official.

When the Supreme Court of the United States relocated to the District of Columbia in 1800, the City of Philadelphia reclaimed the entire building for use as the mayor's office and for meetings of the city councils. Once the Athenæum vacated Philosophical Hall next door in favor of its new building on Washington Square (pages 132–137), the City rented the space from the Philosophical Society and erected a hyphen between the two buildings. Following consolidation of the city and county in 1852, the need for a new city hall became even more pressing, leading ultimately to the construction of the new public buildings at Broad and Market Streets (pages 180–185). The City vacated Old City Hall in the 1890s, and several organizations—the Boy Scouts of America and the Grand Army of the Republic, for example—rented the building. In 1921 the City permitted the American Institute of Architects to restore the building, which was then used as a museum until the restoration was completed by the architects and historians of Independence National Historical Park in the 1960s.

CARPENTERS' HALL

320–322 Chestnut Street, Philadelphia, PA 19106-2708

Robert Smith, master builder, 1770–1773
National Historic Landmark, 1970

Telephone for visitor information: 215.925.0167
www.carpentershall.org

Carpenters' Hall has three rightful claims to landmark status. Architecturally it is admired as one of the finest intact Middle Georgian buildings in North America. Politically it is venerated for its association with the American Revolution. Socially it represents the unparalleled continuity of the Carpenters' Company of the City and County of Philadelphia, the only surviving colonial American craft guild. While located in the heart of Independence National Historical Park, Carpenters' Hall is owned and happily maintained by the builders, architects, and engineers whose predecessors founded the Company more than 250 years ago.

The Carpenters' Company traces its origins to medieval regulations establishing craft guilds in the city of London. These fraternal societies were devoted to

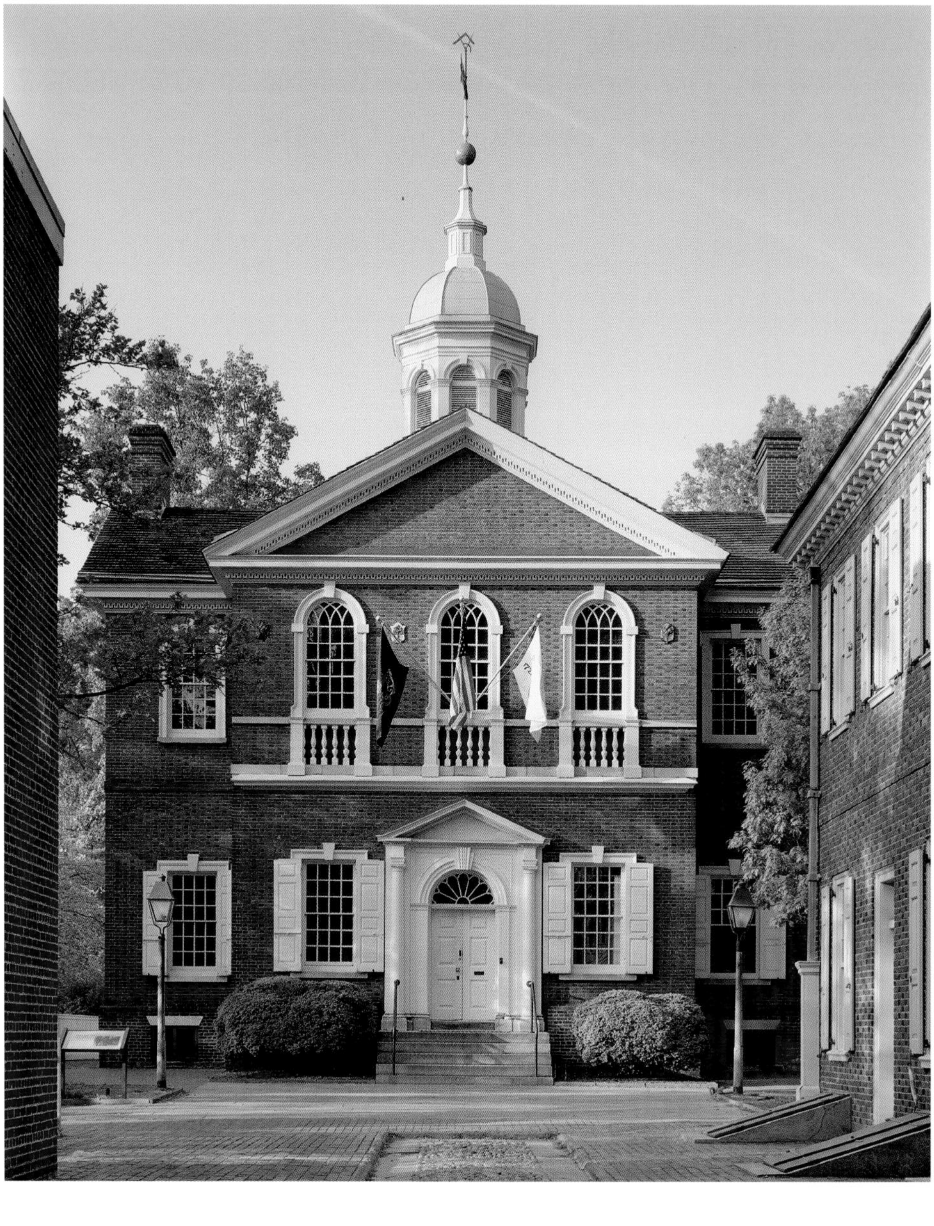

Carpenters' Hall (1770–1773) is sited in the middle of a block and has always been approached by a narrow alley. The buildings on either side of the alley were constructed by Independence National Historical Park to recreate the original setting.

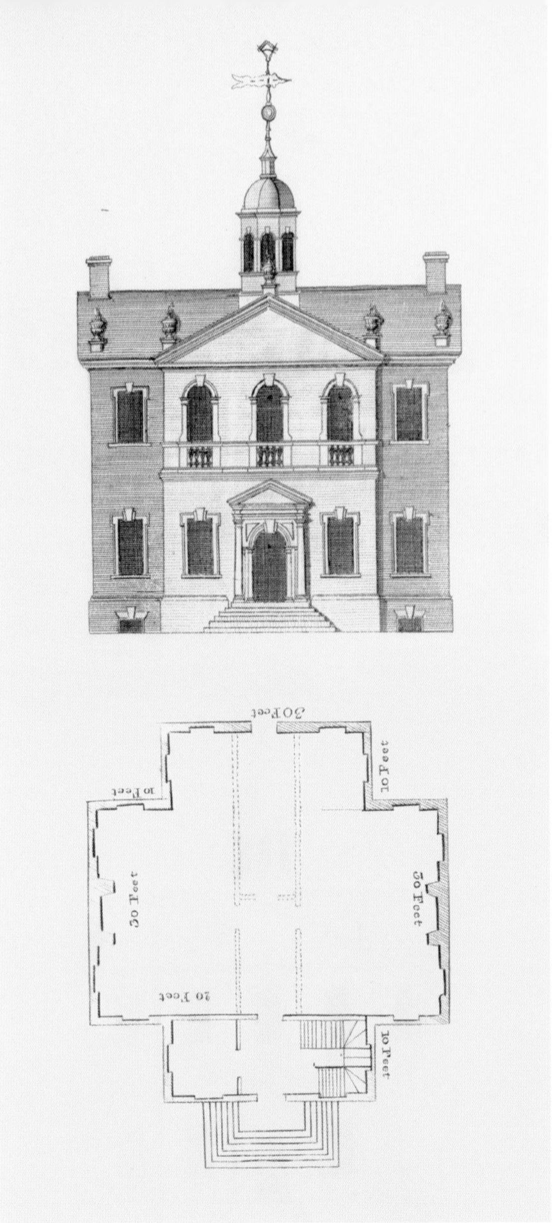

The elevation and ground floor plan of Carpenters' Hall as drawn by Thomas Nevell and engraved by Thomas Bedwell is probably based on Robert Smith's original drawing. It was first published in 1786. There is no evidence the roof urns were ever installed. Athenæum of Philadelphia Collection.

charitable aid—to succor the sick, to bury the dead, and to comfort the survivors of members who happened to share a common craft. In the fifteenth century a loosely organized group of London house carpenters achieved incorporation as the Worshipful Company of Carpenters and was empowered to make its own ordinances "to support their businesses and the matters touching the mystery and brotherhood" of carpentry. These ordinances granted the Company broad authority. Henceforth it would determine which lads would be accepted as apprentices in a city where no one could "exercise the trade of Carpentry unless he should have first been bound apprentice to the same trade, served in the same by the space of seven years at the least." The Company also controlled which carpenters would be granted permission to set up shop in the City, established the standards and prices for building materials, and set the prices charged for carpentry.

Fast forward to late seventeenth-century Philadelphia. Some of the carpenters enticed to America by William Penn had been trained in the London guild system. They probably encouraged their younger colleagues to form a similar guild in the 1720s "for the purpose of obtaining instruction in the science of architecture, and assisting such of their members as should by accident be in need of support." In fact, the Company—through various informal means—gradually gained considerable influence over the Philadelphia building trades, although it never had the official powers granted to the London guild. The Company was able to manipulate what clients paid to build through a closely guarded book of prices, and its members were required to have served a seven-year apprenticeship under a member of the Company and then several years as a successful journeyman before they could be elected to membership and assume the informal title "master builder." Successful master builders—such as Samuel Rhoads and David Evans, who were responsible for the Pennsylvania Hospital, Edmund Woolley, who designed and erected Independence Hall, and Thomas Nevell, whose masterpiece was Mount Pleasant—combined practical skills in building with the ability to coordinate diverse crafts (the equivalent of a modern general contractor) and knowledge of both design and structure (the architect or engineer of today). In the nineteenth and twentieth centuries, these skills became more specialized. As a consequence, the men and women elected to membership in the twenty-first-century Carpenters' Company include the leading builders, architects, and engineers of Philadelphia, who are more likely to hold advanced degrees from our finest universities than to have served apprenticeships.

This is the ground floor room in which the First Continental Congress met in 1774. The tile floor dates from the "restoration" of Carpenters' Hall in the 1850s.

Carpenters' Hall is an outstanding example of Middle Georgian architecture, although its modest scale and location at the end of a narrow alley mean that it can inadvertently be overlooked by tourists setting out to visit Independence Hall and the Liberty Bell. The Company began to plan for its own building in the 1760s as a place "to Transact the Business of Said Company & to Calculate & Settle their private Accounts of . . . Carpenters work." It purchased a lot on Chestnut Street and on April 18, 1768, master builder Robert Smith "exhibited [a] Sketch for a Building to be thereon Erected." Company members contributed cash, material, and labor to erect a two-story cruciform brick building laid in Flemish bond with equal gables at the four points of the compass and a tall octagonal cupola crowned by a weathervane. Work did not actually begin until 1770 but was sufficiently advanced by fall 1773 for Benjamin Franklin's Library Company (pages 192–195) to move into the second floor as a tenant.

It is no surprise that Robert Smith (1722–1777) was selected to design Carpenters' Hall. He clearly was recognized as the first among equals, especially as a designer. For that reason, later historians have long held that he may have been one of the first master builders to make the transition from builder to architect, a common pattern by the 1830s. Smith was born near Dalkeith, Scotland, and migrated to Philadelphia about 1748, already versed in the "mystery" of architecture. He rapidly became the leading master builder in the city, with a reputation that spread to other colonies. The 1750s and early 1760s were prosperous years in Philadelphia, especially after the defeat of France in the French and Indian War. With Philadelphia's rapid expansion in the 1760s, Smith and his colleagues in the Carpenters' Company embellished Philadelphia streets with elegant town houses, substantial civic structures, and a remarkable number of Georgian churches, while notable villas and country houses sprouted along the banks of the Delaware and Schuylkill Rivers. Smith's contributions included the steeple of Christ Church (1751), Saint Peter's Church (1758), Saint Paul's Church (1760), Benjamin Franklin House (1766), Third Presbyterian Church (1766), and Powel House (1765), to name a few of his commissions (see *Historic Houses* and *Historic Sacred Places*).

By the 1770s, revolutionary unrest had cast its shadow over the city. The Carpenters' Company nearly to a man favored separation from the mother country, and provided leaders in the non-importation movement and various revolutionary committees. In September 1774, the Company offered its Hall for the meeting of the First Continental Congress, which had been called in response to the closing of the Port of Boston after the Boston Tea Party. From that meeting came the Articles of Association, a compact among the colonies to boycott British goods. While independence was neither the purpose nor the

The second floor has a long history of use as a library. Benjamin Franklin's Library Company occupied this space in 1774–1784, and it now contains the Company's library of rare architectural pattern books, including some that belonged to Robert Smith.

result of the First Continental Congress, it demonstrated that the radicals had broader support than previously imagined. It also brought together leaders from twelve of the thirteen colonies, many of whom would return to Philadelphia resolved to establish a new nation.

As the Revolution moved from coffeehouse and assembly hall into the streets and onto the battlefields, Carpenters' Company members were found manufacturing arms for the Committee of Safety, building fortifications on the Delaware, and serving in the military—the Company provided at least twenty officers to the patriot cause, nearly a third of its total membership at the outbreak of hostilities.

After the Revolution, Carpenters' Hall was rented to a variety of income-producing tenants, including the First and Second Banks of the United States (pages 60–65, 80–85). The Hall reached its nadir when used as an auction house in the mid-nineteenth century. Historian Benson J. Lossing discovered it in that guise. "What a desecration!" he cried. "Covering the facade of the very Temple of Freedom, with placards of groveling mammon!" Perhaps Lossing's expression of "indignant shame" encouraged the Carpenters' Company in 1856 to declare its intention to renovate the building and "preserve, as much as possible, every feature in said Hall as it now exists indicative of its original finish."

Soon after the renovated Carpenters' Hall was opened to the public, the City of Philadelphia approached the Company to determine whether it "would be willing to convey to the City your proud Monument of Revolutionary memory" to be administered jointly with Independence Hall for public edification. The Company's response established a precedent for a similar request from the National Park Service a century later: "We in common with our fellow citizens venerate [Carpenters' Hall] not only for its associations with the stirring events of the Revolution," but because it represents "a sacred trust committed to us by our predecessors, which nothing shall ever induce us to part with." To this day Carpenters' Hall is Company property, kept open "for the inspection of all who may wish to visit it" without charge and without public funding—one of the earliest American examples of nongovernmental preservation and restoration.

PHILOSOPHICAL HALL

American Philosophical Society
104 South Fifth Street
Philadelphia, PA 19106-3386

William Roberts and David Evans, master builders, 1785–1789
Wilson Brothers & Company, renovation and expansion, 1890
National Historical Landmark, 1965

Telephone for visitor information: 215.440.3400
www.amphilsoc.org

In 1743, Benjamin Franklin published "A Proposal for Promoting Useful Knowledge among the British Plantations in America." His objective was a society of "Virtuosi or ingenious Men residing in the several Colonies, to be called The American Philosophical Society." Since Philadelphia was the "City nearest the Centre of the Continent-Colonies," he reasoned it should "be the Centre of the Society." From this seed emerged what is now the oldest and most distinguished learned society in the United States, since the eighteenth century, located on Independence Square in a hall of its own devising.

From the Philosophical Society's founding through the turbulent years of the Revolution, it wandered from place to place without a building of its own, sometimes meeting in members' homes. In 1785, however, the General Assembly of Pennsylvania granted a rectangular lot 70 by 50 feet on State House Square "for the purpose of erecting thereon a Hall, Library, and such other

buildings or apartments as the said Society may think necessary for their proper accommodation." A building committee headed by merchant, philanthropist, and horticulturist Samuel Vaughan (1720–1802) decided to allocate the entire lot to a two-story building with attic and basement having symmetrical entrances on both Fifth Street and the State House Square leading to a passage that divides the building into equal spaces on each floor. Vaughan is occasionally listed as the

The central passage stair reflects several campaigns of renovation and restoration.

The façade of Philosophical Hall facing onto Independence Square, erected in 1785–1789 by master builders William Roberts and David Evans in the new Federal Style then becoming popular in Philadelphia. The Hall houses the administrative offices of the American Philosophical Society founded in 1743 by Benjamin Franklin.

"architect" of the building, but there is no record of him either having architectural pretensions or designing other buildings. Once the general scope of the project had been determined by the committee, it was left to master builders William Roberts and David Evans to make the actual design decisions. Evans (1733–1817) is known to have worked on the Pennsylvania Hospital (pages 54–59) and designed Old City Hall (pages 38–41) next to the Philosophical Hall site. Vaughan's role was to keep the accounts and pay Evans's invoices for the various subcontractors he coordinated to erect the building.

Work on the new hall began immediately but proceeded in stuttering fits and starts due to fund-raising difficulties. The project was near foundering when Benjamin Franklin stepped in with a loan of £500 to complete the building in 1789. The five-bay brick structure with arched entrances and a low-pitched hip roof into which the Society finally moved is one of the first in Philadelphia to be

The first and second floors now provide public exhibition spaces for the display of the Society's collection of books, manuscripts, and objects. The installation shown here is "The Princess & The Patriot: Ekaterina Dashkova, Benjamin Franklin, and the Age of Enlightenment" (2006).

erected in the newly popular Late Georgian or Federal Style, which would be used for Congress Hall (1787–1789) and Old City Hall (1790–1791) on State House Square, Library Hall across Fifth Street (1789–1790), the grand house intended for the President of the United States (1792–1797) on Ninth Street, and the "center house" of Pennsylvania Hospital (1794–1804) on Pine Street between Eighth and Ninth.

The meeting room as it appeared in 1885 before the new structural system was installed. American Philosophical Society Collection.

In 1789 the American Philosophical Society had no need for a building of 12,000 square feet. Rooms on the second floor were reserved for Society meetings and storage of its modest collection of books and papers; most of the building was rented for the next 150 years to a diverse group of income-producing tenants. Merchant John Vaughan (1755–1841) rented the cellar for storage of wine and liquors; other early tenants included the University of Pennsylvania and the College of Physicians. In 1794, Charles Willson Peale took over virtually the entire building for his museum and residence. When he moved from Philosophical Hall to the long gallery in nearby Independence Hall, artist Thomas Sully rented Philosophical Hall for a residence and picture gallery. In the meantime, The Athenæum of Philadelphia—founded in 1814 by members of the Philosophical Society and Library Company—began its own odyssey of rented rooms. This new library desired to secure space in Philosophical Hall, and in 1818 it was finally able to sublet two rooms from Sully.

When his lease expired, the Athenæum became the Society's principal tenant, occupying the entire first floor and basement until 1847. When the Athenæum departed for its own building on Washington Square (pages 132–137), its former space was rented to provide offices for the mayor of Philadelphia and then city and federal courts.

Library Hall of the American Philosophical Society faces Philosophical Hall across Fifth Street. It was erected in 1958–1959 from designs by Sydney E. Martin. The façade replicates the Library Company of Philadelphia building designed by Dr. William Thornton, which stood on the same site from 1790 to 1887 (page 194).

By 1890 the expansion of the Society library—and the vulnerability of the building to fire—prompted an extensive renovation that included inserting a fire-resistant structural system and erecting a sixteen-foot third floor providing a two-level library designed by Wilson Brothers & Company, one of Philadelphia's leading firms of civil engineers and architects of the time. The visual effect was singularly unfortunate. What had been a delicate Federal composition en suite with the adjoining Independence Hall group had become an overblown Colonial Revival intrusion on the Square. To add insult to disfiguring injury, the Wilson Brothers expansion soon proved inadequate for the

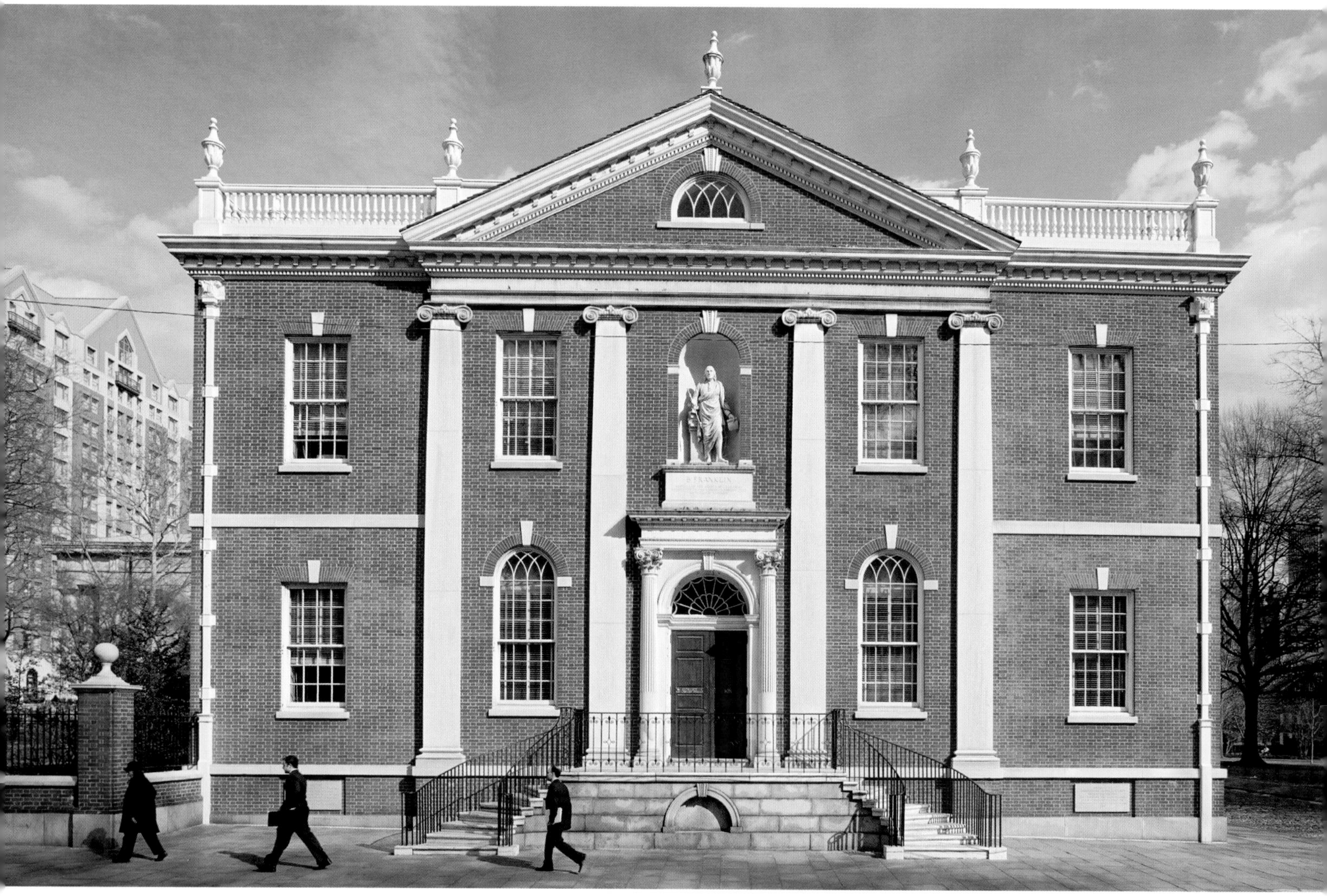

Society's needs. Space for the library had to be found across the street in the Drexel Building.

The realization of Independence National Historical Park in the years following World War II had dramatic impact on several of Philadelphia's ancient cultural institutions. In the case of the American Philosophical Society it encouraged the restoration of Philosophical Hall under the supervision of Sydney E. Martin, FAIA (1883–1970). The Wilson Brothers' third floor was removed and the low-hipped roof and tall chimneys were recreated. At the same time, provision was made for the Society's library and archives in a new building erected directly opposite Philosophical Hall on Fifth Street. The new Library Hall was modeled on the original Library Company of Philadelphia façade, designed by Dr. William Thornton in 1789–1790 and demolished in 1887 to be replaced by the Drexel Building, which was in turn demolished in 1956 to make way for the new Library Hall designed by Martin, Stewart & Nobel.

PENNSYLVANIA HOSPITAL

800 Spruce Street
Philadelphia, PA 19107

Samuel Rhoads, Joseph Fox, and others, master builders, East Wing, 1755–1757
David Evans and David Evans, Jr., master builders, West Wing, 1794–1797, Center House, 1794–1804
National Historic Landmark, 1965

Telephone for visitor information: 215-829-3000
www.pennhealth.com/pahosp/about/

The expansion of Philadelphia in the eighteenth century rapidly transformed William Penn's country town into the largest city in British North America. Estimates vary, but in 1730 there were probably 11,500 Philadelphians and by 1750 nearly 15,000. The total had risen to 40,000 on the eve of the Revolution. From a twenty-first-century perspective, these numbers may seem minuscule, but this accelerating growth in the mid-eighteenth century brought with it social ills exacerbated by the glut of Scotch-Irish and German immigrants disgorged by trans-Atlantic ships. The human cargo too often arrived with little more than the clothing on their backs and a fervent desire for a fresh start in the new world. One observer of this migration complained that, "a large proportion" of the new arrivals are "aged, impotent, diseased."

The Pennsylvania melting pot unquestionably had its dark side. Here, according to one historian, "Europeans, Africans and Indians engaged in free exchange of their respective infections." And if the fears of unknown or poorly understood contagion were not enough, concentrated population also brought increased incidence of mental illness. To Dr. Thomas Bond (1712–1784), the European-trained physician who served as inspector of contagious diseases for the Port of Philadelphia, the need for a voluntary hospital was clearly indicated for both the physically and mentally ill. On January 20, 1751, a petition in the hand of Dr. Bond's friend Benjamin Franklin was presented to the Pennsylvania Assembly favoring a bill "to encourage the establishing of an hospital for the relief of the sick poor of the Province and for the reception and cure of lunaticks." With Franklin's support, more than £2,000 in private subscriptions were raised and

"Pennsylvania Hospital, in Pine Street, Philadelphia," by William Birch & Son, 1799. By the time of the Birch view, both wings had been completed and the center house was under construction. Athenæum of Philadelphia Collection.

matched by £2,000 from the Assembly to create what would become America's first hospital.

While the hospital was briefly housed in a private residence, the managers purchased the eastern part of an undeveloped rectangle of land bounded by Eighth, Ninth, Spruce, and Pine Streets on December 7, 1754, setting the stage for the erection of a building. (In 1767 the proprietors would grant title to the balance of the land.)

The building history of the hospital (1755–1757) is complex, but recent research suggests that the key figures were the master builders Samuel Rhoads (1711–1784), described in the hospital records as the "Undertaker," and Joseph Fox (1709–1779). These two were asked "to prepare plans & to consult with all of the Contributors as are skilled in building." Both men were members of the Carpenters' Company (pages 11–14, 42–47) who had made their fortunes and were devoting most of their energies to political and philanthropic activities; both were also closely associated with Franklin.

In developing the hospital plan, Rhoads and Fox made specific reference to the Hospital of Saint Mary of Bethlehem in London (famously known as Bedlam) and William Adam's design for the Edinburgh Infirmary—both buildings intended by their architects to shelter and treat the sick poor as well as the mentally ill. Philadelphia master builder Robert Smith (1722–1777), who designed and constructed many large-scale institutional buildings such as Nassau Hall in

"A South-East Prospect of Pennsylvania Hospital," by Henry Dawkins and John Sleeper, 1761. This view shows the original Middle Georgian design by Samuel Rhoads for the entire hospital, although only the east wing actually existed at the time. This engraving may have been intended to help raise funds to complete the project. Historical Society of Pennsylvania.

The center building (Pine Street Building) was designed and constructed by David Evans and David Evans, Jr. The east wing (shown on the right) was designed by Samuel Rhoads and Joseph Fox.

Princeton, New Jersey, and the Walnut Street Prison facing Independence Square (page 4), and probably designed the Hospital for Idiots and Lunatics in Williamsburg, Virginia, is also known to have consulted with Rhoads, but as yet he cannot be documented as having actually worked on the site, as has been occasionally suggested. So, for the time being, the original design for the hospital complex must be given to Rhoads, Fox, and other unidentified co-contributors.

Influenced by the London and Edinburgh prototypes mentioned above, the overall hospital edifice would consist of three parts: two symmetrical (T-shaped) wings facing east (Eighth Street) and west (Ninth Street), connected by a "center house" facing Pine Street to the south. The east wing was erected first and occupied on December 17, 1756. It is a typical Middle Georgian, two-and-one-half-story brick building laid in Flemish bond with glazed headers. The hipped roof with dormers has a three-story central pavilion with a flat roof and cupola. The men's ward was on the first floor and the women's ward on the second; the cells for the insane occupied the basement, together with the kitchen, pantry, and baths.

The War of Independence descended on Pennsylvania Hospital in late 1776, when the Council of Safety seized the building "for the sick troops of the Continental Army." Following the Battle of the Brandywine and the fall of Philadelphia to General Howe's British legions on September 26, 1777, the wards were filled with British wounded. After the British army evacuated the city, much space in the wards was occupied by the sick and wounded of Washington's Continental Army. Following the Revolution, however, the hospital gradually recovered and, with grants from the Commonwealth of Pennsylvania in the 1790s, the managers decided to complete Samuel Rhoads's original composition by erecting the west wing and connecting the two wings with a new center house.

By now the master builders responsible for the east wing were long dead. As a consequence, David Evans (1733–1817) was invited to submit estimates to erect the west wing and center house, which he thought could be done "for ten thousand pounds, exclusive of the stone steps and curbstones round the area, and the frontispiece to the outside door." Evans, then in his late fifties, emerged during the Federal era as a master builder with pretensions. He owned English architectural pattern books and was responsible for Old City Hall (pages 38–41) and Philosophical Hall (pages 43–53), although his design for Library Hall was rejected in favor of one by the amateur architect William Thornton. Evans is known to have worked at Library Hall, but serious injuries sustained in a fall from a three-story scaffold in 1790 may have limited his capacity as a builder.

↑ The operating room amphitheater on the third floor of the center house dates from 1804. It is open to the public.

When Evans submitted his estimate to complete the hospital, his son David Evans, Jr., brought in a ground plan and estimate of £3,309 for finishing the west wing interior. At this point most histories of the hospital conflate the elder David Evans and his son, but the manager's minutes state that David Evans, Jr., was "engaged as a principal to undertake the whole building with liberty to employ his own workmen" and to submit a contract to "undertake the work." The elder Evans—clearly pleased that his son had secured the contract—offered "to superintend the work without any compensation."

Construction of the west wing began in 1794 and was completed late in 1797. Because of a shortage of funds, work on the center house would drag on until 1804. While the west wing hewed closely to Samuel Rhoads's original design (albeit a few feet wider and topped by a slightly different cupola), the center building is a fine example of the Late Georgian or Federal Style that the elder Evans had helped introduce to Philadelphia. Rhoads's Middle Georgian design of 1755 called for an institutional version of Mount Pleasant (1763–1765) writ large: a five-bay, three-story brick front with a three-bay projecting pavilion topped by a pediment and a hipped roof with balustrade. The center

↑ The Pennsylvania Hospital Library on the second floor of the center building houses the rare book collection. In 1850 the American Medical Association declared that the hospital's collection of medical books was the largest in the nation. It is open for public tours.

building design by David Evans, Jr., also called for a five-bay, three-story front. But here the façade is flat (no projecting pavilion). The first story is faced with white marble surrounding four arched windows flanking an arched center door with a semicircular fanlight similar to those on the Physick House on South Fourth Street (1786–1788) and Lemon Hill in Fairmount Park (1799–1800)—both important Federal houses whose architect/builders are as yet unidentified (see *Historic Houses*, pages 44–45, 90–93). The second and third stories of the hospital center building are red brick, against which six white marble pilasters with Corinthian capitals are set in high relief. A pediment with oval window spans four of the pilasters behind which rises the skylight drum of the operating room amphitheater.

Today the interiors of the east and west wings have been adapted to meet the contemporary administrative demands of the great metropolitan medical center that has grown up around Dr. Bond's eighteenth-century hospital. The public spaces of the central building have been maintained largely as they were in the nineteenth century, and visitors are welcome to tour the library and the operating theater which have been restored.

In 1800 the hospital managers asked famous artist and Philadelphia native son Benjamin West (1738–1820) to donate an allegorical painting of *Christ Healing the Sick*. West agreed, although the painting was not completed and delivered until 1817. A small brick building facing Spruce Street was erected to house the painting, to which admission was charged. By 1841 nearly $20,000 had been raised from fees. The painting now hangs prominently in a public passage between the Pine Street building and the modern Spruce Street building, appropriately at the very heart of America's first hospital.

FIRST BANK OF THE UNITED STATES

(Bank of the United States; Stephen Girard's Bank)
Independence National Historical Park
120 South Third Street
Philadelphia, PA 19106

Samuel Blodget, Jr., architect (?), 1795–1797
James Windrim & Son, architects, 1901–1902
National Historic Landmark, 1987

Not currently open to the public; proposed site of Civil War and Underground Railroad Museum of Philadelphia

On December 6, 1790, Philadelphia became the capital of the United States; it remained the seat of the federal government until May 14, 1800. No sooner had Congress arrived from New York than Secretary of the Treasury Alexander Hamilton submitted his Report on a National Bank, which recommended the incorporation of an institution to "provide sufficient capital to support an extensive circulation" of currency and to "enhance the current price of government obligations and thereby sustain the government's credit." It would also give the new Treasury Department far-reaching powers to administer the nation's finances by restraining the extension of credit by other banks.

Over the strenuous objections of James Madison and Thomas Jefferson—who were suspicious of expanding the central government through implied constitutional powers—the Bank of the United States was given a twenty-year charter. The managers promptly rented Carpenters' Hall (pages 42–47), where the bank remained until a new building was constructed.

The design for the new bank is usually credited to Samuel Blodget, Jr. (1757–1814), the New England-born East India merchant, speculator in Washington real estate, and promoter of schemes that ultimately led him into bankruptcy, imprisonment, and an obscure death. Blodget may also have fancied himself an architect. In 1792 he entered a hastily prepared design for the United

The Third Street façade of the bank is Pennsylvania marble carved by French stonemasons. The lantern over the banking room door held a whale oil lamp, and the foot scrapers were essential conveniences in a age when horses and unpaved streets were common.

States Capitol featuring a tall dome and four porticos, the latter modeled on the Maison Carrée at Nîmes that inspired Thomas Jefferson's design for the Virginia State Capitol. Although invited by the commissioners of the Federal City—who were meeting in Philadelphia—to submit more finished drawings, Blodget appears to have dropped out of the running; he was, however, appointed superintendent for public buildings in 1793.

The First Bank of the United States (1795–1797) is based on the Royal Exchange in Dublin, Ireland. It may be the earliest classical building with a "giant order" marble portico erected in America.

Blodget's design for the new bank—if indeed it is his design—is almost certainly based on the Royal Exchange in Dublin (1769–1779; now Dublin City Hall) designed by Thomas Cooley (1740–1784). The cornerstone was laid in 1795 and the bank moved from Carpenters' Hall in 1797, although work continued on the building until 1800. The completed seven-bay brick building rises three stories with a marble front and Corinthian hexastyle portico supported by fluted columns and echoing pilasters. It may be the first classical building in America with a marble "giant order" portico. While *retardataire* Palladian by British standards, it was for America quite remarkable at the time. As an example of eighteenth-century Philadelphia architecture, the First Bank of the United States should be better known by the public and more widely celebrated by Independence National Historical Park.

Notwithstanding Benjamin Henry Latrobe's negative reaction to Clodius F. LeGrand's mahogany sculpture in the portico tympanum, it is an elaborate masterpiece of eighteenth-century woodcarving and a remarkable survival.

The attribution of the First Bank to Blodget is based on his remark in *Economica* (Washington, D.C., 1806), that "the plan [of the bank] was by the author of this book; but its brick sides are an injurious deviation." As already mentioned, Blodget had been appointed superintendent of public buildings in 1793, and perhaps his claim is based on "superintendence" rather than authorship. Two Irish architects were present in Philadelphia at the time it was designed. The first of these, Christopher Myers (Jr.), announced himself by placing an advertisement in the *Federal Gazette* for November 20, 1795, claiming to have been "regularly bred under his late father [Christopher Myers (1717– 1789)], Architect of the Board of Works in Ireland, and was clerk to Sir William Chambers, architect, for some years." Myers offered his services providing "plans and elevations for houses from the simple cot[tage] to the most superb town or country residence." Apparently he failed to attract Philadelphia clients and returned to Dublin.

Another, more likely candidate is the Irish architect James Hoban (c. 1762–1831), who actually worked on the Dublin Exchange before coming to America in 1785. Today he is chiefly remembered as the architect of the White House and superintending architect of the Capitol of the United States. It is also known that Hoban designed a hotel for Blodget in Washington in 1793 and could easily have supplied the new superintendent of public buildings with a design to be used for the banking house in Philadelphia.

While we may never know how the Dublin Exchange inspired the Bank of the United States, we can be certain about the actual craftsmen who created this dramatic contribution to Philadelphia architecture. The French sculptor Clodius LeGrand appeared in Philadelphia city directories between 1795 and 1801, where he described himself as a woodcarver, guilder, and stonecutter. On December 14, 1797, LeGrand placed an advertisement in the *Philadelphia Aurora* in which he reported, "having just finished the marble colonnade, sculpture, carving, &c of the portico of the new building of the Bank of the United States, they [he and his sons] are ready to contract for any works of their respective professions, from the plainest to the most extensive job of stone cutting; likewise all sorts of sculpture and carving executed in the marble, wood, plaster of Paris or terra cota; also monuments with figures, &c or plain architecture." In 1803 LeGrand secured a letter of introduction from his countryman Stephen Girard and departed Philadelphia for Santo Domingo.

The new bank was widely praised in the popular press. The *Gazette* hailed it as "the first finished building of any consequence wherein taste and knowledge has been displayed in this country." *Claypoole's Advertiser* trumpeted, "This may safely be pronounced the master-piece of Philadelphia, for beauty and grandeur

NK·AND GIRARD NATIONAL BANK SINCE 1832 · ERECTED·1

of architecture. The front is covered entirely with elegant polished marble, decorated with superb specimens of sculpture; and a great piazza [portico] is finished, the top of which is supported by marble pillars of immense size and height." Perhaps it is no surprise that Benjamin Henry Latrobe, who had just come to town to build the nearby Bank of Pennsylvania (pages 3, 74–75), would be unimpressed. "The white marble columns of the bank are full of bluish and yellowish veins," he wrote, "but they have not withstanding, a very beautiful appearance. Sufficient attention has not been paid to the successive heights of the blocks, nor are the joints level. The plain workmanship is well executed. The sculpture is not good." Later he referred to the bank as "only a copy of a European building of indifferent taste, and very defective in its execution." Many critics also complained that only the Third Street façade had been clad in marble, leaving the other three exposed red brick. This is the origin of Blodget's criticism in 1806 that the red brick sides are an "injurious deviation" from the original intent, probably to save on construction costs.

In 1811 the bank's charter expired and was not renewed; individual state banks had long chafed under the restraining hand of the Bank of the United States, which translated into hostility on the floor of Congress. Stephen Girard (pages 110–111), wealthy Philadelphia merchant and largest stockholder of the Bank of the United States, purchased the building, hired most of its staff, and reopened it as Girard's Bank which he operated until his death when the building was rented to a new bank chartered by the Commonwealth of Pennsylvania. In 1901 James Hamilton Windrim (1840–1919), architect of the Masonic Temple (pages 172–179), graduate of Girard College, and long-time architect for the Girard Estate, remodeled the bank interior by removing the original barrel-vaulted banking room ceiling and inserting in its place a circular rotunda topped by a domed skylight. The building ceased to be used as a bank in 1929 and was rented to various tenants. It was acquired as part of Independence National Historical Park in 1955 and the exterior restored, most notably the copper-clad hipped roof. It is presently used for INHP offices, but as this book goes to press plans have been announced to use the building as the Civil War and Underground Railroad Museum of Philadelphia.

The circular Corinthian-columned rotunda that rises within the first and second floors was inserted by architect James Windrim in 1901–1902. The banking room ceiling was originally barrel vaulted. This photograph was taken while the space was being temporarily used for public exhibitions now installed in the nearby Second Bank of the United States.

NEW MARKET

(Head House Square)
Second and Pine Streets
Philadelphia, PA 19106

National Historic Landmark, 1966

City of Philadelphia, Commissioner of Public Property

↑ This view looks north along the New Market stalls on Second Street as restored in the 1960s. Looming in the distance are the Society Hill Towers (1958–1964) by I. M. Pei & Associates.

City residents have always depended on food markets kept stocked by others. This certainly included the first settlers of Philadelphia who looked eagerly to the fertile farms of the West Jersey Quakers just across the Delaware River. From the earliest days of settlement, these farmers were informally allotted space at Front and High (Market) Streets to display their produce. In 1692, a formal market was staked out at Second and High Streets that was open on Wednesday and Saturday. Farmers were forbidden to sell on their way to the market, hucksters who fanned out into the neighborhoods to peddle fresh fruit and vegetables from wagons were not allowed to buy until the market had been open for two hours, and farmers were charged for each animal they brought to be slaughtered on site. (The term shambles—which Philadelphians sometimes applied to the market sheds—originally meant a meat market but came to refer to a slaughterhouse.)

"High Street Market," by William Birch, 1800. This view of the interior of the old market shambles on High (Market) Street gives some idea how the New Market on Second Street would have looked at the end of the eighteenth century. Athenæum of Philadelphia Collection.

In 1709 a town hall was erected in the middle of High Street at Second Street, and the first permanent market sheds with roofs extended westward nearly to Third Street. As shown in the famous "High Street Market" engraving by William Birch, these sheds were modest affairs consisting of brick columns supporting a simple gable roof. Racks with iron hooks were provided for hanging cuts of meat, small game, and fowl. Over the following decades these sheds were extended, reaching Eighth Street by 1816. In the meantime, the original "Jersey Market" extending from Front to Second Street—specializing in fruit and vegetables—was also roofed over, and, in 1822, given a terminal building with a fanciful domed roof bracketed with decorative carved cornucopia. This jumble of sheds extending from Front to Eighth was demolished in the mid-nineteenth century.

As Philadelphia's population expanded south along the Delaware River toward Southwark—the part of the city below Cedar (South) Street—the need for another, more accessible market became obvious. Second Street between Pine and Cedar seemed a likely location, but the typical fifty-foot width of Philadelphia's north-south streets was hardly adequate for market sheds similar to those on High Street. The solution was to purchase a strip of land from individual property owners on both sides of Second Street from Pine to Cedar, which was assembled by 1745. Two investors, Edward Shippen and Joseph Wharton, proposed to erect "Sixteen Stalls in the New Market place,

Viz. [namely] Eight Stalls in Second Street to the Southward of Lombard Street, and Eight Stalls to the Northward of said Lombard street . . . at their own Costs and Charge." The new market would be "Built after the same Modell as the present Stalls in the West Side of the Court house of this City" on High Street. Both Shippen and Wharton were major landowners in the area, and they doubtless thought a new market would enhance property values. They operated the market until the City of Philadelphia bought them out in 1772. Then the Revolution intervened.

The decorative "Jersey Market" terminal at Front and High Streets was erected in 1822. All the High Street Market sheds were demolished in the mid-nineteenth century. Photograph by Thomas S. Hacker. Athenæum of Philadelphia Collection, gift of George Vaux.

There were no changes in the New Market on Second Street until 1795, when the Common Council approved extending the 1745 stalls of the market that were south of Lombard Street and erecting a two-story firehouse crowned by a cupola. This is the Cedar Street "head house" shown in William Birch's engraving "New Market in South Second Street" dating from 1799. Expansion of the Society Hill neighborhood caused the Common Council to take similar action in 1804 by ordering that the market be extended again "in complete uniformity with the part already erected, to within thirty feet of the south line of Pine Street with the addition of two fire engine houses . . . to be built of the same materials as the aforesaid market house." The resulting "head house" that survives today was to accommodate two fire companies and their engines. The second floor room was to be "for the use of such fire companies as may think proper to meet therein." The north wall was to have "an aperture . . . suitable to fix a clock in," and there should be "on the top of said building a cupola sufficiently high and strong, on which to hang an alarm bell."

"New Market in South Second Street," by William Birch & Son, 1799. This view is looking south from Pine Street toward the fire house with cupola on Cedar (South) Street, erected c. 1795 to accommodate the Southwark Hose company. The present "head house" was built on the vacant lot in the foreground in 1804. Athenæum of Philadelphia Collection.

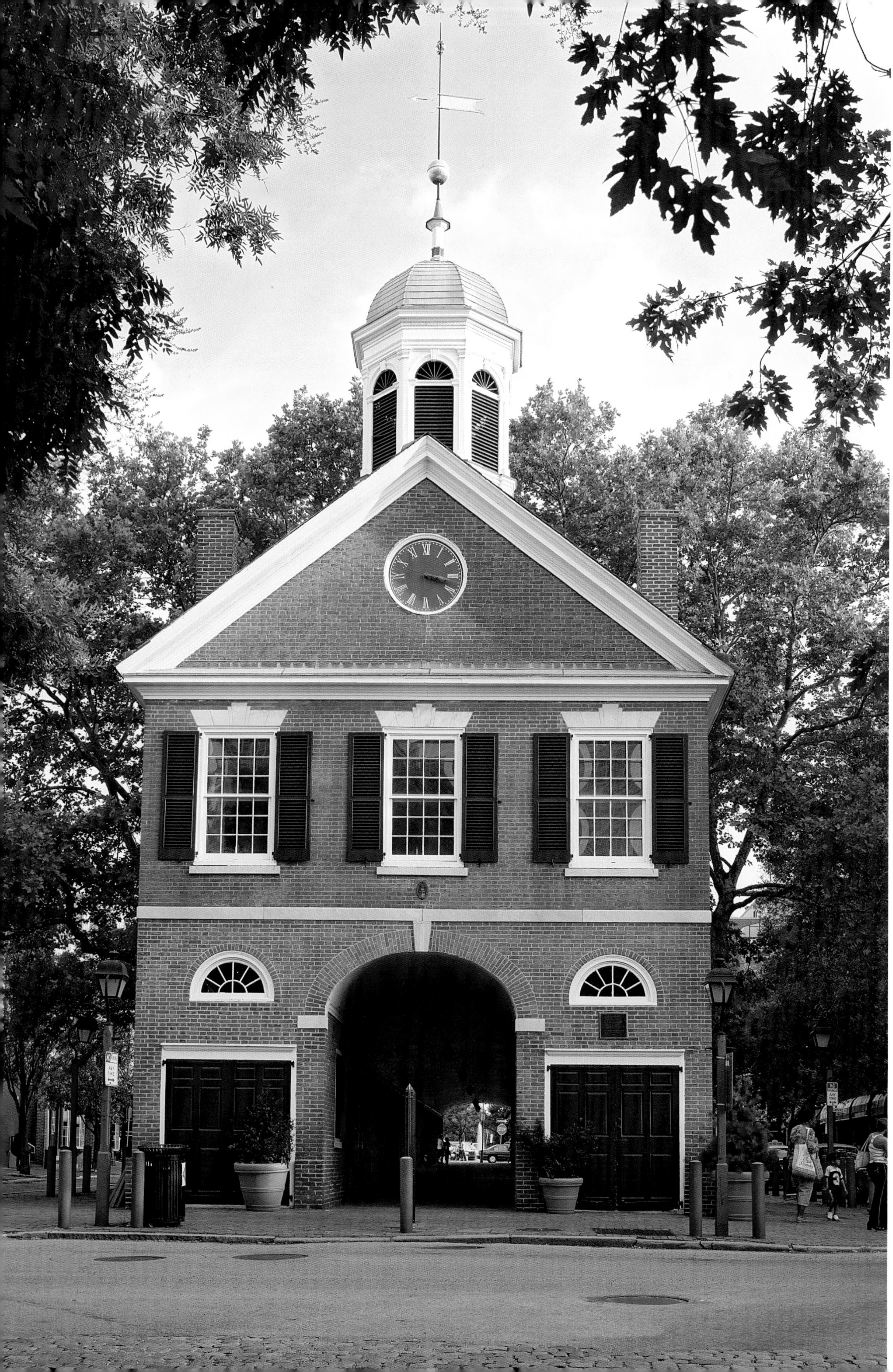

By the mid-nineteenth century the decline of the river ward residential neighborhoods, and changes in marketing and sanitation, caused the Second Street market gradually to decline. The firehouse on Cedar Street dating from 1799 was demolished by 1860. But the stalls south of Lombard survived until 1956, when they were demolished as part of urban renewal. Today the site of those stalls provides parking spaces for busy South Street businesses. Fortunately the original stalls of the 1745 market and the head house of 1804 north of Lombard survived. In 1959 architect G. Edwin Brumbaugh (1890–1983) prepared a plan to restore the section north of Lombard for the Philadelphia Historical Commission. Both the head house and the market stalls—the earliest surviving market structures in America—were restored in the early 1960s. Thirty years later a not-for-profit friends group, The Head House Conservancy, was formed to repair and maintain the structure.

The head house at the north end of New Market was added to the shambles in 1804 "in complete uniformity with the part already erected." The two large doors accommodated the fire engines of Fellowship Engine Co. No. 29 and Hope Hose Co. No. 6.

STEPHEN
WHO ORIGINATED
AND ENDOWED
THIS COLLEGE.

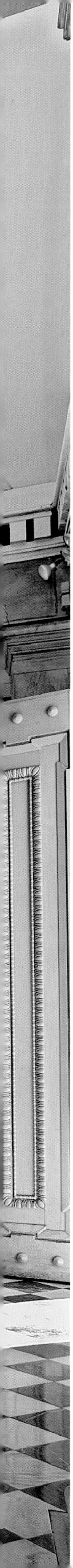

CLASSICAL PHILADELPHIA

Fairmount Water Works

Second Bank of the United States

Eastern State Penitentiary

Dorrance Hamilton Hall, University of the Arts

Walnut Street Theatre

United States Naval Home

Merchants' Exchange

Founder's Hall, Girard College

Atwater Kent Museum

Philadelphia Contributionship for the Insurance of Houses from Loss by Fire

Philadelphia Club

Founder's Hall at Girard College (1833–1847) by Thomas Ustick Walter was called "a perfect, chaste specimen of Grecian architecture." The entrance hall contains the tomb of Stephen Girard.

FAIRMOUNT WATER WORKS

640 Water Works Drive
Philadelphia, PA 19130

Frederick Graff, 1812–1815, 1819–1822
National Historic Landmark, 1976

Telephone for visitor information: 215.685.0723
www.fairmountwaterworks.org

Unlike many other American cities, Philadelphia has never suffered a catastrophic fire, earthquake, or flood. That partly explains why so many historic buildings survive. Our city was, however, visited by a plague of appalling and far-reaching consequence. It struck with near biblical suddenness in August 1793, when Philadelphia was the capital of the new United States and its largest city. The pestilence killed one in ten of her citizens in little more than 100 days. The cause was the female mosquito, *Aëdes aegypti*, whose bite spread yellow fever. Of course, no one at the time knew what caused the deadly contagion, or its re-occurrence in 1798. But some physicians in that age before pathogens were understood suspected that Philadelphia's wells were contaminated by the even more numerous and unregulated cesspools and privies. Clearly a reliable source of fresh, pure water was needed.

For advice on a how to supply that water, the city fathers turned to America's first professional architect and engineer, Benjamin Henry Latrobe (1764–1820),

a recent immigrant from England, where he had worked in the offices of John Smeaton (1724–1792), probably the leading English civil engineer of his time, and S. R. Cockerell (1754–1827), an architect whose work was noted for its powerful classical simplicity. In 1798 Latrobe secured a major commission to design the Bank of Pennsylvania, resulting in America's first Greek Revival building. The following year he designed Sedgeley, a picturesque *cottage orné* on the banks of the Schuylkill River, the first American villa in the Gothic Revival style. Now he would give America another first: a waterworks.

Latrobe recommended that water be pumped from the Schuylkill River and distributed throughout the city in mains of hollowed logs. Motive power would come from a steam engine pumping the water from the river to a reservoir and then via a brick tunnel running to Center Square, the present location of City Hall. At this point a steam engine would raise the water to reservoirs in the pump house, from which elevation it would flow by gravity to the mains. Latrobe's water system went into operation in 1801. Unfortunately, it proved inadequate to the task of supplying the rapidly growing city.

With Latrobe otherwise engaged, Philadelphia's Watering Committee turned to his assistant, architect and engineer Frederick Graff (1774–1847), to improve on his master's innovative—albeit flawed—design. The son and grandson of builders, Graff had served his apprenticeship in Latrobe's office and in 1805 was appointed superintendent of the waterworks. Graff's solution also exploited Schuylkill water, but now it would be raised from the river by steam engines to a three-million-gallon reservoir cut into the rocky heights of Fairmount (now site of the Philadelphia Museum of Art), the highest point near the center of

The restoration of the Fairmount Water Works complex and opening of the Interpretive Center and a restaurant have once again made the site a popular promenade.

"The Water Works, in Centre Square Philadelphia," by William Birch & Son, 1800. Designed by Benjamin Henry Latrobe, the pump house enclosed a steam engine that lifted Schuylkill River water into a reservoir, from which it flowed into the underground mains of America's first municipal water system. Athenæum of Philadelphia Collection.

town. From the Fairmount reservoir, gravity would carry the water throughout the mains already laid under the city streets. Work began on Graff's handsome stucco-over-stone neoclassical pump house at the base of Fairmount in August 1812; its two steam engines went into operation in 1815.

By 1817 Graff's new system was supplying 32 miles of pipe connected to 3,500 houses; Philadelphia quickly gained the reputation as the cleanest city in America. Unfortunately the steam engines were expensive to fuel and maintain.

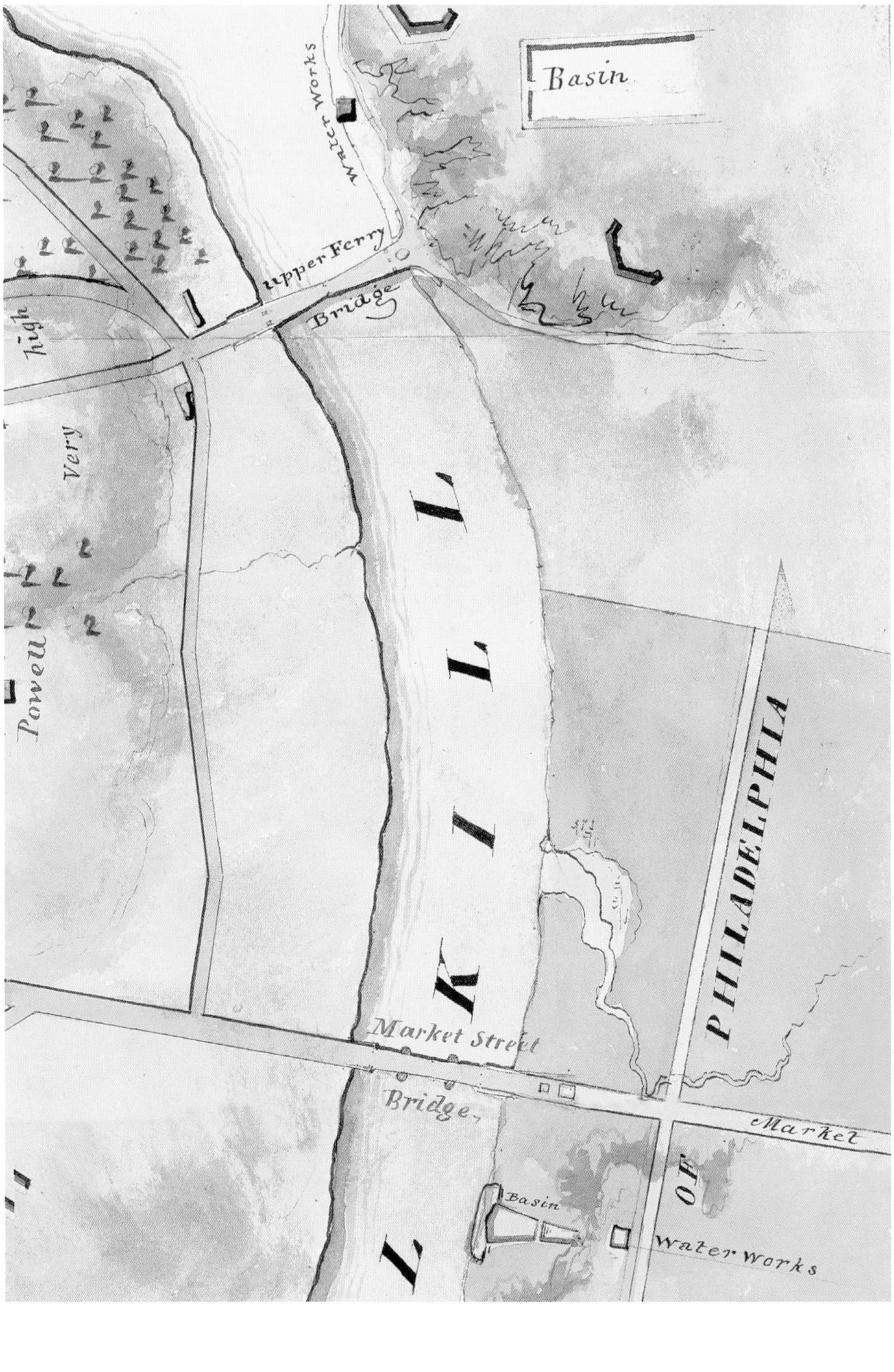

↞ The locations of the Latrobe reservoir ("basin") south of Market Street (1801) and Graff's reservoir ("basin") on Fairmount (1812) are shown on this detail of a military map drawn by William Strickland in 1814. American Philosophical Society Collection.

Graff realized that a hydraulic system using waterwheels would be cheaper—provided the water itself could be harnessed to fill the reservoir. To supply a steady head of water, a 1,250-foot crib dam was constructed across the Schuylkill River. Water was backed up, creating a pool (see Boathouse Row, pages 206–211) that conducted the water into a forebay behind the mill buildings, where it filled the waterwheel buckets, causing them to turn clockwise and empty the water at river level below the dam. Then the rotary motion was converted to reciprocating motion, which operated the pumps to raise the water to the reservoir. Virtually overnight the waterworks became profitable.

Once the decision to convert from steam engine to waterwheel had been made, Graff designed a 238-foot-long mill house that ultimately would contain eight breast waterwheels sixteen to eighteen feet in diameter. The mill house stylistically harmonizes with the neoclassical engine house and creates the handsome architectural composition that rapidly became one of the most published views of nineteenth-century Philadelphia.

Replaced by waterwheels, the steam engines fell silent in 1822 and the engine house became the center of a public garden providing visitors with refreshments. Recognizing the interest in the waterworks, the mill house was

Thomas Birch, *The Fairmount Waterworks*, 1821. Pennsylvania Academy of the Fine Arts, Philadelphia. Bequest of Charles Graff.

designed so the public could be admitted to marvel at the massive waterwheels silently moving the water. One visitor recorded:

> It is impossible to examine these works without paying homage to the science and skill displayed in their design and execution; in these respects no hydraulic works in the Union can compete, nor do we believe they are excelled by any in the world . . . , the whole operation of forcing up daily millions of gallons into the reservoirs on the mount, and thus furnishing in abundance one of the first necessaries of life to an immense population—was performed with less noise than is ordinarily made in working a smith's bellows! The picturesque location, the neatness that reigns in the buildings, the walks around the reservoirs and the grounds at large, with the beauty of the surrounding scenery, render the name of this place singularly appropriate.

To heighten the public appeal of the Fairmount site, the Watering Committee commissioned a variety of fountains and sculptures to adorn the grounds. Two large figures by William Rush, *Allegory of the Waterworks (The Schuylkill Freed)* and *Allegory of the Schuylkill River in Its Improved State (The Schuylkill Chained)*, were also commissioned for the mill house in 1825. (The original carved wood figures, now at the Philadelphia Museum of Art, have been copied and reinstalled in their original locations.) European visitors such as Frances Trollope and Charles Dickens—both highly critical of America—were here impressed by what they saw. Dickens commented in 1840, "Philadelphia is most bountifully

William Rush, sculptor, *Allegory of the Waterworks (Schuylkill Freed)*. Commissioned by the City of Philadelphia, on loan to the Philadelphia Museum of Art. A fiberglass replica of Rush's famous carved wood figure painted white, dating from 1825, has been installed in the original location atop the mill house.

provided with fresh water. . . .The Water-works, which are on a height near the city, are no less ornamental than useful, being tastefully laid out as a public garden, and kept in the best and neatest order."

The rapid expansion of the water system throughout Philadelphia brought previously unknown luxury and comfort to her citizens. Sidney George Fisher recorded in his diary for December 20, 1852,

> My habits now are to rise at 7. I go to my dressing room which is in the back building & is very comfortable, having a bath with hot & cold water & a water closet adjoining, also a sink to carry off waste water & slops, all which are among the modern improvements which add so much to the comfort of life & which are now contained in houses of moderate cost. . . . I take not a cold bath, which is too severe, but make the water from 60 to 65, about the temperature that it is in the summer or early autumn. It is a great luxury, exhilarating & refreshing, & diffuses over the body a fine glow & sensation of health & vigor, and is far preferable to my old fashion of sponging bath which I used because I had no other in the old house.

As the mid-nineteenth century approached, concern over the quality of the water being supplied to Philadelphians prompted the purchase of the Lemon Hill and Sedgeley villas to protect the land above the waterworks from industrial development. Lemon Hill was preserved; Latrobe's innovative Sedgely was demolished, as had been all vestige of his original waterworks design. These acquisitions eventually led to the formation of the Fairmount Park Commission in 1867 and the assembling of the great urban park we know today, mainly to protect Philadelphia's potable water supply.

The eventual introduction of hydraulic turbines caused further additions to the waterworks complex, but the limitations of the site and increasing pollution of the Schuylkill in the late nineteenth century ultimately forced the closure of the Fairmount Water Works in 1909. The mill site was turned into a public aquarium and the reservoirs became the site of the Philadelphia Museum of Art. In the late 1970s a study by the Historic American Engineering Record of the U.S. Department of the Interior helped stimulate public interest in this neglected and decayed National Historic Landmark and its potential value to the city of Philadelphia. Subsequent restoration of the historic complex and development of the Fairmount Water Works Interpretive Center as a partnership of the Fairmount Park Commission and the Philadelphia Water Department has once again made this site and its handsome complex of buildings a major cultural and recreational resource.

Independence National Historical Park
420 Chestnut Street
Philadelphia, PA 19106

William Strickland, architect, 1818–1824
National Historic Landmark, 1987

Telephone for visitor information: 215.597.8974
www.nps.gov/inde/archive/second-bank.html

Americans historically have a love-hate relationship with central banks, a tension tangibly expressed in two landmark buildings within Independence National Historical Park. These extraordinary structures, designed and erected in the early days of our republic, both housed banks intended to serve as the national government's depository and regulator of currency. The First Bank of the United States (pages 60–65), chartered by Congress on the recommendation of Alexander Hamilton, failed to be rechartered in 1811. Without the central bank's restraining hand, the number of local banks rapidly increased. They issued currency of uncertain—and only regional—value while enthusiastically extending inadequately secured credit, causing the entire system to collapse during the War of 1812. To remedy this financial chaos, a new Bank of the United States (the "second bank") was chartered in 1816, again for a term of twenty years. The bank was promptly, although unsuccessfully, challenged on constitutional grounds in *McCulloch v. Maryland* (1819), one of the most famous Supreme Court cases of the nineteenth century, wherein Justice John Marshall famously proclaimed, "the power to tax is the power to destroy."

In the meantime, the directors of the new bank, like those of the first bank, rented Carpenters' Hall for temporary offices and advertised in the *Philadelphia Gazette* (May 12, 1818) for architects to submit "appropriate designs and elevations for a Banking House."

Portrait of William Strickland (1788–1854) by John Neagle (1796–1865), Philadelphia, 1829. In the background is the Second Bank of the United States. Yale University Art Gallery, Mabel Brady Garvan Collection.

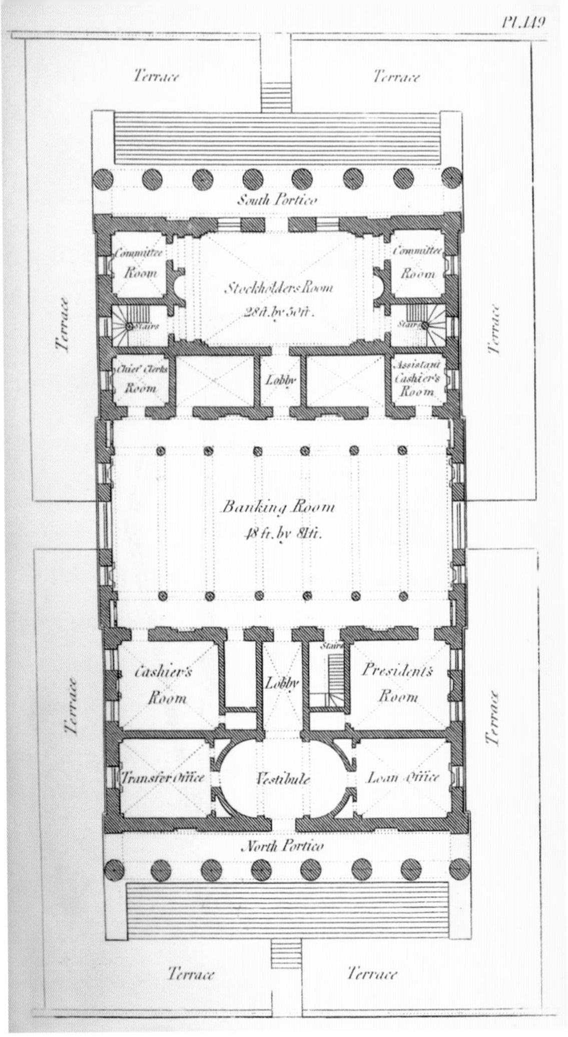

⇷ Original floor plan of the Second Bank provided by William Strickland for an article on the bank that appeared in *The Port Folio* in 1821. Athenæum of Philadelphia Collection.

> The building will be faced with marble, and have a portico on each front, resting upon a basement or platform of such altitude as will combine convenience of ascent with due proportion and effect.

Several architects, including Benjamin Henry Latrobe, perhaps the recent English immigrant John Haviland, and the French immigrant Maximilian Godefroy, submitted designs. But when the winning design was announced, it was from the hand of a young and relatively unknown former apprentice of Latrobe's by the name of William Strickland.

Strickland (1788–1854) was the eldest son of John Strickland, master carpenter. From 1798 to 1801 the elder Strickland had worked on Latrobe's Bank of Pennsylvania; this brought young William—who exhibited a precocious talent for drawing—to Latrobe's attention, leading to his being accepted as an apprentice in 1803. After two years with Latrobe, Strickland supported himself as an artist and draftsman until receiving his first major commission as an architect—the Masonic Hall in Philadelphia (1808; burned 1819). During the War of 1812, he was primarily concerned with defense work, but after the war he secured several commissions, culminating in the Bank of the United States that proved to be a turning point in both his career and the course of American architecture.

Responding to the call for "a chase [chaste] imitation of Grecian Architecture in its simplest and least expensive form"—which certainly implied a preference for the Doric order over the more complex and expensive Ionic or Corinthian orders—Strickland based his design on the Parthenon in Athens that was possibly influenced by Latrobe's similar submission. Whether the idea originated with the master or the pupil is less important than the impact of the bank as a seminal work in the history of the Greek Revival in America. It also established Strickland's position in Philadelphia, both personally and professionally; a growing number of architectural and engineering commissions followed, and he was elected to the American Philosophical Society, the Athenæum of Philadelphia, the Franklin Institute, and the Musical Fund Society. In 1826 his design for the United States Naval Home (pages 100–103) was accepted, as were his designs for the First Unitarian Church (1828), the Arch Street Theater (1828), the United States Mint (1829; page 10), and the Merchants' Exchange (1832; pages 104–109). In addition, he recreated the steeple of Independence Hall (1828), one of the earliest examples of restoration in America (page 30)

By the mid-1830s, William Strickland had done more than any other architect to shape the look of Philadelphia; from the Delaware to the Schuylkill his

South façade of the Second Bank of the United States by William Strickland, 1818–1824. The identical north and south façades consist of two-story Doric octastyle porticos—eight fluted columns in a row supporting the pediment running the full width of the building. The marble came from Montgomery County, Pennsylvania, and the mason was Philadelphian John Struthers (1786–1851), whose firm was responsible for many of Strickland's most important buildings.

monumental marble buildings housing our city's leading citizens, congregations, and institutions could be encountered along the streets of Center City. At a banquet celebrating the completion of the Philadelphia Merchants' Exchange in 1833, this toast was offered in Strickland's honor, "He will realize the boast of the ancient emperor [Augustus speaking of Rome]. He found us living in a city of brick, and he will leave us in a city of marble."

Ironically, the Exchange would be his last major Philadelphia building; Strickland was encountering serious competition. While he may have benefited from Robert Mills's move to Washington and John Haviland's bankruptcy, Strickland was losing major commissions to younger men. His former student Thomas Ustick Walter (pages 110–115) and the immigrant Scot John Notman (pages 132–143) took the Girard College, Laurel Hill, and Athenæum commissions over Strickland's submissions, for example. Other projects, such as a grand library and museum complex to house the Academy of Natural Sciences, the Athenæum, the Library Company, and the Philosophical Society failed to mature. Then, during the depression following the financial collapse of 1837, a period when building virtually ceased in Philadelphia, Strickland accepted an offer to design and build the Tennessee State Capitol in Nashville, where he enjoyed a revitalized career and lived out the final years of his life. He is buried in the Tennessee State Capitol.

But for now let us look at the Second Bank of the United States. The most obvious ancient Greek attributes of Strickland's design for the bank are the north and south porticos in the Doric order based on engraved plates of the Parthenon from James Stuart and Nicholas Revett, *Antiquities of Athens* (London, 1762–1816). Strickland is reported to have said of this "bible" of American neoclassicism, "the student of architecture need go no further than the *Antiquities of Athens* as a basis for design."

The heart of the building is the handsome banking room, 81 feet long and 48 feet wide, that runs east and west and is dramatically lined with parallel rows of six fluted marble columns in the Ionic order. The ceiling is a barrel vault and at each end large Palladian windows echo the vaulting and provide a flood of natural light. This dramatic space survives largely as designed. The bank was completed in 1824 at a cost of nearly half a million dollars, a significant sum for the time.

Nicholas Biddle, who will be encountered later in the context of Girard College (pages 110–115), became a director and then third president of the bank. Given his well-documented role in shaping the final design of Founder's Hall at Girard College and the renovation of Andalusia, his country villa on the Delaware River—both in the Greek Revival style—it is tempting to look for

FOUNDED A.D. MDCCXCV.
SCIENCE

Biddle's hand in Strickland's design of the Second Bank. However, Biddle was not a director of the bank when the call for submissions was published in May 1818, nor when the final design was selected by the directors in September. He became a director in January 1819, and the cornerstone was laid on April 19, 1819, so it is unlikely he had any official role in shaping the competition or refining the design. Nonetheless, Biddle must have agreed with the directors' decision; he was Philadelphia's most vocal advocate for classical architecture—having visited Greece in 1806 and published articles by advocates of Greek architecture in *The Port Folio*, which he edited.

Unfortunately for Biddle, who became president of the Bank of the United States in 1823, the prejudices that brought down the first bank gained passionate advocates during the presidency of Andrew Jackson in the 1830s. As summarized by historian Bray Hammond, the Jacksonians disliked the bank for five reasons.

> Wall Street's jealousy of Chestnut Street, the business man's dislike of the federal Bank's restraint upon bank credit, the politician's resentment at the Bank's interference with states' rights, popular identification of the Bank with the aristocracy of business, and the direction of agrarian antipathy away from banks in general to the federal Bank in particular.

The second bank, like its predecessor, failed to be rechartered. Biddle was able to secure a state charter from the Commonwealth of Pennsylvania, but that bank failed in 1841 during the financial panic that began in 1837. Strickland's handsome building, one of the finest and most widely imitated examples of Greek Revival architecture in America, remained vacant until acquired by the United States Customs Service in 1845. It served as the Custom House for the Port of Philadelphia until the agency moved to the new Custom House designed by Ritter and Shay in 1935 (pages 258–263). The National Park Service took over the building from the Treasury Department in 1939, eventually using it as an exhibition gallery. In 2002 the Park Service launched an extensive restoration and reinterpretation of the building, which was completed in late 2004. The Second Bank now houses a permanent exhibition inspired by Charles Willson Peale's museum that once occupied the long gallery of Independence Hall. Writing in the *Wall Street Journal*, critic Ada Louise Huxtable praised the new installation as expressing the early national period's "highest aspirations of symbolism and style. The combination of place and people magically erases time, giving powerful presence and meaning to the past. We are in their world, not ours, immersed in a reality that puts all of Disney's patriotic animatronic fakes to shame."

→ The original colors of the banking room have been restored, and this dramatic space now contains a permanent exhibition devoted primarily to early national period portraits of the founding fathers, mainly by Charles Willson Peale.

(Cherry Hill Penitentiary)

2124 Fairmount Avenue, Philadelphia, PA 19130

John Haviland, architect, 1822–1836
National Historic Landmark, 1965

Telephone for visitor information: 215.236.3300
www.EasternState.org

↑ The front building or "keepers' house" of Eastern State Penitentiary was designed by John Haviland in the Gothic Style he called "Anglo Norman" (1822–1836). The entrance that obscures Haviland's Gothic arch was added in 1937–1938.

If asked to name a famous prison, most Americans might come up with Alcatraz in San Francisco Bay, Sing Sing at Ossining, New York, the Bastille in Paris, or the French penal colony off Devil's Island in French Guiana. It is doubtful that many would mention Cherry Hill in Philadelphia. Yet in the pantheon of world prisons, Philadelphia's Eastern State Penitentiary, as it is now known, is among the most influential American buildings of the nineteenth century. And how this came to be is a fascinating story that deserves to be better known.

Before the late eighteenth century, corporal punishment was common, even for what today would be considered minor offenses. At the time of Philadelphia's founding, a person could be executed for nearly two hundred crimes in England. Those unfortunates who were arrested to await trial and sentencing would be confined under conditions of squalor and filth; men, women, and children together, often without bedding, heat, or running water—and where they were likely to be infected with typhus-like "gaol fever." Only gradually was imprisonment itself, rather than sanguinary execution, mutilation, or transportation in servitude to climates likely to ensure a brutish early death, seen as punishment.

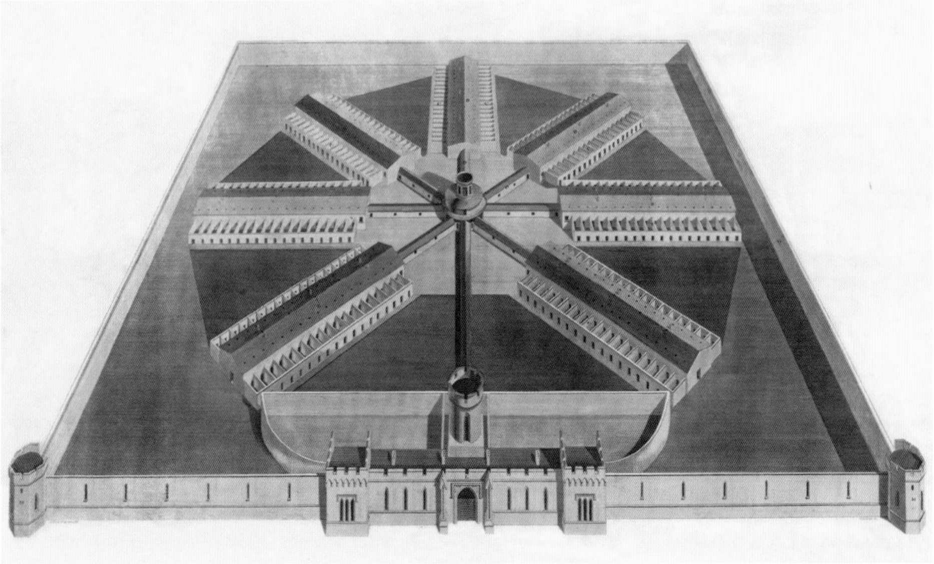

"Bird's Eye View of the New State Penitentiary, Now Erecting Near Philadelphia," by C. G. Childs, c. 1829. The radial "hub-and-spoke" plan would make the building one of the most influential prisons in the world. Free Library of Philadelphia, Print and Picture Collection.

To William Penn and other early Quakers, imprisonment came to be viewed as a humane alternative to corporal punishment, even though Philadelphia's overcrowded Old Stone Prison at Third and High (Market) Streets was considered a "sink of wickedness." Consequently, the Pennsylvania Assembly authorized the purchase of a prime lot of ground on Walnut Street opposite the State House yard (Independence Square) in 1774 on which to erect "a new Gaol, Work-House and House of Correction." The master builder Robert Smith (1722–1777) was selected for this important civic project (pages 4, 45). The Walnut Street Prison was available just in time to become infamous for the inhumane housing of American prisoners captured at the battles of the Brandywine and Germantown, who died in large numbers from starvation, maltreatment, and want of medical care during the winter of 1777–1778.

Following the war—and encouraged by the new Philadelphia Society for Alleviating the Miseries of Public Prisons—the Commonwealth passed an Act to Reform Penal Laws (1790) to encourage the introduction of solitary confinement, as well as separation of men from women and debtors from felons. No matter how well intended these reforms, the Walnut Street Prison was simply inadequate to cope with overcrowding, let alone to maintain solitary confinement. By 1820 the prison population gathered from all across Pennsylvania had reached more than eight hundred inmates. Pressed by the Prison Society (as it came to be called), two new prisons were authorized, a Western State Penitentiary at Pittsburgh in 1818 and an Eastern State Penitentiary in 1821.

The site selected for the new penitentiary at Philadelphia was a cherry orchard north of the city; henceforth the facility would popularly be known as Cherry Hill. Here inmates would be kept in solitary confinement, a concept in

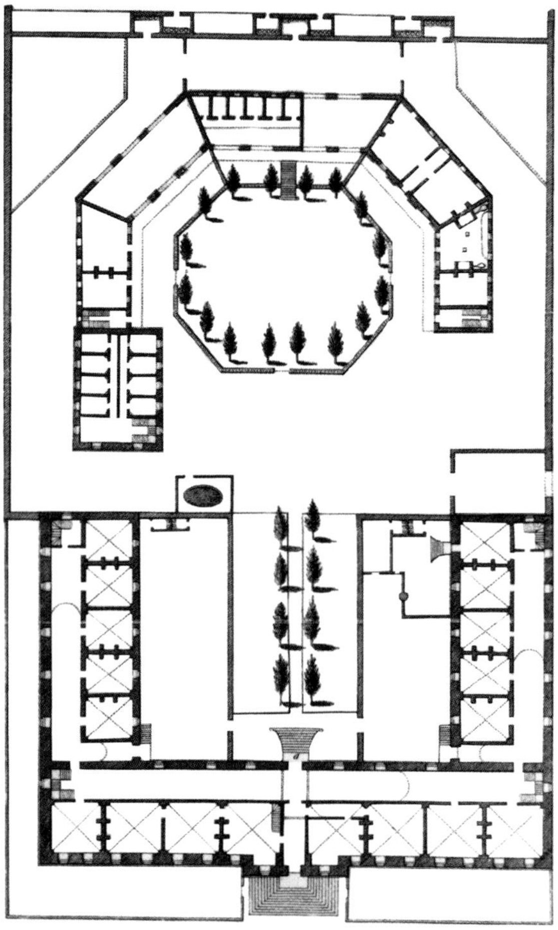

Plan of the Walnut Street Prison, by Joseph Bowes. The prison was designed and constructed by master builder Robert Smith, 1774–1775, and expanded in an effort to provide solitary cells and workshops around a central courtyard, 1798. Athenæum of Philadelphia Collection.

the penal code much favored by the Quaker reformers of the Prison Society and which would come to be known as the "Pennsylvania system." According to Alexis de Tocqueville, who studied American prisons, "thrown into solitude . . . [the prisoner] reflects. Placed alone, in view of his crime, he learns to hate it; and if his soul be not yet surfeited with crime, and thus have lost all taste for any thing better, it is in solitude, where remorse will come to assail him." Thus the prisoner, penitent of his antisocial behavior, could hopefully be returned to civil society.

To provide healthy, secure, and solitary cells for large numbers of prisoners placed unusual demands on the architect. John Haviland (1792–1852) ultimately was awarded the commission for a radial, or hub-and-spoke, plan based largely on the latest British prison designs. Before migrating to America he had studied with James Elmes (1782–1862) who was already designing prisons influenced by the writings of the British reformer John Howard (1726–1790) whose commentary on British and European prisons had also motivated Philadelphia prison reformers. The hub-and-spoke plan, Haviland remarked, would promote "*watching*, *convenience*, *economy* and *ventilation*." The original plan called for an octagonal center (the "hub") connected to seven cellblocks (the "spokes") with double-loaded corridors, that is, with cells off both sides, each having its own exercise yard. Cherry Hill opened in 1829 with three cellblocks designed to confine 250 prisoners; by the time it closed in 1970 there would be fourteen cellblocks accommodating 900 prisoners.

The exterior style of a solitary penitentiary, in the words of the building commissioners, "should exhibit as much as possible great strength and convey to the mind a cheerless blank indicative of the misery which awaits the unhappy being who enters within its walls." Haviland favored the castellated Gothic Style for the front building, with massive crenelated towers pierced by lancet windows and a central entrance with a massive wrought-iron portcullis and double oak doors studded with iron rivets. The psychological message, while not quite Dante's "All hope abandon ye who enter here," was undoubtedly intended to be grim.

John Haviland was on his way to becoming a successful Philadelphia architect by the time he won the Cherry Hill commission over William Strickland (see pages 81–83). But at the peak of his career Haviland was nearly brought down by a fatal combination of bad luck and poor judgment. He began to speculate in his own projects, most notably commercial arcades in Philadelphia (1825–1828)

One of the two-story cellblock corridors. The building was originally designed for seven single-story cellblocks, but the demand for additional cells dictated two-story blocks. Ultimately there were fourteen cellblocks within Haviland's original walls.

and New York (1826–1827) and an ill-conceived amusement park called the Labyrinthine Garden (1828). Threatened by bankruptcy, Haviland diverted funds to cover some of his debts from the Naval Hospital (1826–1833) at Port Nelson, Virginia. These monies proved insufficient for his needs, and Haviland was forced into bankruptcy and full disclosure. He would never secure another major federal commission. His career passed under a cloud in Philadelphia.

Elsewhere Haviland's reputation as a designer of prisons brought him important commissions. At the New Jersey Penitentiary (1833–1836) he again used the radial plan developed for the Eastern State Penitentiary, and he introduced Egyptian motifs that also appeared at the New York City Halls of Justice and House of Detention (the "Tombs," 1835–1838). Haviland's reputation as a designer of prisons also secured him prison commissions for Missouri, Rhode Island, and Arkansas.

Ultimately the Pennsylvania system of solitary confinement proved to be a failure, but Haviland's radial plan used at Cherry Hill and then at the New Jersey Penitentiary became the most influential American building on other continents. Governments as far ranging as China, Russia, Brazil, and Prussia sent delegations to examine Cherry Hill. As late as the mid-twentieth century, radial hub-and-spoke prisons were still being erected throughout the world.

Eastern State Penitentiary closed in 1970, and was virtually abandoned until stabilization and preservation began in 1991. In the mid-1990s the penitentiary opened for public tours on a regular schedule with interpretive exhibitions and trained guides, and the World Monument Fund placed the site on its list of the one hundred most important endangered landmarks in the world. An extensive program of stabilization, preservation, and public programming is ongoing and Cherry Hill has become a major tourist attraction.

Central to the Pennsylvania system was solitary confinement in cells such as this unrestored example. Late eighteenth-century prison reformers favored solitary confinement, but not all visitors agreed. Charles Dickens called it "rigid, strict, and hopeless . . . , cruel and wrong."

DORRANCE HAMILTON HALL, UNIVERSITY OF THE ARTS

(Pennsylvania Institution for the Deaf and Dumb)
320 South Broad Street
Philadelphia, PA 19102

John Haviland, architect, 1824–1825
National Register of Historic Places, 1971

Telephone for visitor information: 800.616.ARTS
www.uarts.edu

Many Philadelphia landmarks are monuments to the city's heritage of philanthropy. Pennsylvania Hospital, Girard College, and the Institute of the Pennsylvania Hospital buildings immediately come to mind. The Pennsylvania Institution for the Deaf and Dumb building is less likely to be recognized because the handsome classical temple at Broad and Pine Streets was sold in 1893 to the Pennsylvania Museum and School of Industrial Art and then in 1964 to the Philadelphia College of Art, and is now known as the Dorrance Hamilton Hall of the University of the Arts.

The Pennsylvania School for the Deaf—as it is now known—was founded in 1820 and chartered by the Commonwealth as a charitable institution "to reclaim the deaf and dumb" by founding "an asylum and school in the city of Philadelphia, where the children . . . labouring under the privation of the faculty of speech are maintained and educated." Like most newly established institutions, the school occupied various rented houses for its first years of existence. In 1824, however, the directors purchased the northwest corner of Broad and Pine Streets and engaged John Haviland to design a building, which

↟ The University of the Arts now occupies John Haviland's building on the Avenue of the Arts.

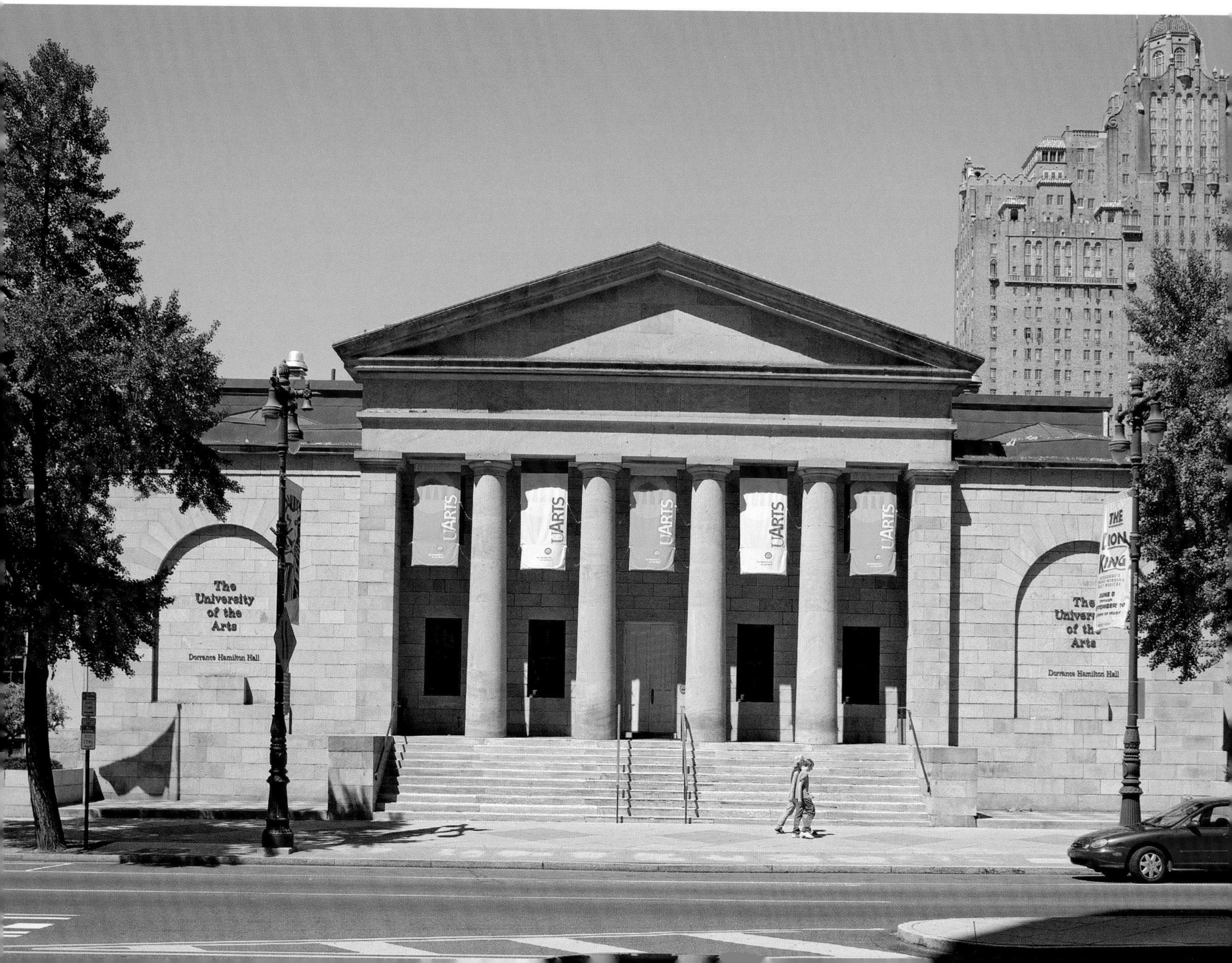

was completed by the end of 1825. English-born and trained, Haviland had established an office in Philadelphia by 1818, and following the publication of his *Builder's Assistant* (Philadelphia, 1818–1821) began to secure important projects, including First Presbyterian Church (1820), Eastern State Penitentiary (1822), and Saint Andrew's Episcopal Church (1822). Just as the Pennsylvania Institution for the Education of the Deaf and Dumb was being completed he was awarded the Franklin Institute commission (pages 116–119). These years would mark the high point of his career, making him one of the most influential architects in Philadelphia.

According to Haviland's extensive notebooks, which survive at the University of Pennsylvania, he worked through six different designs for the school, finally settling on a plan in the shape of an E. The foundations were laid in May 1824 and the building completed in fall 1825 at a cost of $80,000. The archaic Greek Doric portico (known as the "center building") is flanked by pavilions that are exactly proportional, the entire composition stretches 100 feet on Broad Street, the colonnaded portico is 50 feet wide, and each of the flanking astylar pavilions is 25 feet wide. The wings of Haviland's design project 92 feet

John Haviland's perspective view of the Pennsylvania Institution for the Deaf and Dumb, Broad and Pine Streets, Philadelphia, c. 1824. Athenæum of Philadelphia Collection.

Graduates
UARTS
UARTS
UARTS
hi mom!
LOVE REDEEMS BEAUTY REVIVES
push it
BANG!
PLAYER
CHEESE
yo meat HOOK!
POW
402 Pine
MAY THE FORCE BE WITH YOU
LIVE THE 4TH
LOYOLA DONS
UARTS VIDEO
MAKE IT RAIN
BE free!
From VA Jazz Dance To PA 2008!
Mexico
DO YOU!
NILES
GIMMEGIMME MT!
C-TOWN ROCKS
It Don't Mean A Thing If It Ain't Got That "DING"! ~MT '09

to the west behind the pavilions. These would eventually be extended to 176 feet and a second story added. A chapel occupied the courtyard between the wings to complete the E plan. Two small pavilions would also be added to either side of the façade.

Rapid expansion of the school dictated the need for even more space by the 1870s. Efforts to find an appropriate suburban location failed, and the directors opted instead to erect a large, utilitarian addition stretching from Haviland's building along Pine Street to Fifteenth Street designed by Frank Furness (1874–1875). By 1890, however, the directors had decided to move to a sprawling campus in Mount Airy. Following the relocation in 1893, the Haviland-Furness complex was sold to the Pennsylvania Museum and School of Industrial Art. This organization had been founded in 1876 in response to the Centennial Exhibition and eventually separated into the Philadelphia Museum of Art (pages 278–283) and the Philadelphia College of Art, the latter organization assuming full responsibility for the historic buildings in 1964. Fourteen years later the Philadelphia College of Art and the Philadelphia College of the Performing Arts joined to become the Philadelphia College of Arts, which was granted university status in 1987.

Every other year the class of students gather in the courtyard to have their photograph taken.

WALNUT STREET THEATRE

825 Walnut Street
Philadelphia, PA 19107-5107

John Haviland, architect, 1828–1829; John M. Dickey, restoration architect, 1970–1972
National Historic Landmark, 1962

Telephone for visitor information: 215.574.3550
www.wstonline.org

American theater history begins in Philadelphia, although the first public performance by a company of actors in 1724 was not actually in the town but in the southern liberty known as Southwark, the better to circumvent protests by various religious denominations against theatrical productions. In 1749 Messrs. Thomas Kean and Walter Murray were able to produce Joseph Addison's *Cato, a Tragedy* within the town limits. This performance was staged in a warehouse belonging to a future mayor, William Plumsted. A decade later, the Society Hill Theater, a modest frame structure, made its appearance on Cedar (South) Street, but after a brief season was forced to close. Not until 1766 was the Southwark Theater, the first permanent performance space in Philadelphia—and the first in the English colonies—erected on Cedar Street west of Fourth

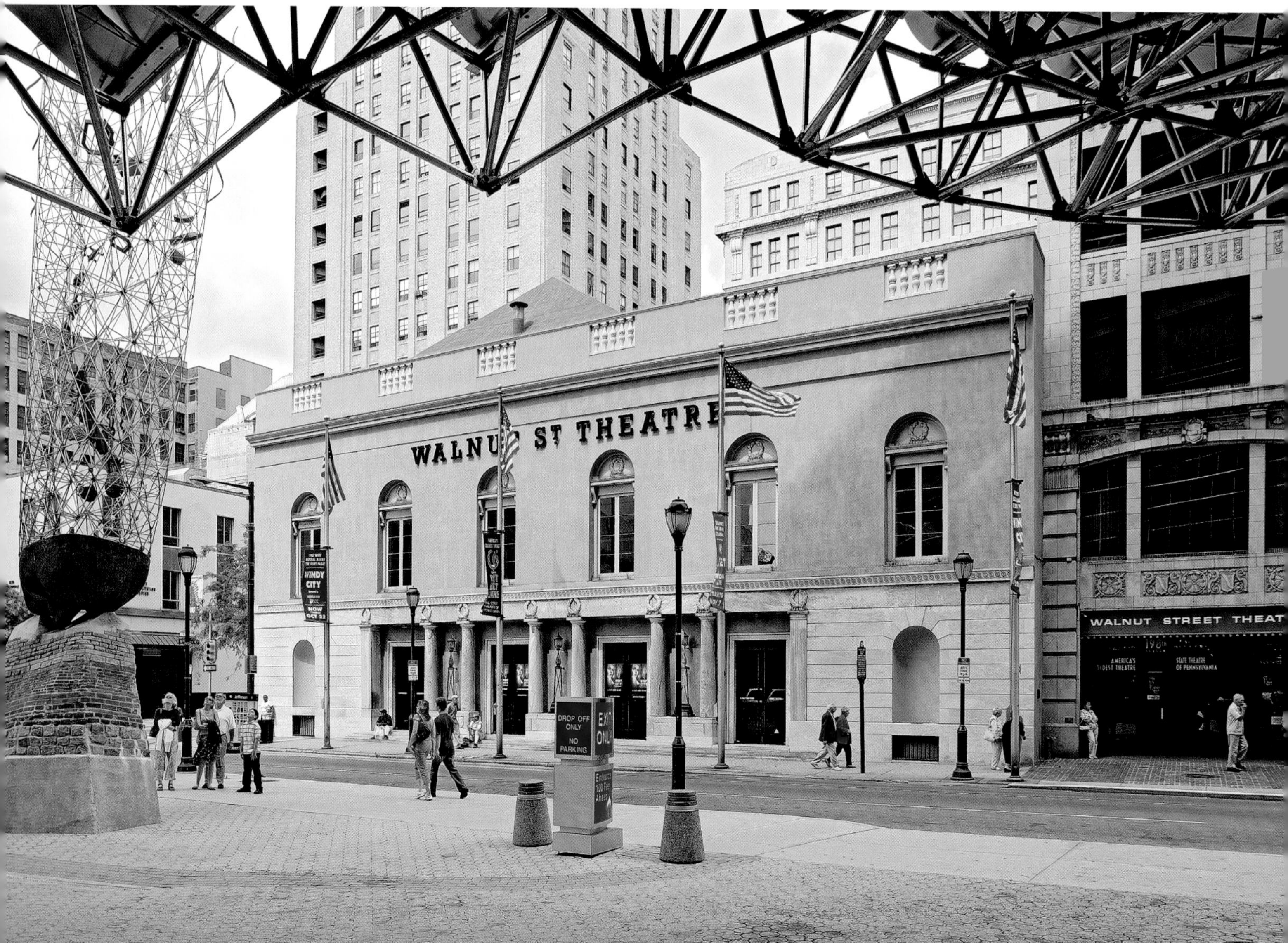

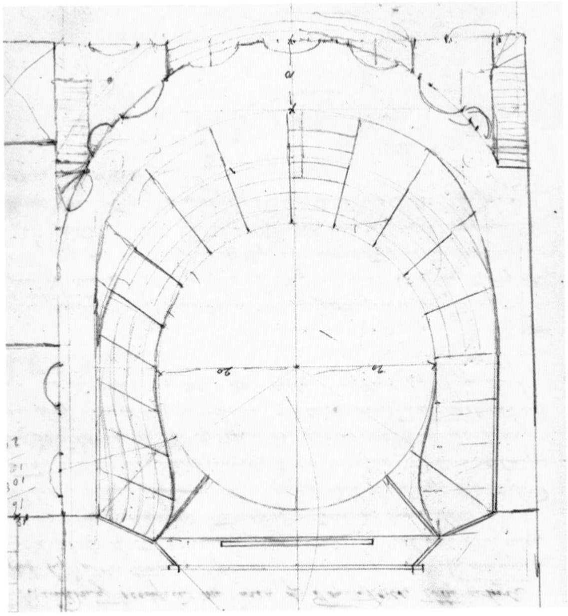

John Haviland's design sketch for the interior of the Walnut Street Theatre (c. 1828). Rare Book Collection, Van Pelt Library, University of Pennsylvania.

Street by David Douglass; it avoided the laws prohibiting theater performances by being on the *south side of the street* and arguably "out of town." The Southwark continued to function as a legitimate theater until the early nineteenth century.

Prohibitory acts against theaters were not repealed until after the Revolution, permitting the construction of a new theater on Chestnut Street (1791–1794, burned 1820; reopened 1822, demolished 1855) near Independence Hall. On the southwest corner of Sixth and Chestnut Streets, directly across from the Chestnut Street Theater, was Rickett's Amphitheatre (1795; burned 1799), where both circus acts and plays were performed. The Walnut Street Theatre, now celebrated as the oldest continuously operating theater in the English-speaking world, also began as a circus, opening its large elliptical arena for equestrian and acrobatic exhibitions—including chariot races—on February 2, 1809, under the name the New Circus. A stage for such theatrical embellishments as historical melodramas and patriotic pantomimes was added to the north in 1811. Most of this disappeared when the owners decided in 1828 to hire John Haviland, the architect of three other landmarks discussed in this book: Eastern State Penitentiary (pages 86–91), Dorrance Hamilton Hall, University of the Arts (pages 92–95) and the building now occupied by the Atwater Kent Museum (pages 116–119). As reported in the popular periodical known as *The Casket*, Haviland transformed the "large old dilapidated building . . . into one of the most imposing, elegant and convenient dramatic temples ever seen." The circus ring became an auditorium with balconies in a horseshoe arrangement as shown in his sketch reproduced here.

The Walnut Street Theatre as it appears today. John Haviland's façade was recreated by restoration architect John Dickey c. 1971.

HESNUT STREET THEATRE
MELODEON
CELEBRATED
TROUPE
DANCERS
SHOOTING GALLERY
SHAKSPEARE
BOWLING
SALOON
MELODEON!
FULL HOUSES
EVERY EVENING
DANCERS
TROUPE
DANCERS
EVERY
EVENING
LAST NIGHT
JULIA DALY
FAINT HEART
16
STRING JACK

Throughout subsequent decades other architects were engaged to update the theater, including the insertion of storefronts at the ground floor level and the suspension of an electric motion-picture-house projecting marquee sign. These excrescences were swept away in a 1920–1921 renovation by architect William H. Lee (1884–1971), whose successful career included several theaters and academic buildings for Temple University, Franklin and Marshall College, and Eastern Baptist College (now Eastern University). Lee removed the storefronts, marquee, and disfiguring fire escapes from the Walnut Street façade. While not a restoration, Lee's work certainly respected Haviland's original design. On the interior, however, all vestiges of Haviland's work disappeared.

From the 1920s to 1969, when the building was purchased by the public-spirited Haas Community Funds, the Walnut Street Theatre remained an important legitimate venue managed by the Shubert Brothers. But fifty years had taken a toll. Consequently, the interior was renovated to meet the needs of a modern performance hall, and the Haviland exterior was returned as closely as possible to its classical appearance in 1828 by restoration architect John M. Dickey (1911–1990). The renovation/restoration has assured that this National Historic Landmark will continue to function well into the twenty-first century, claiming to be "the oldest living Theater in the English-speaking world."

The first major theater building erected in Philadelphia after the Revolution was the celebrated Chestnut Street Theater near Independence Hall—variously known as the New Theater, Old Drury, and the Philadelphia Theater (1791–1794). It burned in 1820 and was redesigned as shown here by architect William Strickland and reopened in 1822 (demolished 1855). The figural sculptures depicting Tragedy and Comedy—which survive—are by William Rush. Athenæum of Philadelphia Collection.

UNITED STATES NAVAL HOME

(United States Naval Asylum)
2420 Grays Ferry Avenue,
Philadelphia, PA 19146

William Strickland, architect of Biddle Hall (1826–1833), Governor's Residence and Surgeon's Residence (1844)
National Historic Landmark, 1976

Private residential development

Painful memories of the Revolutionary War had hardly faded when the newly established United States found itself drawn into armed conflict with its former French allies. Their privateers were seizing American ships, and the United States had no standing navy to defend its ports and merchant shipping. Congress, meeting in Philadelphia, authorized the president to acquire, arm, and man naval squadrons to harry the privateers. Realizing that a navy sent in harm's way meant casualties, a Board of Commissioners of Naval Hospitals was eventually created to buy or build hospitals, one of which was to be an asylum for "decrepit and disabled naval officers, seamen, and marines." It was to design such a facility that the commissioners engaged architect William Strickland in 1826.

In addition to having completed the highly visible Bank of the United States (pages 80–85), Strickland had recently returned from a tour of the United Kingdom as an agent of the Pennsylvania Society for the Promotion of Internal Improvement. His *Reports on Canals, Railways, Roads and Other Subjects* (Philadelphia, 1826) had just been published and widely distributed, especially among departments of the federal government. It also didn't hurt that his good friend, the East Indian trader-turned-philanthropist Robert Ralston (1761–1836), wrote to the secretary of the navy on November 1, 1826, recommending Strickland. "Three large buildings," Ralston remarked,

↓ Lithographed view of the Naval Asylum by John Casper Wild (Philadelphia, 1838). Athenæum of Philadelphia Collection.

> the Orphan Asylum, the Indigent Widows' and Single Women's Asylum, and the Mariners Church have been constructed and erected under his direction, in each of which, I have had to make all the payments, and consequently have derived information which enables me to bear testimony to the skill, good judgment, punctuality, and fidelity of Mr. Strickland.

What more could a client hope for? Strickland submitted his estimate on Christmas Day, 1826, and was awarded the commission.

The land selected for the new Naval Asylum was in Passyunk, the site of a colonial-era Schuylkill River villa formerly owned by the prominent Quaker merchant James Pemberton (1723–1809) (for the Schuylkill villas, see *Historic Houses*, pages 60–70). The Navy purchased the villa and about twenty-three acres, and the asylum cornerstone was laid on April 3, 1827. On that occasion, Commodore William Bainbridge remarked, "A home thus will be established for the faithful tar who has been either worn out or maimed in fighting the battles of his country. A comfortable harbor will be secured, where he may safely moor and ride out the ebb of life, free from the cares and storms by which he has been previously surrounded."

The resulting three-part, three-story building stretches 385 feet parallel to Grays Ferry Avenue, set back approximately 200 feet from an iron fence. The central block is dominated by a pure Greek Revival pedimented, octastyle portico (that is, eight columns across the front). Strickland was again inspired by the drawings of Athenian antiquity he first exploited at the Bank of the United States, but here he adopted an Ionic order based on a small temple on the banks of the Ilissus, a stream that flowed through Athens, published by Stuart and Revett in the eighteenth century. Symmetrically placed to either side of the central block are two dormitory wings with open verandas—or piazzas as they were typically called in Philadelphia—across the back and front that are supported by iron columns, an early and innovative example of this material used structurally in America. The plan provided for 180 dormitory rooms "each of which is well lighted and ventilated, being calculated for the reception and accommodation of about four hundred men." This structure would later be named Biddle Hall after the first governor of the Naval Asylum, Commodore James Biddle, who supervised the institution from 1838 to 1842.

Fireproof masonry construction was used throughout with arched, barrel, and groin vaulting rather than the cheaper and vulnerable wood framing that was still common at the time. (When the building was set on fire by an arsonist in 2003, only the wood roof rafters burned.) The basement was granite, and the upper floors and portico were Pennsylvania marble shaped and erected by

William Strickland's United States Naval Asylum (1827–1833) was renamed the United States Naval Home in 1889. It has been converted for private residential use as part of a gated community called Naval Square, developed by Toll Brothers Inc.

John Struthers (pages 108–109), who had worked with Strickland on the Bank of the United States and would collaborate with him on several future projects.

Strickland originally estimated the cost at $118,760, including $11,520 for the eight Ionic marble columns. But delays in navy appropriations slowed construction through 1828 and into 1829. The building was not occupied until the close of 1833. Meanwhile the amount paid for goods and services increased and change orders pushed costs higher. When the Board of Commissioners of Naval Hospitals complained, Strickland responded in phrases that clients ranging from ancient Thebes to the modern Pentagon would recognize. "It very rarely happens in the construction of public works of this kind that some excess beyond the estimated cost does not take place; in this case it is owing eventually to a strong desire to produce not only durability, but a suitable and defined architectural finish." He would later say that the Naval Asylum cost less "than is required to build and fit out a frigate." When the building was ready for occupancy, the total cost had ballooned to $276,332.

Strickland continued to be involved at the Naval Asylum, and in 1844 he designed two residences on the grounds set equidistant to either side of Biddle Hall to house the governor and the surgeon. Both are simple, late classical, two-story structures stuccoed over brick with verandas supported by cast-iron pillars.

During the Civil War the demand for a naval hospital overwhelmed the available space within Biddle Hall, prompting a call for the construction of a dedicated facility on the grounds designed by the Philadelphia architect John McArthur, Jr. (1823–1890), who would later crown a long and successful career with Philadelphia's City Hall (pages 180–185). McArthur was an obvious choice to design the hospital that would be known as Laning Hall; he had designed and erected twenty-four temporary hospitals as architect for the Quartermaster General's Department in Philadelphia during the late war, after which he became architect of the Navy and in 1871 superintendent of all federal buildings under construction in the city. By this time contemporary taste had turned against the Greek Revival Style. One navy doctor referred to Strickland's building in 1883 as being "in the bastard classic style which was all the fashion at the period of its erection." Warming to this prejudice he continued, "The architects of banks, colleges, churches, and even private residences, all went to Greece and Rome for their architectural inspiration. This fashion has fastened upon the country a great number of solid and costly buildings, utterly unsuited to our climate, as well as being unsightly, from the very lack of fitness." McArthur's Laning Hall (1868, now demolished) reflected the then current taste for Second Empire design, most notably by adopting the mansard roof that would be used to good effect a few years later by Henry Fernbach on the Victory Building (pages 196–199) and McArthur's own City Hall.

The United States Naval Asylum was renamed the United States Naval Home in 1889 and continued to serve its intended purpose until 1976, when new quarters were provided in Gulfport, Mississippi. The site was advertised for sale by the General Services Administration and eventually sold in 1988 with protective covenants on the three Strickland buildings, incorporated into the subsequent development of the site as a residential complex that opened in 2005.

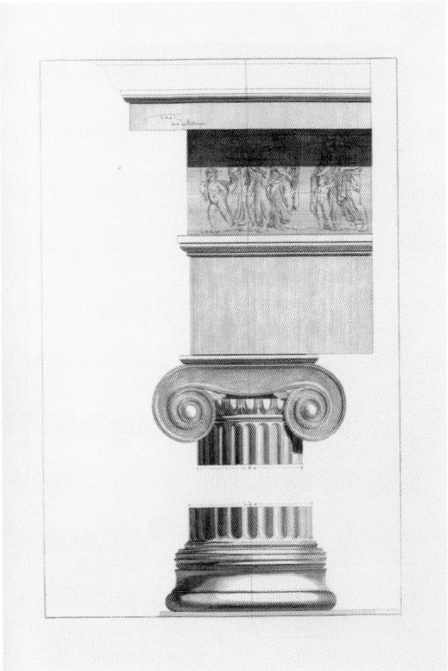

The portico is based on this Ionic capital, column base, and entablature from a fifth-century B.C.E. temple on the banks of the Ilissus River. James Stuart and Nicholas Revett, *The Antiquities of Athens* (London, 1762–1816), 1: 2, plate VI. Athenæum of Philadelphia Collection.

MERCHANTS' EXCHANGE

(Philadelphia Merchants' Exchange)
Independence National Historical Park
143 South Third Street
Philadelphia, PA 19106

William Strickland, architect, 1832–1834
National Historic Landmark, 2001

Not open to the public

Readers opening their copy of the *Philadelphia Album* for May 14, 1831, found this declaration: "Philadelphia is truly the Athens of America; in its public institutions, in its benevolent and charitable societies, in its literary reputation—in its site, the beautiful regularity of its streets—its buildings both public and private—in every particular . . . we are superior, without a doubt to every other City in the Union." Architecturally, at least, the Athenian metaphor might not have seemed far-fetched, given the predilection of Philadelphians for buildings in the Greek Revival Style. Benjamin Henry Latrobe's Bank of Pennsylvania (1798) and William Strickland's Bank of the United States (1818) had led the way, followed by the latter's United States Naval Asylum (1826) and United States Mint (1829). There were also John Haviland's First Presbyterian Church on Washington Square (1820), Saint Andrew's Episcopal Church (1822), the Asylum for the Deaf and Dumb (1824), the Franklin Institute (1825), and, on the east bank of the Schuylkill, Frederick Graff's Fairmount Water Works (1812–1822)—to mention a few examples that appear elsewhere in this book or in *Historic Sacred Places*. Philadelphia, more than any other city in antebellum America, helped shape Greek Revival as the national architectural style, and in 1831 it

↑ The Philadelphia Merchants' Exchange (London: George Virtue, 1839). Print and Picture Collection, The Free Library of Philadelphia.

was about to gain another Greek building, designed by no less a master than William Strickland (pages 80–85). It would be his last Philadelphia building of consequence—and probably his best.

By the 1830s many American cities—Charleston, Baltimore, and New York, for example—had commercial exchanges where merchants could meet to sell their cargoes. To supply a similar structure for Philadelphia, a group of prominent businessmen, including Stephen Girard, acquired a wedge-shaped lot of ground bounded by Walnut, Third, and Dock Streets that was conveniently sited near the waterfront and the major banking houses. Dock Street acquired its name from Dock Creek, which was formed by several streams flowing from the center of town to the Delaware River. Little more than an open sewer by the late eighteenth century, the creek had been arched over, thereby forming the wide street that today is paved with granite stones. It provides an unexpected urban plaza meandering across the "beautiful regularity" of Philadelphia's uncompromising grid from Third Street below Chestnut to Front Street. William

Demolition of the buildings that once occupied at the northwest corner of Third and Walnut Streets now permits William Strickland's handsome west façade to be appreciated from a distance.

Strickland was appointed architect for the new Exchange and the cornerstone was laid on the centennial of George Washington's birth (February 22, 1832).

The lot on Dock Street was potentially difficult. How to position a symmetrical structure on an asymmetrical site? But as is often the case, the constraints of the site can bring out the best in an architect. Strickland's solution was to design a rectangular classical building with a *semicircular portico* at the narrow end of the triangle. This feature alone makes his Exchange one of the most familiar historic landmarks in Philadelphia.

From the time of its completion in 1834, the east portico was a public attraction. Visitors climbed the cupola for views over the city, and omnibus service carried tourists from the Exchange to the Fairmount Water Works and, by the 1840s, to Girard College.

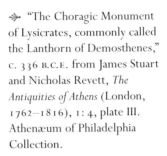

"The Choragic Monument of Lysicrates, commonly called the Lanthorn of Demosthenes," c. 336 B.C.E. from James Stuart and Nicholas Revett, *The Antiquities of Athens* (London, 1762–1816), 1: 4, plate III. Athenæum of Philadelphia Collection.

The "Choragic Monument of Lysicrates," plate VI, illustrates the capital and antefix used by Strickland at the Merchants' Exchange. Athenæum of Philadelphia Collection.

The entire three-story structure rests on a basement story supporting the *piano nobile* and the attic. The main entrance to the lobby, stairs, and hence to the Exchange Room above, was from Third Street. Unfortunately the Third Street façade suffers because it rises flush to the lot line on a narrow street without the setback of platform and stairs Strickland provided at the Second Bank or Haviland did at Saint Andrew's Episcopal Church. Thus the handsome Corinthian portico can only be fully appreciated today as a consequence of the demolition by the Park Service of the buildings on the opposite side of Third Street. Strickland kept the entire Third Street façade in this single plane; the portico is what architectural historians call "in antis" (among the pilasters), so the crowning pediment is visually supported by four columns between two flat pilasters. On either side of the portico there are tripartite windows, a pattern of fenestration that carries around to the otherwise plain flank elevations. On the ground floor a dozen doors provided access to the post office and spaces rented to insurance companies and banks.

Today we can stand at the intersection of Dock and Walnut Streets looking northwest—just as Strickland must have done when first studying the site. In the distance is the First Bank of the United States (pages 60–65), based on the Dublin Exchange with a classical portico of Roman Corinthian columns. As he had done previously—and would do in the future—Strickland turned to Athenian architecture for inspiration, specifically from his favorite source book, Stuart and Revett's *Antiquities of Athens*. Here the direct inspiration is the Choragic Monument of Lysicrates, which he followed meticulously. Not only is the monument with its circular colonnade reproduced as the distinctive tower, but it animates the entire semicircular portico. Twin stairs curve up from the ground to doors leading to the Exchange Room.

So visually appealing is this east portico that many writers have declared that Strickland intended it to be the main entrance (as opposed to the Third Street entrance). This seems unlikely, given the exposure of the stairs to the weather. In addition, the Philadelphia Contributionship insurance survey of 1848 strongly suggests that most persons coming and going to the building favored the Third Street entrance.

The marble work was a tour de force. As at the Second Bank, the United States Mint, and the Naval Asylum, the principal mason was the Scot immigrant

The pair of marble lions on the east portico were carved in Philadelphia by Messrs. Fiorelli and Battin in 1838.

John Struthers (1786–1851) whose name appears with Strickland's carved into the rotunda plinth, as it does under the portico at the Second Bank. For the fine detail sculpture, particularly the complex Corinthian capitals, skilled Italian-trained artisans were engaged; their names appear carved on the columns: "Petrus et Philipus Bardi de Cararia Fecurunt 1832" (made by Pietro and Filippo Bardi of Carrara, 1832). The recumbent lions at the top of the exterior stairs to the Exchange Room were a later addition. According to the *United States Gazette* (March 21, 1838), "a pair of lions [is being] sculptured by Messrs. Fiorelli and Battin, 3 Dock St., to be placed in front of the Merchants' Exchange." The following month the *Gazette* reported that "one of the marble lions sculptured by Signor Fiorelli, assisted by Mr. Battin, has been put in place." Probably due to their similarity to Antonio Canova's heraldic lions for the tomb of Pope Clement XIII (1783–1792) at St. Peter's in Rome, the Merchants' Exchange lions were traditionally believed to have been imported from Italy—as stated in countless guidebooks.

The original interior of the Exchange no longer survives, forcing us to rely on written accounts, most exclaiming on the grandeur of the Exchange Room. According to one article from 1835, the Exchange Room "is on the east front, extending across the whole building, and occupying an area of 3300 superficial feet. The ceiling extending to the roof, is of the form of a dome, and supported by several marble columns. Its panels are ornamented with splendid fresco paintings, representing Commerce, Wealth, Liberty, etc. beautifully executed, appearing to have as striking a relief as sculptural work." Samuel Breck of Sweetbriar identifies the artist for us, recording in his diary (May 22, 1834): "A Roman painter named Monachesi is acquiring reputation by painting the ceiling of the principal hall of the New Exchange in Phila. It is splendidly executed in Fresco. The foreshortening of the figures is admirable. If I mistake not, this ceiling will be one of the greatest attractions in Phila. The artist receives two thousand dollars for the work." Nicola Monachesi (1795–1851) immigrated from Rome to Philadelphia in 1831 and over the following decades he decorated Saint John's, Saint Mary's, Saint Joseph's, Saint Augustine, and Saint Philip's Roman Catholic churches.

In the decades following the Civil War, as business moved west toward Broad Street, the Exchange building was allowed to decline until 1901–1903, when the Philadelphia architect Louis C. Hickman (1863–c. 1917) removed the Strickland work and redesigned the interior. From 1922 until 1952, when the building was acquired by the National Park Service, it served as the Produce Exchange. The exterior has now been restored to its appearance in the 1830s and the interior renovated as National Park Service offices.

FOUNDER'S HALL, GIRARD COLLEGE

2101 S. College Avenue
Philadelphia, PA 19121-4857

Thomas Ustick Walter, architect, 1833–1847
National Historic Landmark, 1969

Telephone for visitor information: 215.787.2600
www.girardcollege.com

Founder's Hall, Girard College, by Philadelphia architect Thomas Ustick Walter (1833–1847). Nicholas Biddle called it "a perfect, chaste specimen of Grecian architecture." It follows the order of the Choragic Monument of Lysicrates (c. 336 B.C.E.) near the Acropolis of Athens, as published in James Stuart and Nicholas Revett's *Antiquities of Athens*—a copy of which Walter is known to have owned.

When the French-born Philadelphia merchant and financier Stephen Girard (1750–1831) died, he may have been the richest man in America. Personally modest to the point of diffidence, inspired by Benjamin Franklin's civic activism, and deeply influenced by his adopted city's tradition of philanthropy, he made liberal bequests to local charities such as the Pennsylvania Hospital (pages 54–59), the Pennsylvania Institution for the Deaf and Dumb (pages 92–95), and the Orphan Asylum of Philadelphia. But Girard's principal gift—six million dollars—went to the City of Philadelphia to build and operate in perpetuity a residential school for "poor white male orphan children." At the time it was the most generous act of philanthropy in American history. When the college was completed and opened, fully a third of the bequest, two million dollars, had been spent on construction, most of it to erect Founder's Hall, making it the most costly building in America, second only to the United States Capitol.

News of a client with deep pockets had spread rapidly among America's architects; more than twenty individuals or firms entered the design competition, including most of the leading practitioners in the nation: William Strickland and John Haviland from Philadelphia; Edward Shaw and Isaiah Rogers from Boston; and Town, Davis & Dakin from New York. All the submissions were exhibited at Independence Hall. Much to everyone's surprise, the winning design

came from Thomas Ustick Walter (1804–1887), one of the youngest competitors, who was just beginning his long and distinguished career.

Born in Philadelphia, the son of a bricklayer, Walter worked in the office of William Strickland (pages 80–82), attended lectures by John Haviland (pages 116–117), and learned watercolor technique from the landscape artist William Mason—what Walter called a "liberal, though not collegiate" education. He also served a practical, hands-on apprenticeship with his father and by 1831 had begun actively to practice architecture. He first gained local attention with his Gothic-style Moyamensing Prison (1832–1835) and the Wills Hospital for the Relief of the Indigent Blind and Lame (1831–1832). Hundreds of commissions both at home and abroad followed, leading ultimately to his successful competition entry for the wings and dome of the United States Capitol. Of course, all this was in the future when young Walter's handsome perspective rendering for Mr. Girard's new college went on display.

In February 1833, it was announced that Walter's design had been awarded the first premium by the Select and Common Councils of Philadelphia, and the following month he was appointed architect of Girard College. At this point

When Stephen Girard died, the contents of his Philadelphia townhouse at 21–25 North Water Street were carefully inventoried and stored. Following the completion of Founder's Hall, the furniture, paintings, silver, glass, porcelain, and textiles spanning c. 1780–1820 were moved to the new building where they remain on display. Shown here is a suite of ebony parlor furniture made by Ephraim Haines in 1807, for which the original invoice survives. Next to the portrait bust of Napoleon I by Antonio Canova—given to Girard by Joseph Bonaparte—is a musical *secrétaire à abattant*.

Walter encountered Nicholas Biddle (1786–1844), the newly elected president of the Girard College trustees. Biddle came from a respected Delaware Valley family of means. After graduating from Princeton and reading law, he traveled abroad in the party of General John Armstrong, newly appointed United States minister to France. During the three years he spent in Europe, Biddle witnessed Napoleon's coronation as emperor, met the artists Jean-Antoine Houdon and John Vanderlyn, and, during the summer of 1806, visited Greece—which aroused in him what was to be a lifelong interest and appreciation of classical architecture. By 1833 Biddle was one of the leading citizens of Philadelphia. For a decade he had been president of the Bank of the United States housed in

The entrance hall follows the Ionic order and contains the sarcophagus and marble statue of Stephen Girard, the latter by French sculptor Nicholas Gevelot, who had executed *William Penn's Treaty with the Indians* (1827) in the United States Capitol Rotunda. He received the Girard commission in 1833 but did not complete the work until 1845. Girard's sarcophagus was designed by Philadelphia architect and engineer Frederick Graff.

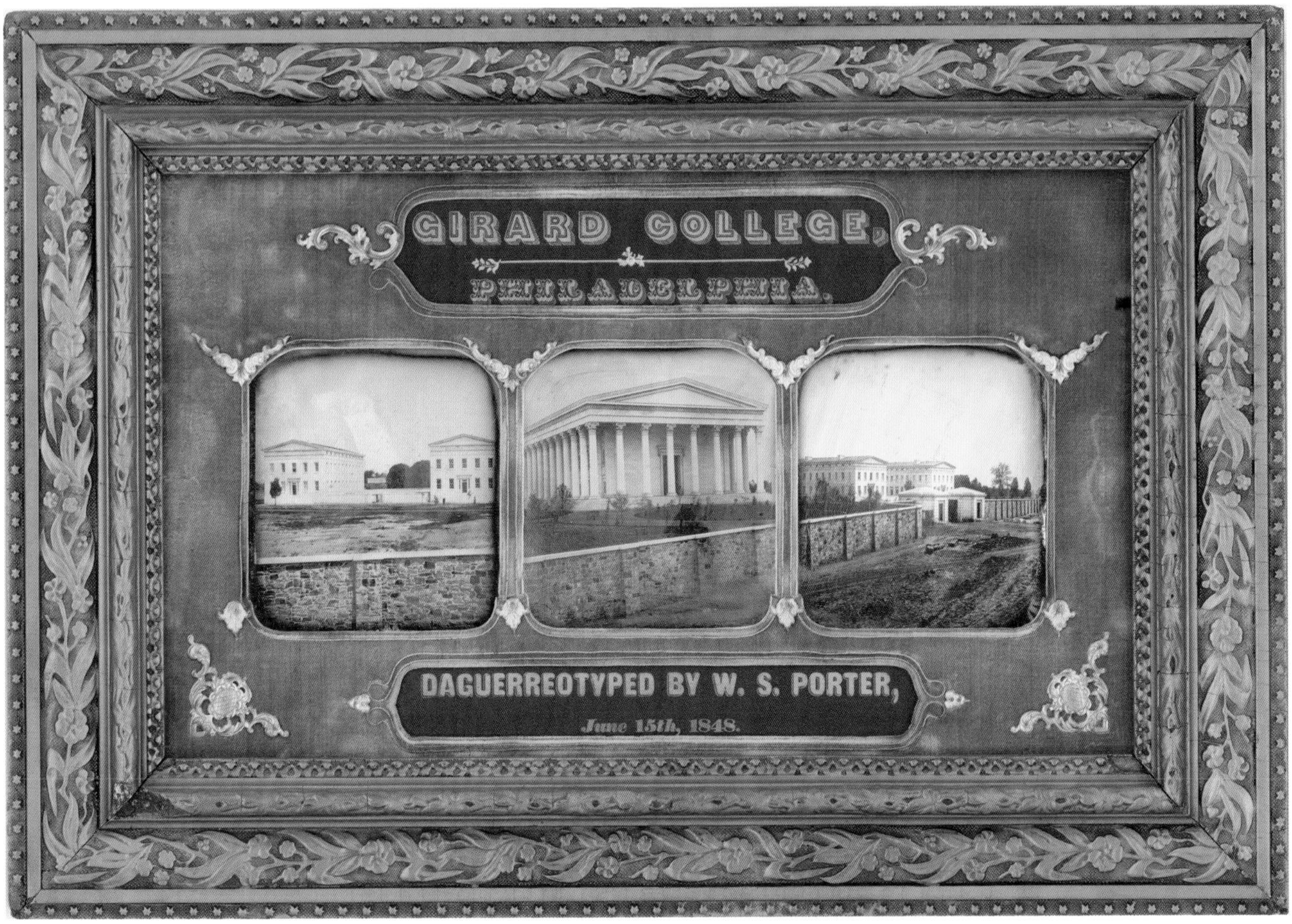

William Strickland's Parthenon on Chestnut Street (pages 80–85), a building he greatly admired.

Biddle was disdainful of Walter's winning design for Girard College. He recorded that it was "a large showy building, wanting simplicity + purity—but not ill-adapted to please." Walter had pasted together a three-part composition that juxtaposed La Madeleine with flanking buildings inspired by Ange-Jacques Gabriel's mid-eighteenth-century twin *hôtels particuliers* from the Place de la Concorde, Paris. Biddle set out "to wean Mr. Walter from his plan . . . to excite his ambition to achieve . . . the opportunity of immortalizing himself by a perfect chaste specimen of Grecian architecture." Walter was tractable, according to Biddle: "he renounced his own plan and came at once into my views, and prepared all the necessary drawings, and seconded me with great cordiality." It should also be mentioned that about the same time Biddle gave Walter the commission to greatly expand Andalusia, his villa on the Delaware River (see *Historic Houses*, pages 154–57).

The resulting Founder's Hall design is, as Biddle wanted, a full peristyle Greek temple—that is, with columns on all four sides. And what columns. Ultimately

Three-plate daguerreotype of Girard College by William Southgate Porter, June 15, 1848, in the original presentation frame. Girard College Collection.

"Philadelphia from Girard College," lithograph by B. F. Smith, 1850. The building rose one hundred feet and was on an elevated site to the northwest of the city, making the view from the marble roof a popular tourist destination. Two other nineteenth-century landmarks, Eastern State Penitentiary and the Fairmount Water Works, can just be seen in the distance. Girard College Collection.

there were 34 marble columns with fluted shafts and Corinthian capitals, eight across the north and south fronts, eleven on each flank—costing in themselves nearly $500,000. The stone was excavated from a quarry in Chester County, Pennsylvania, and transported to the building site by rail cars. Walter recorded in his diary, "What a man can do with money!!!"

Construction of the college moved slowly. Controversy over what some critics considered profligate expenditure on a building Girard had believed should be constructed "avoiding needless ornament," labor unrest, economic depression, failure of the Bank of the United States, and efforts by Girard's relatives to overturn the bequest, all caused delays. Charles Dickens remarked in his *American Notes* (1842),

> Near the city is a most splendid unfinished marble structure for the Girard College . . . which if completed according to the original design, will be perhaps the richest edifice of modern times. But the bequest is involved in legal

> disputes, and pending them the work has stopped; so that, like many other great undertakings in America, even this is rather going to be done one of these days than doing now.

Two years later the courts upheld Girard's will and work proceeded to the point that the building committee could declare that the college is "an edifice unsurpassed in this country, whether we regard the chaste and beautiful character of its architecture or the great strength and solidity of its construction,—a temple of elegance worthy of the noble purpose for which it is to be dedicated." Girard College accepted its first one hundred pupils on January 1, 1848.

The clause in Girard's will that his college would benefit "poor white male orphan children" came under increasing scrutiny after the 1954 Supreme Court *Brown v. Board of Education* decision, leading ultimately to the admission of four African American boys in August 1968. The first girls were admitted in the 1980s. Today there are 720 children enrolled, evenly divided between boys and girls, and 80 percent African American. Since Girard College opened, twenty-one thousand children have benefited from Stephen Girard's estate, and Founder's Hall remains an extraordinary monument to his philanthropy.

ATWATER KENT MUSEUM

(formerly the Franklin Institute)
15 South Seventh Street
Philadelphia, PA 19106

John Haviland, architect,
1825–1826
National Register of Historic Places, 1979

Telephone for visitor information: 215.685.4830
www.philadelphiahistory.org

↑ Erected in 1825–1826 for the Franklin Institute from designs by John Haviland, the building now houses the Atwater Kent Museum.

Most great institutions begin modestly, and the Franklin Institute is no exception. Established in 1824 "for the promotion of the mechanic arts," the founders, in the words of one historian, "were reformers in an era of reform, democrats in the age of Jackson, and entrepreneurs at a time of burgeoning economic opportunity." They set out to diffuse knowledge of mechanical science by sponsoring public lectures, gathering a library and model collection, and by awarding prizes for improvements in the arts.

To house the new mechanics' institute and, in particular, as a venue for their lecture programs, the managers rented Carpenters' Hall (pages 42–47), and shortly thereafter established a mechanical drawing school taught by the architect John Haviland. By the spring of 1825, the need for a building to house the Institute's rapidly expanding collections and multifaceted educational programs had become obvious. Consequently, instructor Haviland prepared plans for a neoclassical building that would exhibit, according to the *United States Gazette* (June 9, 1825), "purity of design and solidity of construction."

English-born and trained John Haviland (1792–1852) ranks among the most important Philadelphia architects of the early nineteenth century. In short order,

Portrait of John Haviland by John Neagle, 1828. Haviland holds a copy of Stuart and Revett's *Antiquities of Athens*. On the drawing board are an elevation and plan of Eastern State Penitentiary. Metropolitan Museum of Art, The Alfred N. Punnett Endowment Fund, 1938. Image © 1994 The Metropolitan Museum of Art.

after arriving here in 1816, he married the widowed daughter of his first Philadelphia patron, established an architectural office, and promoted himself by producing a book. The landmark *Builder's Assistant* (1818–1821) is significant as the earliest American architectural pattern book to contain both Greek and Roman orders. In 1825 Haviland was probably the most successful architect in Philadelphia. (His Saint Andrew's Episcopal Church, 1822, now the Greek Orthodox Cathedral of Saint George, is discussed in *Historic Sacred Places*; his Pennsylvania Institution for the Deaf and Dumb is discussed on pages 92–95 and his Eastern State Penitentiary on pages 86–91.)

For the Franklin Institute commission, Haviland turned for inspiration to the principal source book for the Greek Revival style in America, James Stuart and Nicholas Revett's *Antiquities of Athens* (London, 1762). Stuart and Revett's work was so important to Haviland that John Neagle portrayed him clutching a copy. In his *Builder's Assistant*, Haviland argued that classical Greek buildings were the best "models of imitation and confessed standards of excellence" for the modern

↠ Haviland based his design on the ancient Greek Choragic Monument of Thrasyllus, Athens, from James Stuart and Nicholas Revett, *The Antiquities of Athens* (London, 1762), the principal source book for the Greek Revival Style in America. Athenæum of Philadelphia Collection.

American democracy. So it is not surprising that the main façade of the Institute building is loosely based on the austere marble porch of the Choragic Monument of Thrasyllus from the Athenian Acropolis. Haviland reduced the number of wreaths in the frieze and created a three-bay façade by adding a second pier and making both piers thicker than the single pier of the Choragic Monument. The result was a monumental balanced composition within a relatively small and confined sixty-foot urban lot. He also suggested that a statue of Benjamin Franklin be installed at the attic floor level directly above the front door, as a further echo of the classical prototype. Cooler heads prevailed and the statue was omitted, most likely as a cost saving. The central entrance is approached by marble stairs flanked by cast iron lamps, themselves remarkable survivors from an age when such illumination was commonly part of the design for public buildings.

The cornerstone was set in place on June 8, 1825, and the three-story building costing $35,000 opened the next year. To provide income for operating costs, the second story was rented to the U.S. marshal for the district courts; the Institute's lecture hall occupied most of the ground floor. For the next century Haviland's building served the Institute without significant alterations, except for a new wing added in 1897 that was later removed. By the 1920s, however, the Institute had outgrown its building, and in 1933 it moved to its present quarters on the Benjamin Franklin Parkway (page 274), leaving Haviland's building standing vacant.

At the suggestion of Frances A. Wister, president of the Philadelphia Society for the Preservation of Landmarks (see *Historic Houses*, pages 17–18), and encouraged by Mayor S. Davis Wilson and other community leaders, the radio manufacturer Atwater Kent purchased the old Franklin Institute building in 1938. While little remembered today, Atwater Kent (1873–1949) developed a highly successful business in the first decades of the twentieth century manufacturing electrical parts for automobiles. In the 1920s he realized the potential market for residential radio sets, and by 1925 his factory on Wissahickon Avenue was the largest manufacturer of radios in the United States. His factories closed in 1936 during the Great Depression.

Kent renovated the interior of the Franklin Institute building to be used as a museum named for himself and dedicated to the history of Philadelphia. The Atwater Kent Museum opened in 1941 and continues to function as a museum of Philadelphia.

First floor lecture hall, 1922. From the Historical and Interpretive Collections of the Franklin Institute, Inc., Philadelphia.

PHILADELPHIA CONTRIBUTIONSHIP FOR THE INSURANCE OF HOUSES FROM LOSS BY FIRE

212 South Fourth Street
Philadelphia, PA 19106

Thomas Ustick Walter, architect, 1835–1836
Collins and Autenrieth, additions and alterations, 1866–1867
National Historic Landmark, 1977

Telephone for visitor information: 215.627.1752
www.contributionship.com

As the largest city in pre-Revolutionary America, it is no surprise how many "firsts" Philadelphia can legitimately claim. Among these is the first successful property insurance company, founded by Benjamin Franklin and his friends in 1752. (There had been an earlier effort in Charleston, South Carolina, but the great conflagration of 1740 in that town caused the fledgling company to fail.) The Contributionship was founded as a mutual insurance company, patterned on the Amicable Contributionship of London (1696), which functioned on the principle that policyholders mutually share the risks all face from catastrophic loss by fire. Thus the famous fire mark used to identify insured properties features the "hand in hand" fireman's carry.

Designed by Thomas Ustick Walter and erected in 1835–1836, the Contributionship building was significantly altered by the firm of Collins & Autenrieth in 1866–1867.

Walter's late neoclassical design differed little from a typical "first rate modern house" of the time in Philadelphia. Philadelphia Contributionship for the Insurance of Houses from Loss by Fire.

Several fundamental principles of modern insurance were first introduced to America by the company: the careful selection or rating of risks based on property inspections, setting charges according to risk, and the accumulation of financial reserves to pay for losses. From the beginning, the Contributionship used "surveyors" to inspect properties before issuing policies. The first of these were Joseph Fox (1709–1779) and Samuel Rhoads (1711–1784), both prominent master builders and members of the Carpenters' Company (pages 42–47). As practical builders, these two and their successors, most of them Carpenters' Company members, would carefully record in the policies both the materials and the quality of finishes of any building to be insured. These policies survive to this day as part of the Contributionship archives and are of invaluable use to modern homeowners and architectural historians.

The Contributionship influenced the nature of building in early Philadelphia when, in 1769, the managers decided no longer to insure wooden buildings or those lacking brick fire walls and, in 1781, to issue no new policies for buildings surrounded by trees—on the theory that trees interfered with firefighting. (This regulation led to the formation of a rival company, The Mutual Assurance Company, which adopted a fire mark featuring a "green tree.")

From 1752 to 1836 the Contributionship had no permanent headquarters, business being conducted in the courthouse, taverns, or from the home of whoever was the company clerk or treasurer. This changed in 1835, when the company purchased a lot of ground on the west side of Fourth Street just south of Walnut for $26,000 on which to erect a business office and dwelling for the company treasurer and his family. The directors hired Thomas Ustick Walter (1804–1887) as architect. Walter's rapid rise to prominence in Philadelphia after establishing an independent practice in 1831 has been noted elsewhere (pages 104–115). By the time he was awarded the Contributionship commission in 1835 he had already made his mark in the city with his Gothic-style Moyamensing

Prison (1831–1835) and the monumental Greek Revival Founder's Hall of Girard College (1833–1848).

According to Walter's diary, which survives at The Athenæum of Philadelphia, he met with the Contributionship committee in early July 1835, and two weeks later submitted the design illustrated here and a bid of $20,500 to "furnish the building complete with all the convenience and beauty customary in a first rate modern house, the whole to be delivered ready to accommodate the office and a family on or before the first of June next." This proposal was accepted on August 4, 1835, and the masons began laying foundation stone immediately. The three-story red-brick building (50 feet wide by 54 feet deep) with marble portico was completed in 1836. Walter received his final payment for extras in January 1837.

In 1866 the Contributionship Committee on Repairs and Improvements hired the German-trained architects Edward Collins (1821–1902) and Charles M. Autenrieth (1828–1906). They had arrived in Philadelphia in the late 1840s and formed a partnership in time to enter unsuccessfully the Academy of Music competition (pages 154–159). Together they would later design the Lit Brothers store on Market Street. Collins and Autenrieth removed Walter's Grecian roof cresting and supplied a fashionable mansard fourth floor. In addition, because Walter's portico was found to be "second quality marble," which "had perished to become friable to so great a degree as to be unfit for the partial restoration

↑ Behind the Contributionship is a modern formal garden.

Recent renovations of the ground floor include a small display of fire insurance artifacts, including early fire marks.

previously agreed," the committee directed the architects "to build it of Pennsylvania marble of first quality in the existing form in all its parts, modified as to the steps and pilasters." Consequently, most of what we see today dates from the 1866–1867 reworking, particularly the double curved steps and balustrade.

Internally the building has been reworked over several campaigns, most recently to create a museum space on the ground floor. Tours of the building, the small display of early company memorabilia, and the large formal garden to the rear are by special appointment only. Like so many of the institutions founded by Benjamin Franklin and his friends, The Contributionship continues to thrive, protecting businesses, cultural institutions, and thousands of homes in the Philadelphia region.

PHILADELPHIA CLUB

1301 Walnut Street
Philadelphia, PA 19107

Architect unidentified, Daniel R. & Robert Knight, builders, 1838
Furness, Evans & Co., expansion, 1888–1889

Not open to the public
Telephone for information: 215-735-5924

↞ The Philadelphia Club, the oldest gentlemen's city club in the United States, has occupied the Butler House at the corner of Walnut and Thirteenth Streets since 1850. With the exception of an addition by Frank Furness dating from 1888, the clubhouse appears much as it did when erected in 1838.

The Philadelphia Club could easily pass for the private residence of a prosperous early nineteenth-century family who for generations had married and invested well and then—when the internal combustion engine replaced horses and carriages—resisted the temptation to abandon the city for the sylvan suburbs of the Main Line and Chestnut Hill. There is little, save a modest monogrammed awning at the entrance, to suggest that for more than 150 years this substantial seven-bay red-brick house has sheltered the oldest gentlemen's city club in the United States. And that is just the way the members would prefer that it remain.

The Philadelphia Club originated with two groups of congenial friends who met to play cards at coffee houses on Fifth Street not far from three cultural institutions to which most of them belonged: the American Philosophical Society, the Athenæum, and the Library Company (pages 48, 132, 192). In 1834 they moved to the Adelphi Building on Fifth Street below Walnut Street and temporarily called themselves the Adelphi Club, but soon they organized formally as The Philadelphia Club. The first published *Rules and Regulations for the Government of the Philadelphia Club* (1834) lists the names of sixty-two members and declares, "this Club shall be termed the 'Philadelphia Club,' and its object shall be the encouragement of social intercourse." In thus organizing, they became the first city gentlemen's club in Philadelphia and the oldest of its kind in the United States. (The Union Club in New York City was founded in 1836 and the Somerset in Boston in 1851.)

In 1835 the Board of Directors rented the handsome house at 260 South Ninth Street that had been occupied by Joseph Bonaparte, elder brother of Napoleon I and former king of Spain, who styled himself Comte de Survilliers during his long exile in America. A few years later the club moved again, this time to Walnut Street below Tenth Street, and in 1850 the directors purchased the present building on the northwest corner of Walnut and Thirteenth Streets, which had been commissioned from an as yet unidentified architect by Thomas Butler, son of the Irish-born South Carolinian Pierce Butler (1744–1822)—not to be confused with his grandson of the same name who married the famous actress and abolitionist Fanny Kemble. Butler died in 1838 leaving the house to be completed by his trustees, who paid Daniel R. and Robert Knight for the construction. In the 1830s Walnut Street just east of Broad Street was a fashionable neighborhood of substantial late Federal residences; and the new house was leased to a variety of tenants, including a young ladies' boarding school. Initially the Philadelphia Club offered to rent the Butler house but in 1850 the property was purchased for $30,000.

Today the Butler House reflects several alterations and additions undertaken by the Club, mostly prior to World War I. In 1850 the first floor double parlors

Equality forum
ONE WAY
NO TURN ON RED
metro

overlooking Walnut Street were connected by sliding doors and gas lighting was introduced; a few years later a one-story billiards room was added to the north. In 1888, the firm of Furness, Evans & Company raised the billiard room extension to three stories with a mansard roof and an elliptical bay window looking to the east. This provided the spacious second floor dining room which to this day

is the heart of the Club. Additional alterations by Horace Trumbauer and the firm of Mellor, Meigs & Howe continued the Club's long tradition of hiring leading architects. The first floor War Memorial tablet dating from 1918, for example, was designed by Club member Wilson Eyre (1858–1944) and his partner John Gilbert McIlvaine (1880–1939).

The net effect of this architectural fine tuning—as opposed to replacing or substantially expanding the clubhouse as both the Union League (pages 166–171) and the Racquet Club (pages 244–247) have done—has been the preservation of the intimate residential scale of the clubhouse. Nathaniel Burt, in describing the ideal of the Philadelphia house, remarked that it should be

> large enough for dignity, spaciousness, generosity, elbow room, small enough for comfort, easy keeping, modesty. Large enough to be a significant architectural monument, small enough to be the living quarters of a purely private person. Large enough for aristocracy, small enough for democracy . . . it [should be] impressive without the slightest hint of cumbrousness, elegant without the least affection.

As for interior decoration, the Philadelphia Club reflects a kind of "Philadelphia taste" that takes many generations to lay down, an effect that is well beyond simulation by the most skilled decorator. As Burt remarks in *The Perennial Philadelphians*, "most Old Philadelphians prefer to live with the furniture that God, abetted by will and testament, gave them in houses approximating as closely as possible the Old Family Place." Over 150 years the house committee has preserved a residential ambiance of oriental carpets, portraits, prints, and well-polished furniture while eschewing shabby chic or the latest hotel decorator fad.

Which is not to suggest that the Club hasn't flirted with moving up town. As Walnut Street east of Broad Street declined as a residential area, the Philadelphia Club, like other institutions (the American Philosophical Society and the Athenæum, for example), considered a move during the real estate boom of the 1920s. The membership voted in 1927 to acquire land on the Parkway at Eighteenth Street and to erect thereon a new building by the New York society architects William Adams Delano (1874–1960) and Chester Holmes Aldrich (1871–1940), who had designed homes and clubs for the Astor, Vanderbilt, Whitney, and Rockefeller families. Fortunately nothing came of this scheme. In light of what happened to city clubs in the decades after the Depression and war of the 1930s and 1940s, those institutions and clubs that remained in their landmark buildings are inclined today to be self-congratulatory.

When the Philadelphia Club moved into the Butler House, the two parlors were joined by sliding doors, the east room designated as the reading room or library, the west room as the drawing room. Lighting gas was introduced in 1850 for fixtures supplied by the Cornelius Company of Philadelphia.

Like all city clubs, the Philadelphia Club suffered from changing demographics in the twentieth century. One club historian remarked in 1935, "the automobile, interest in out-door sports, the removal of residence to the suburbs and country of practically all the members of the Club . . . have changed the life of the Club—not only this Club, but city clubdom in general." One change was the criteria for election to membership. According to club historian F. Markoe Rivinus, writing in 1995, "despite little ethnic and religious prejudice in its early decades, the Philadelphia Club by the end of the [nineteenth] century had become 'exclusive.' Parochial considerations of ancestry in a social connotation

In 1888 architect Frank Furness added a three-story extension to the rear, which created this second floor dining room with an elliptical bay window on the east end.

became the key to acceptance" to membership. This changed in the second half of the twentieth century, when the Philadelphia Club began "accepting as members persons who contributed to the life and culture of the city. The Philadelphia Club no longer concerns itself with the race, religion, or national origin of perspective members," thereby assuring that this oldest of America's gentlemen's clubs will—in the words of Owen Wister (1860–1938), author of *The Virginian* and a club member—continue "the tradition, patriotic, social and civilized, of an honorable and happy past."

VICTORIAN PHILADELPHIA

Athenæum of Philadelphia

Laurel Hill Cemetery

Freedom Theatre

Institute of the Pennsylvania Hospital

Academy of Music

Wagner Free Institute of Science of Philadelphia

Union League of Philadelphia

Masonic Temple

Philadelphia City Hall

Pennsylvania Academy of the Fine Arts

Philadelphia High School for Creative and Performing Arts

Victory Building

Memorial Hall

Boathouse Row

Philadelphia Zoological Gardens Gatehouses

Anne and Jerome Fisher Fine Arts Library, University of Pennsylvania

Philadelphia and Reading Railroad Terminal Head House and Shed

The main reading room of the University of Pennsylvania Library and Museum (1888–1891) was designed by Frank Furness.

ATHENÆUM OF PHILADELPHIA

East Washington Square
219 South Sixth Street
Philadelphia, PA 19106-3794

John Notman, architect / builder, 1845–1847
National Historic Landmark, 1976

Telephone for visitor information: 215.925.2688
www.PhilaAthenaeum.org

The Athenæum of Philadelphia is a member-supported special collections library founded in 1814 to collect materials "connected with the history and antiquities of America, and the useful arts, and generally to disseminate useful knowledge." The founders were the intellectual and literary leaders of the city, many of whom were also members of the American Philosophical Society (pages 48–53) and the Library Company of Philadelphia (pages 192–195). In that age before tax-supported free public libraries, member-supported libraries were organized as private stock companies (in which the purchase of a share made one an owner) or as associations of dues-paying members. When sufficient funds had been raised, these libraries rented or erected buildings, purchased books, and paid their librarians with the proceeds from dues, annual share assessments, or rental fees.

For nearly three decades, the Athenæum occupied the first floor of Philosophical Hall on Independence Square, during which the library grew in prestige, membership, and the number of books and periodicals available to its members. After visiting the reading rooms in 1825, Jonathan P. Sheldon of New York City declared, "N. York has no institution of the kind to compare with it.

↞ The Grand Stair rises four stories. At the *piano nobile* are Corinthian columns with matching pilasters marbled in Venetian red.

↠ The Athenæum building faces Washington Square. Designed by John Notman and erected in 1845–1847, it is one of the earliest brownstone structures in Philadelphia and the first American building in the Italianate Renaissance Revival palazzo style.

A comparison of the Libraries of the two cities, and especially the situation of each as to pecuniary matters, would place N. York far behind her rival in matters of correct taste and liberality." The rapidly expanding collection soon filled the rooms at Philosophical Hall, and the directors began setting aside funds "to erect an edifice, of chaste and simple architecture, conveniently situated, and of ample dimensions" to accommodate the library.

Once $25,000 had been accumulated, the directors searched for a nearby lot of ground and announced an architectural competition. Initially they hoped to build at the southeast corner of Walnut and Sixth Streets, a brief walk across Independence Square from their rented rooms. Designs for this site were received from William Strickland, John Haviland, and Thomas Ustick Walter—three of the leading American architects of the day—and a young Scot immigrant, John Notman, who had recently arrived in Philadelphia. But the economic depression following the Panic of 1837 caused the members to resolve "it is inexpedient at present to erect such a building."

← The members' reading room is little changed from its 1847 appearance. The original color scheme of white walls and ceiling, oak-grained woodwork, and Sienna-marbled Corinthian columns, pilasters, and pillars was restored in 1975. The gasoliers and furniture are original to the room, although the floor was covered in the nineteenth century with ingrain carpeting laid wall to wall. The east windows open onto a cast-iron balcony overlooking the garden.

Finally, in 1845, the Athenæum building committee recommended the purchase of a long and narrow lot of ground (50 by 175 feet) on Sixth Street facing Washington Square, half a block south of the Sixth and Walnut Streets corner they originally had favored. This site had been occupied by the Revolutionary-era Walnut Street Prison, which a developer had acquired and demolished after John Haviland's Eastern State Penitentiary opened (pages 86–91). Another architectural competition resulted in the acceptance of a proposal from John Notman (1810–1865), who by this time had established himself as a promising architect by designing such significant structures as the gate house at Laurel Hill Cemetery (pages 138–143) and a building for the Academy of Natural Sciences. He would later design four major center city churches: Saint Mark's, Saint Clement's, Calvary Presbyterian, and Holy Trinity Rittenhouse Square (see *Historic Sacred Places*, pages 158–177).

In part because the Athenæum ground had such a narrow frontage on Washington Square, Notman took his inspiration from a style of urban palaces that had evolved in northern Italy during the Renaissance for just such a valuable center city location. So far as is known, Notman never traveled to Italy, but he had familiarized himself with the Italianate Renaissance Revival style introduced by William Henry Playfair in his native Scotland (and with whom Notman may have studied) and by Charles Barry at the Travellers' Club (1829) in London. The design Notman presented to the Athenæum building committee consisted of a three-story façade of reddish brown sandstone from quarries in northern New Jersey. A stone balcony was to overlook Washington Square, while a massive wooden cornice painted to simulate stone would boldly declare the palazzo

heritage to which the entire composition owed its origins. Such a building might have passed unnoticed in Florence or Rome, but in Philadelphia it appeared quite revolutionary. While probably not the first brownstone building in the city—as has often been claimed—it is most certainly the earliest and most widely published Italianate Revival style building of the palazzo mode to be erected in the United States. In a few years it would be the most popular urban style in Victorian America. Notman modestly wrote, "It is an excellent specimen of the Italian style of architecture, treated with spirit and taste. It has a bold and imposing appearance from the simplicity and unity of the design, and a perfect expression of its purpose."

By fall 1847 the library had occupied its new building. Member Sidney George Fisher confided to his diary that the building was "the handsomest edifice in the city . . . the two reading rooms are very large, with lofty ceilings, beautifully finished & proportioned, well carpeted, most comfortably furnished with convenient tables & easy chairs, and heated by flues and lighted by gas. A more quiet and agreeable place for lounging reading one could not have."

Declared a National Historic Landmark in 1976, Notman's splendid Athenæum building serves the community as a busy not-for-profit cultural institution—albeit greatly expanded and mechanically updated. After the founding of the tax-supported Free Library of Philadelphia (pages 288–291), the need for member-supported libraries declined. Where once there were hundreds of such institutions across America, now there are fewer than two dozen; most went out of business or were absorbed by their local public library. In post-World War II Philadelphia, however, heightened interest in the Independence Hall group (pages 24–41) and the renewal of the Society Hill neighborhood called attention to the importance of the Athenæum building as a seminal structure in the history of American architecture. At the same time the rich legacy of the library's collections of rare books, periodicals, a quarter million architectural drawings, prints, and 300,000 historic photographs became appreciated, especially as the library emerged as a leader in electronic dissemination of information. In the twenty-first century The Athenæum of Philadelphia has achieved international recognition as a special collections library and archives documenting American architecture and design. It could justly be said that the building continues to serve as its creators intended, as the home for collecting "antiquities of America, and the useful arts, and generally to disseminate useful knowledge."

The Henry Paul Busch Reading Room was originally intended for the display and reading of newspapers. It now serves as a research and reference room for visiting scholars who have applied for access to the rare book, manuscript, and architectural drawing collections. The pink and gray colors, oak-grained woodwork, and Sienna-marbled pillars and pilasters replicate the original decorative scheme. The double-level book stack dates from 1990.

LAUREL HILL CEMETERY

3822 Ridge Avenue
Philadelphia, PA 19132

John Notman, architect, 1836–1839
National Historic Landmark, 1998

Telephone for visitor information: 215.228.8200
www.thelaurelhillcemetery.org

In the first three decades of the nineteenth century, the population of Philadelphia nearly trebled—and with that explosive growth came an enormous increase in the numbers of the dead. Alarmed civic leaders realized that "the practice of burying in populous cities is becoming more objectionable" and believed it contributed to the contagions that regularly savaged urban populations. Some reasonable alternative to the city's churchyards and burial grounds had to be devised. These "repositories for the dead," it was argued, "once consecrated by the tears of the bereaved, and for awhile preserved in decent keeping by grateful affection," are increasingly "left to neglect and forgetfulness, and with every prospect of being ultimately disturbed" by development. The answer they found was the garden cemetery.

Among American cities, Boston had led the way by establishing Mount Auburn Cemetery on a 72-acre tract along the Charles River near Cambridge, ten miles from the city center, in 1831. The organizers involved the Massachusetts Horticultural Society in an effort to create a "garden of graves" set in romantically landscaped grounds "where the beauty of nature is heightened by the care of man, where the gloom of death cannot sadden the hearts of the living, nor the labor of life stand in too close contrast to the stillness of the dead." Even the word "cemetery"—from the ancient Greek word meaning "put to sleep"—came into wide usage for the first time.

The Laurel Hill gatehouse as it appears today.

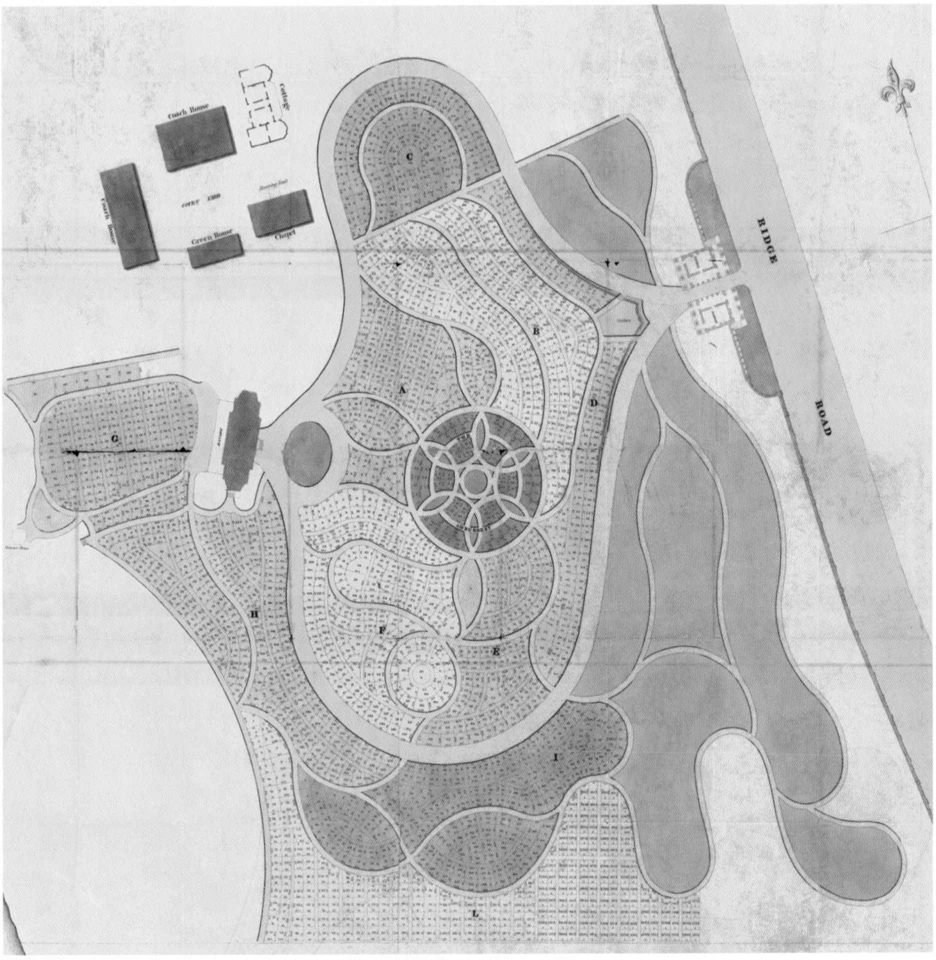

Plan of the Laurel Hill Cemetery, near Philadelphia. Surveyed by Philip M. Price and engraved by J. T. Hammond, 1836. Athenæum of Philadelphia Collection, gift of George B. Tatum.

The garden cemetery movement in both England and America traces its origins to Père Lachaise—the world's first garden cemetery—founded in 1804 by the French government in response to overcrowded Paris churchyards. Located on the former estate of François d'Aix de la Chaise, the picturesque setting with spectacular views of Paris soon became a tourist attraction, a place of fashionable garden promenades and displays of monumental good taste that might also demonstrate a family's social and financial distinction.

In 1836 the founders of what would become Philadelphia's first garden cemetery purchased Laurel Hill, the Schuylkill villa and gardens of the wealthy merchant Joseph Sims (1761–1851) on Ridge Avenue, approximately four miles north of Philadelphia near the East Falls neighborhood. The picturesque site overlooks the Schuylkill River from a plateau of "deep, dry and well-drained" soil. The subsequent purchase of three additional parcels of land brought the total to 74 acres. The resulting cemetery would become an important landmark in the history of burial reform and a notable example of American architecture, landscape gardening, and funerary art.

Vignette from the Plan of the Laurel Hill Cemetery, illustrating John Notman's gatehouse (1836) and probably based on his original drawing, now lost.

Unlike Mount Auburn, Laurel Hill Cemetery was to be laid out by a professional architect. Design proposals were received from William Strickland, Thomas Ustick Walter, and recent Scot immigrant John Notman, whom we met in the discussion of the Athenæum. Notman carried the day with a "gardenesque" design based on Henry E. Kendall's scheme for London's Kensal Green Cemetery. Notman would later prepare a similar proposal for Cincinnati's Spring Grove Cemetery (1845)—which was not realized—and for Hollywood Cemetery in Richmond, Virginia, which remains that city's most celebrated garden cemetery—or, to use the American term, "rural cemetery." So far as historians have been able to determine, Laurel Hill was Notman's first Philadelphia commission; it launched a remarkable career that would later prompt Thomas Ustick Walter to declare him the best architect in Philadelphia.

Notman's romantic plan of the cemetery found favor with horticulturalist Andrew Jackson Downing (1815–1852), the principal American advocate for the gardenesque theories of the Scottish gardener and landscape architect John Claudius Loudon (1783–1843). Perhaps Notman was acquainted with Loudon or his publications, and perhaps that association helped him obtain the Laurel Hill commission. (Unfortunately, no link other than nationality has been discovered to cloak this intriguing theory with substance.) Notman also designed several structures to adorn the grounds; the Roman Doric style gatehouse facing Ridge Avenue is the most significant of these to survive. (His cottage and Gothic chapel have been demolished.) He may have based the gatehouse on the Chelsea Physic Garden in London, and it vaguely conveys the sense of a Roman triumphal arch, with octastyle portico bracketing the coffered, barrel-vaulted entry passage. While the building itself is stone, stuccoed and scored to simulate ashlar, the fluted columns are wood, painted and sanded to match the walls.

The two flanking wings were intended as habitations for the gardener and the porter; the north lodge, however, was modified early in the twentieth century for use as the cemetery superintendent's office, a retrofitting that greatly detracts from the symmetry of Notman's design and could easily be reversed.

Directly opposite the entry is another Notman structure housing the figures of "Old Mortality and His Pony" by the self-taught Scottish sculptor James Thom (1799–1850). This literary illusion to Sir Walter Scott's itinerant craftsman who traveled the countryside re-cutting tombstone inscriptions probably escapes most twenty-first-century visitors, but to the founders of Laurel Hill Cemetery it was intended as a reminder to their successors "to keep the place in perpetual repair, and to transmit it undefaced to a distant date."

The founders understood their potential clients and how to market; virtually from the beginning the enterprise was successful. To lend *gravitas* and the patina of patriotic association, the bones of Charles Thomson (1729–1824), secretary of the Continental Congress, were disinterred from an unmarked grave in the private Harriton graveyard—in what is now Bryn Mawr—and buried under an imposing obelisk at Laurel Hill. (Or so they thought. The family believes that the

The marble tomb of Joseph Saunders Lewis (1778–1836), designed by John Notman. Lewis was chairman of the Watering Committee when the Schuylkill River was dammed for the Fairmount Water Works. According to the inscription, Lewis's "remains fitly repose in this spot, on the River rendered by his labors a source of Prosperity, Health and Safety to his Native City."

body moved was that of a household servant, and that Thomson still rests peacefully in Lower Merion.)

In a review of American rural cemeteries published in 1849, Andrew Jackson Downing observed,

> The great attraction of these cemeteries, to the mass of the community, is not in the fact that they are burial places, or solemn places of meditation for the friends of the deceased, or striking exhibitions of monumental sculpture, though all these have their influence. All these might be realized in a burial ground, planted with straight lines of willows, and somber avenues of evergreens. The true secret of the attraction is in the natural beauty of the sites, and in the tasteful and harmonious embellishment of these sites by art . . . richly wooded with fine planted trees, like Laurel Hill.

Lacking large parks accessible to urban areas, Victorians were attracted to rural cemeteries where they would find, in the words of one Laurel Hill founder, "a school of instruction in architecture, sculpture, landscape-gardening,

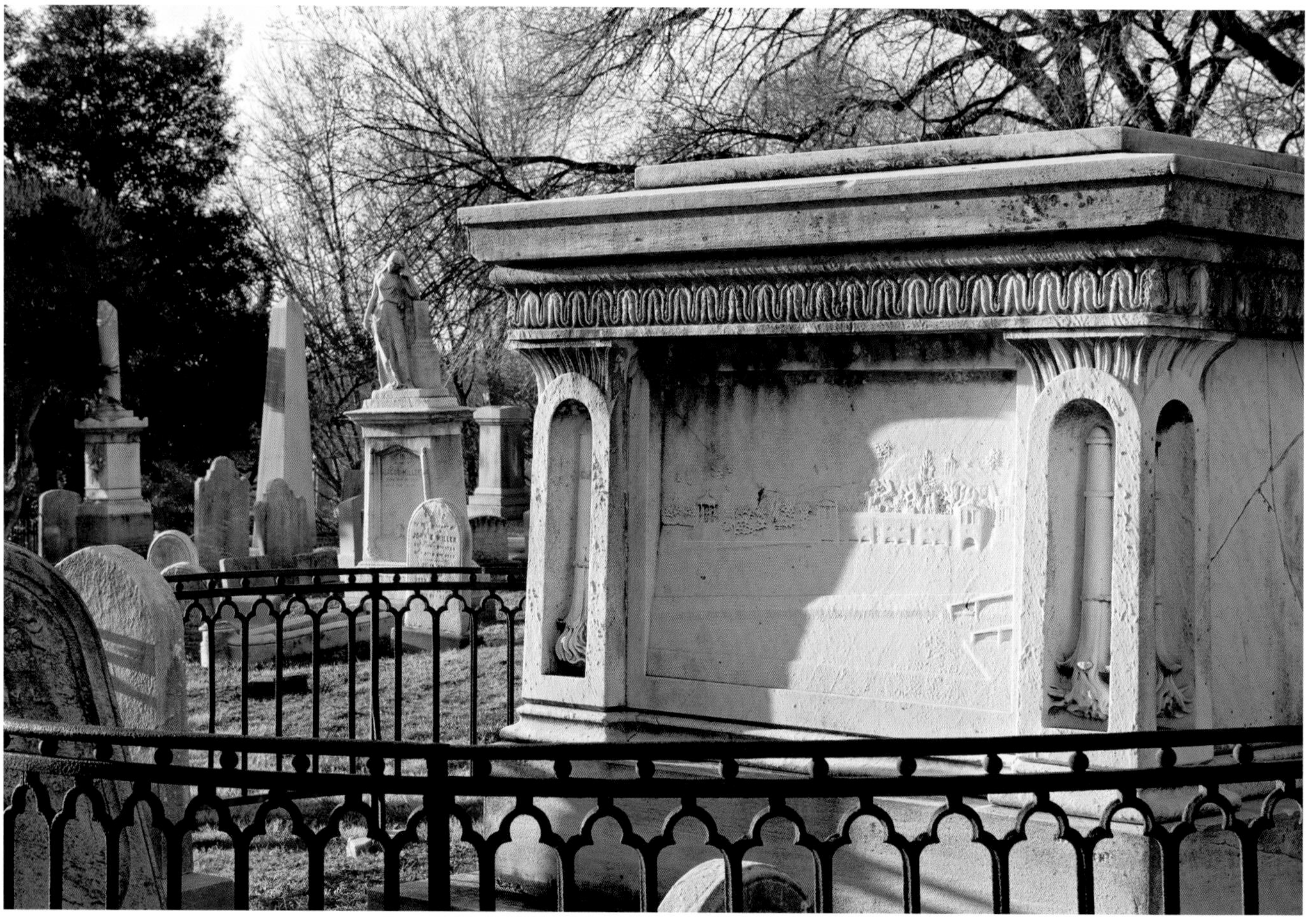

The south side of the Joseph Saunders Lewis tomb carries a relief of the Fairmount Water Works and Dam carved by John Hill of the John Struthers firm.

Mausoleums in "Millionaires Row."

arboriculture, [and] beauty." So popular did Laurel Hill become that Downing reported visitation of nearly 30,000 between April and December 1848, and by 1860 140,000 people toured Laurel Hill in a single year.

Throughout the nineteenth century Laurel Hill enjoyed a reputation as Philadelphia's premier cemetery; during later decades nouveau riche millionaires vied with each other in erecting mausoleums reviving all the exotic architectural modes—Egyptian, Gothic, Moorish, Eastlake, French Renaissance, Classic, and Art Nouveau—on a scale the founders could never have anticipated. In the twentieth century, however, as the surrounding neighborhood declined and wealthy families abandoned the city for the suburbs, Laurel Hill began to lose its appeal in favor of West Laurel Hill across the Schuylkill and countless memorial parks throughout the region. As with many older cemetery companies, the income from conservatively invested perpetual care accounts failed to keep pace with post-World War II inflation; as annual maintenance costs escalated, income from new interments declined. As a result, the well-manicured environment that had been central to the appeal of a garden cemetery suffered, only adding to the downward spiral.

In the last quarter of the twentieth century, however, the renewed interest in Victorian-era art, architecture, and design prompted the founding of the Friends of Laurel Hill Cemetery, who sponsor tours, lectures, special events (the "Gravediggers' Ball"), and publications. The Friends have successfully marketed this landmark as an "underground museum" where the public is now invited to "bury its mind in history."

FREEDOM THEATRE

(Edwin Forrest House, Philadelphia School of Design for Women)
1346 North Broad Street
Philadelphia, PA 19121-4397

Stephen D. Button, architect (attributed), 1853–1855
James H. Windrim, architect of rear addition, 1880
National Historic Landmark, 1993

Telephone for visitor information: 215.765.2793
www.freedomtheater.org

The diverse history of the handsome Victorian-era Italianate brownstone house at the corner of North Broad and Master Streets provides a metaphor for the evolution of its neighborhood over the past 150 years: elegant mansion of a celebrated thespian, theater, restaurant, and—for much of its existence—the first American school of industrial design for women. And now it shelters Pennsylvania's oldest African American theater.

William Penn's dream that the crossing of High (Market) and Broad Streets would one day be the center of Philadelphia became a reality in the mid-nineteenth century. Beginning from the future site of City Hall on Center Square, handsome blocks of residential properties marched north and south along Broad Street, soon to be followed by sacred places, clubs, and cultural institutions. In 1853, the wealthy Philadelphia brewer William Gaul commissioned a substantial city house in the latest Italianate Revival Style that had been introduced to Philadelphia by John Notman at the Athenæum in 1845 (pages 132–137). Gaul's probable choice for an architect was Stephen Decatur Button

Edwin Forrest as "Metamora," c. 1860. Mathew Brady Studio. National Portrait Gallery, Smithsonian Institution; gift of the Edwin Forrest Home for Retired Actors.

(1813–1897), a native of Connecticut who in the late 1840s had relocated to the Philadelphia area, where he fully embraced the picturesque, eclectic, and flexible Italianate style that would characterize his most important commissions, such as the Spring Garden Institute on North Broad Street (1851–1852) and the First Baptist Church (northwest corner of North Broad and Arch Streets, 1853–1856; demolished). He also entered the competition for the Academy of Music (pages 154–159), securing the second premium after the winning design by Le Brun and Runge. He appears to have been much in demand as the designer of houses along Broad Street, and the Gaul house is typical of his work.

Gaul never occupied the house, however, selling the unfinished structure in 1855 to the Philadelphia-born actor Edwin Forrest (1806–1872), who is often characterized as "the first true star of the American theater." Smitten by acting as a young man, Forrest made his first public appearance at the Walnut Street Theater (pages 96–99) in 1820, and from that point he enjoyed a meteoric and highly remunerative career throughout the United States and in London. He specialized in dramatic interpretations from the classical repertoire—Macbeth,

The handsome five-bay façade of the Edwin Forrest House on North Broad Street was probably by architect Stephen D. Button (1853–1855). The extensive addition on Master Street was designed in 1880 by James Hamilton Windrim for the Philadelphia School of Design for Women, now Moore College of Art and Design.

Othello, King Lear—and other roles that are (perhaps fortunately) rarely performed, such as the lead in the 1829 play *Metamora; or, The Last of the Wampanoags* by the aspiring Philadelphia playwright John August Stone (1801–1834). From the beginning of Forrest's career, according to one biographer, "his youth, his robust and manly physique, his clear resonant voice, his fair and handsome face" won favor with audiences both at home and abroad.

Forrest's lifelong devotion to the theater reached beyond acting. He encouraged American playwrights by offering generous prizes for plays by Americans, and he concentrated his testamentary philanthropy on creating a safe haven for elderly actors at his summer retreat called Springbrook in the Holmesburg section of Philadelphia. The retirement home operated from 1876 to 1988, when its assets were merged with the Actors Fund to construct a nursing facility in Englewood, New Jersey, named the Edwin Forrest Wing.

The main entrance of the Italianate style Forrest House survives virtually intact from the 1850s.

Following Forrest's death and the liquidation of his estate, the house at North Broad and Master Streets briefly became a restaurant and then a church. Finally, in 1880, it found an institutional owner that would fully occupy and considerably expand the building over the next eighty years: the Philadelphia School of Design for Women. The school had opened as an informal "Female School of Design" in 1848 to provide "needy and deserving" young women with marketable skills in industrial design for the wallpaper, carpet, floor tile, textile, and wood engraving industries of Philadelphia, all of which were dependent on expensive imported design sources. The founding of such a school was the perfect symbiotic relationship, combining philanthropy with a practical solution to the need for a domestic source of industrial design. It was the first such institution in the United States, soon to be emulated in Boston, New York, Pittsburgh, and Cincinnati. The school was granted a charter in 1853 under the name Philadelphia School of Design for Women, and by 1880 it needed the much larger quarters the Forrest house could provide, especially after the architect James Hamilton Windrim (1840–1919) more than doubled the house with a major addition extending along Master Street. We'll soon meet Windrim as architect of the Philadelphia Masonic Temple on North Broad Street (pages 172–179), and following his addition to the Philadelphia School of Design for Women he served as chairman of the Spring Garden Institute Committee on Art Schools (1881– 1882) and the Committee on Schools of Design and Drawing (1883–1884).

In 1921 the Moore Institute was established by the estate of Joseph Moore, Jr., to provide for the education of the "gentler sex"; in 1932 the Institute merged with the Philadelphia School of Design for Women. With the school now on a secure financial footing for the first time in its history, it was renamed the Moore Institute of Art, Science, and Industry—today Moore College of Art and Design. The renamed school received accreditation from the Pennsylvania State Council on Education (1933) and awarded its first degrees the following year. Moore College had long owned land on Logan Square and in 1959 the North Broad Street building was abandoned for the new campus.

After Moore College vacated the historic Forrest house, responsibility for the property passed to Heritage House, a neighborhood art and music center. In 1966 John E. Allen, Jr., founded the Freedom Theatre at the Forrest house; it is now Pennsylvania's oldest African American theater. A performing arts training program was launched in 1971, and in 1993 a professional repertory performing company known as Freedom Rep was established. In forty years the Freedom Theatre has grown from a neighborhood program to a nationally recognized, award-winning institution. Without question Edwin Forrest would be pleased.

INSTITUTE OF THE PENNSYLVANIA HOSPITAL

(Pennsylvania Hospital for the Insane)
111 North Forty-Ninth Street
Philadelphia, PA 19139

Samuel Sloan, architect, 1854–1859
National Historic Landmark, 1965

Telephone for visitor information: 215.471.2600
www.kirkbridecenter.com

The Pennsylvania Hospital's founders declared their intention in 1751 for the care of "the sick poor of the Province and for the reception and cure of lunaticks" (pages 54–59). Unfortunately for the latter, the emphasis was on reception rather than cure. In the eighteenth century the insane were thought to be forsaken by God or possessed by the devil; treatment often meant chains or other restraints, confinement to cages or cells, bloodletting, blistering, purging, or repetitive plunging into hot or cold water. At the Pennsylvania Hospital insane patients were housed in the basement where the cruel or merely curious could pay a modest admission fee to stare at or tease the unfortunate inmates.

By the early nineteenth century, Quaker reformers were calling such methods into question. They would have far-reaching influence on the treatment of the insane, just as they had led in prison reform (see Eastern State Penitentiary, pages 86–91). Pennsylvania Quakers, encouraged by the teachings of the British Quaker merchant William Tuke and his grandson Samuel Tuke, founded the Friends Asylum in Frankford (now Friends Hospital) in 1817. The Asylum was the first hospital in America intended exclusively for care of the mentally ill. It became a model for other mental facilities, particularly for the humane housing of patients in a linear structure that gave light and ventilation to every room. In his *Account* of the asylum in 1825 Robert Waln remarked, "the free circulation of air, the great supporter of life, is of primary importance; without proper ventilation, the resources of medicine may be developed in vain; the miserable sufferers are suffocated in the effluvia of their own bodies, and [a] long train of physical evils are added to their mental miseries." (In 1999, in recognition of the hospital's seminal role in the moral care of the mentally ill, it was declared a National Historic Landmark.)

At the same time the managers of the Pennsylvania Hospital on Pine Street were grappling with a cruel fact: *more than half their patients* were numbered among the insane. To relieve this overcrowding, the hospital managers purchased a farm two miles west of town on which to erect a facility for the mentally ill, and to design the new hospital they selected English-born architect Isaac Holden (fl. 1830s–1884). Little is known of Holden's career, except that he worked briefly for John Haviland at a time when his countryman was preparing a model design for three naval hospitals. At first the Pennsylvania Hospital managers planned to erect the new building across Pine Street from the eighteenth-century hospital complex, and competition designs were received in 1833 from several architects, including Haviland, Strickland, and Walter. Nothing came of the Eighth and Pine Streets scheme, and on June 22, 1836, the cornerstone was laid for Holden's new Pennsylvania Hospital for Mental and Nervous Diseases near what would become the intersection of Forty-Fourth and Market Streets.

⋞ The Greek Revival style central pavilion of the Institute of the Pennsylvania Hospital was designed and erected under the supervision of Philadelphia architect Samuel Sloan, 1854–1859.

Serving as his building superintendent was a promising young master carpenter named Samuel Sloan. Halfway through the construction, Holden returned to England, leaving Sloan to complete the hospital building in 1841.

At this point it is necessary to introduce Dr. Thomas S. Kirkbride (1809–1883), a member of the Society of Friends and the most influential advocate for the moral treatment of the insane in the mid-nineteenth century. Kirkbride believed the mentally ill could be cured if they were treated in a proper environment, which required a particular building design. Summarizing his approach in an 1847 article titled *Remarks on the Construction and Arrangements of Hospitals for the Insane* (issued in book form in 1854), Kirkbride argued:

> Most other diseases may be managed at home. . . . It is not so, however, with insanity; for the universal experience is that a large majority of all such cases can be treated most successfully among strangers, and . . . only in institutions specially provided for the management of this class of diseases. It is among the most painful features of insanity, that in its treatment, so many are compelled to leave their families.

Kirkbride argued that these ideal hospitals should always be constructed on at least fifty acres in open country where therapeutic farming and gardening could be conducted. The hospital should be sited so patients will have "the most extensive view and most agreeable scenery, and that every possible advantage may be derived from the prevailing winds of summer."

As for the building itself, "apartments are required for the resident offices of the institution, and for the family of its medical superintendent—for all the domestic operations of the house, and those engaged in carrying them out, and for the comfortable accommodation of at least five, (preferably of seven), distinct classes of patients of each sex." The best arrangement would be a central section for staff and administration with narrow wings at right angles to the central pavilion to which an infinite number of wings could be added, each stepping back from the first pair to give every ward access to natural light and cross ventilation.

It has been said that Kirkbride had the Holden-designed building in mind because he was appointed to preside over that West Philadelphia institution. But when Kirkbride received his appointment in 1840 the Pennsylvania Hospital was nearing completion on its narrow lot at the Forty-Fourth Street site; it would ultimately be demolished because it lacked the setting advocated by Kirkbride and did not permit the expansion that was required within a few years. Kirkbride would first realize his ideal hospital design in consultation with

John Notman at the New Jersey State Lunatic Asylum (Trenton Psychiatric Hospital) designed in 1845.

Meantime, what of Samuel Sloan? Having completed the Holden building in 1841, and perhaps on Kirkbride's recommendation, Sloan secured the commission to design the symmetrical, linear plan Alabama Insane Hospital in Tuscaloosa (1852) with flanking pavilions set back *en échelon*. Kirkbride's shallow V-shape rapidly became the standard for American hospitals for the insane, especially after the appearance of *On the Construction and Arrangement of Hospitals for the Insane*, which was illustrated with an unnamed hospital, actually Sloan's Alabama Insane Hospital. That same year the managers of the Pennsylvania Hospital decided to erect a near *duplicate* of the Holden/Sloan building at Forty-Fourth Street on a larger plot of ground at Forty-Ninth Street with Samuel Sloan as architect. (These two buildings were superficially so similar that architectural historians have tended to conflate them.) The surviving structure of 1854–1859 at Forty-Ninth and Market Streets is in the Greek Revival style, with a central gable-roofed pavilion, a central dome, and a two-story pedimented portico with wings—as shown in the accompanying plan.

While the Institute of the Pennsylvania Hospital is his only Philadelphia National Historic Landmark, Samuel Sloan (1815–1884) was one of the leading Philadelphia-based architects of the mid-nineteenth century with a national

Influenced by the philosophy of Dr. Thomas S. Kirkbride, the plan of the hospital was designed to provide ample light and fresh air to all the wards. Samuel Sloan, *Architectural Review and American Builders' Journal* (1869). Athenæum of Philadelphia Collection.

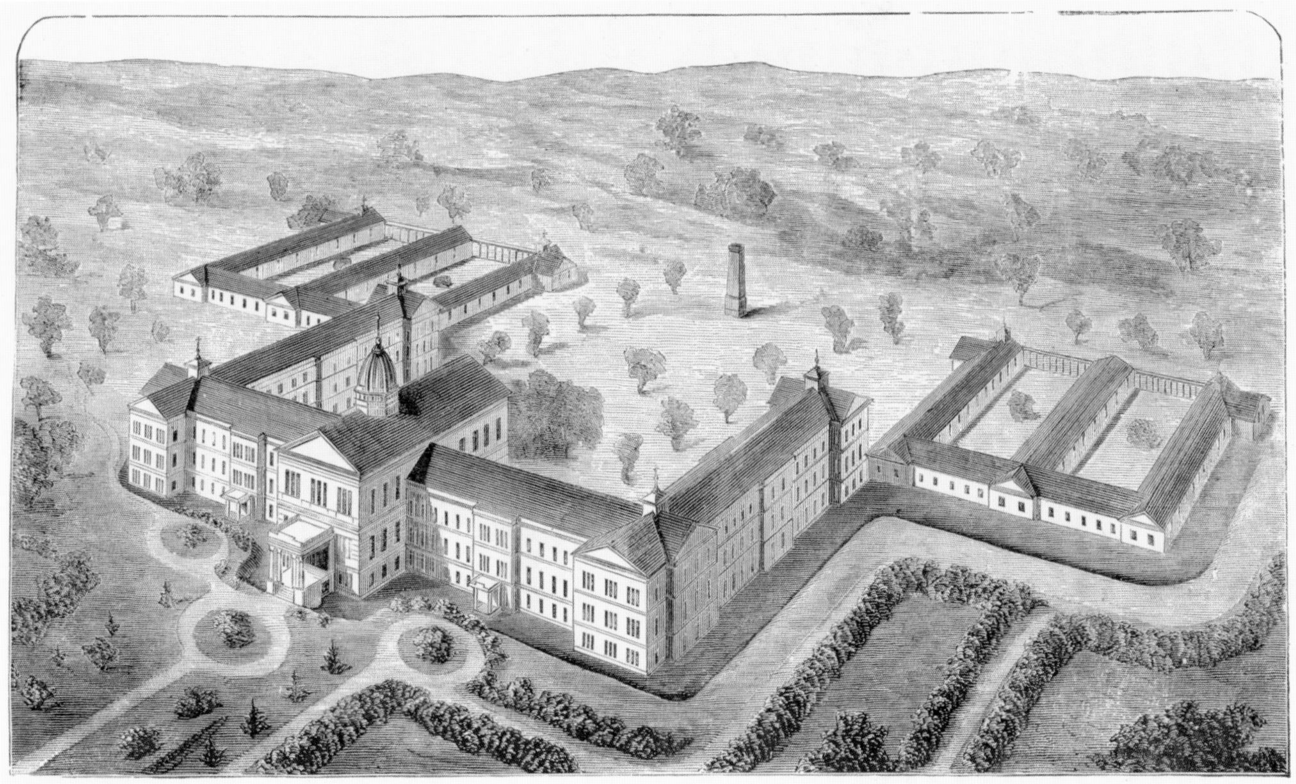

⚘ Plan of Isaac Holden's Pennsylvania Hospital (1836–1841), which provided a prototype for Samuel Sloan's design of the present hospital (1854–1859). Athenæum of Philadelphia Collection.

practice. Sloan has been characterized by his biographer Harold N. Cooledge as "brash, opportunistic, inventive, a quick learner and a driving worker who was hungry for success and who had, throughout his life, an abiding belief in America's destiny." Trained as a carpenter, Sloan came to Philadelphia from his native Chester County in the mid-1830s and is said to have worked at the Eastern State Penitentiary (pages 86–91) before becoming Isaac Holden's superintendent of construction at the Pennsylvania Hospital for Mental and Nervous

Diseases. Throughout the 1830s and 1840s Sloan listed himself as a carpenter in the Philadelphia city directories and only styled himself as an architect from 1851 after winning commissions for the Delaware County, Pennsylvania, courthouse and jail (1849) and an Italianate style villa for Andrew M. Eastwick on the site of Bartram's Garden in Philadelphia (1850–1851; see *Historic Houses*, pages 74–76).

Early in his career Sloan began to publish the series of books that would make him one of the most prolific American authors on architecture of the mid-nineteenth century. Significantly, it was his writings that the author of Sloan's obituary in *American Architect and Building News* selected as his most enduring contribution. His *Model Architect* began to appear in 1851 in parts and was published as bound volumes in 1852–1853, to be followed by *City and Suburban Architecture* (1859) and five other titles, most of which enjoyed multiple editions. Louis Godey also began to publish designs by Sloan in his *Lady's Book* in the 1850, which gave him additional national exposure through the most popular magazine for women in pre-Civil War America.

Throughout the 1850s Sloan enjoyed a rapidly expanding practice, particularly as an architect of hospitals for the insane; his office turned out designs for asylums in Georgia, Illinois, Maine, Michigan, Missouri, Maryland, Massachusetts, and Kentucky, in addition to Alabama and Pennsylvania. However, the financial panic of 1857–1858, the hiatus in building caused by the Civil War, and a political scandal relating to the Philadelphia City Hall competition (pages 180–185) combined to suppress his Philadelphia practice. In the 1870s his most important work was outside Pennsylvania, again designing hospitals for the insane in Indiana, Connecticut, South Carolina, and North Carolina, where he designed the Western State Asylum for the Insane.

ACADEMY OF MUSIC

(The American Academy of Music)
Broad and Locust Streets
Philadelphia, PA 19102

Napoleon Le Brun and Gustav Runge, architects, 1855–1857
National Historic Landmark, 1962

Telephone for visitor information: 215.893.1999
www.academyofmusic.org

Few Philadelphia landmarks are as universally beloved as the Academy of Music. Like the Teatro alla Scala in Milan and Charles Garnier's Théâtre de l'Opéra in Paris, historic opera houses elicit a frisson of anticipation, first from the pomp and ceremony inherent in the coming performance, and then architecturally by the processional entry through highlights of glittering gold and reflected illumination. Long before the house lights dim and the strains of Mozart or Verdi rise from the pit, we are transported to another time, and because this is opera, perhaps to a higher plane.

Prior to the construction of the Academy of Music, Philadelphia had no adequate venue for opera. Musical Fund Hall on Locust Street, designed by William Strickland (1824) and enlarged by Napoleon Le Brun (1847), was not suitable for grand opera, nor could the superannuated Walnut Street Theatre (1809,

Main auditorium of William Strickland's Musical Fund Hall as it appeared at the time of the Academy of Music competition. This drawing is attributed to John Skirving (fl. 1835–1865), who specialized in the warming and ventilating of public buildings. Athenæum of Philadelphia, Thomas U. Walter Collection.

pages 96–99), Chestnut Street Theater (1822), or Arch Street Theater (1828) serve that purpose. By the early 1840s, as Philadelphia began to emerge from the crippling economic depression that since 1837 had halted virtually all civic building and bankrupted our best architects, a group of community leaders, "friendly to the project of erecting a dramatic edifice to be devoted to the representation of operas," began meeting. They even commissioned drawings for an opera house from John Haviland (pages 116–119). But economic clouds still threatened. Not until 1851, perhaps motivated by successful efforts to erect opera houses in Boston and New York, did the Philadelphia committee redouble its effort. Public notices were published, subscriptions solicited, and an option taken on a lot of ground.

Just as the city consolidated the whole of Philadelphia County in 1854—doubling its population—the Academy's committee advertised for a "Design . . . for an Opera House, to be erected at the southwest corner of Broad and Locust streets." More than a dozen submissions from architects in Baltimore, Boston, New York, and Philadelphia were received for a building of a "simple but imposing style of architecture."

Ultimately the committee settled on the design submitted by a newly formed partnership consisting of Napoleon Le Brun (1822–1901) and Gustav Runge

Academy of Music at the corner of Broad and Locust Streets.

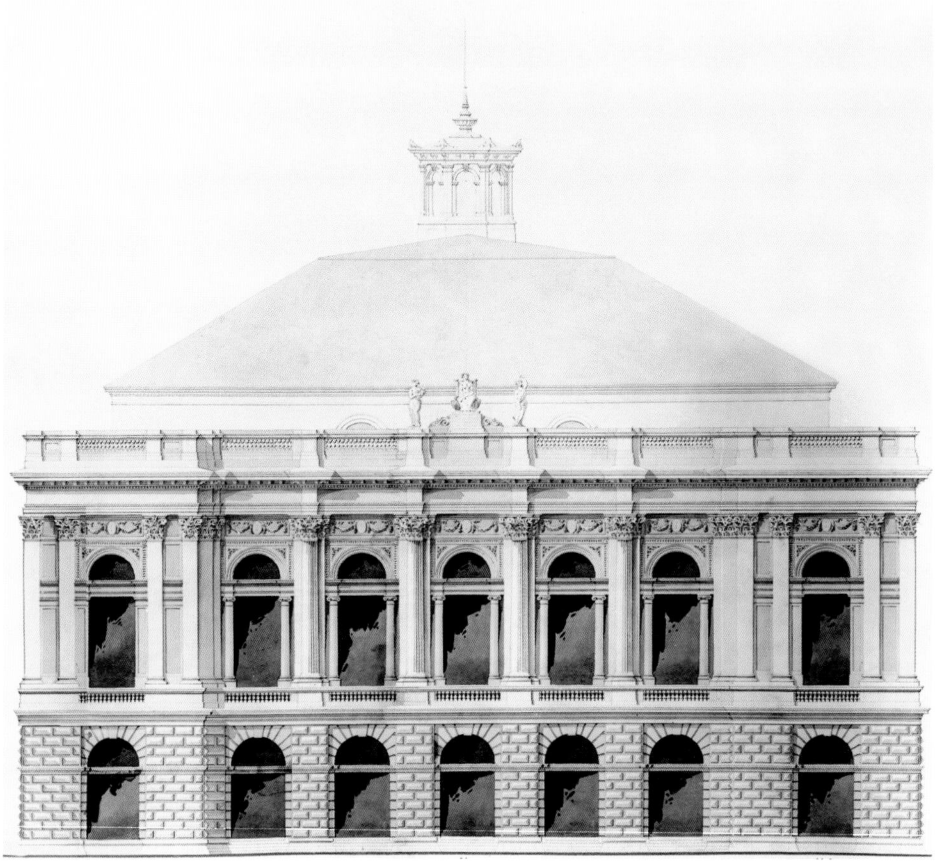

Original competition design for the Academy of Music by Napoleon Le Brun and Gustav Runge (1854). This elegant Venetian façade was simplified for reasons of economy. From a restored photograph of the lost original drawing. Athenæum of Philadelphia Collection, gift of George B. Tatum.

(1822–1900). Le Brun was born in Philadelphia, the son of French-born Catholics, and apprenticed around 1836 to Thomas Ustick Walter, where he remained until around 1841, at which time he opened his own office. His early commissions were Catholic churches, three of which (Saint Philip Neri, Saint Augustine's, and the Cathedral Basilica of Saints Peter and Paul) are discussed at length in *Historic Sacred Places*. A few years earlier he had expanded Musical Fund Hall, a commission that would certainly have brought him favorably to the attention of the Academy committee. Gustav Runge, on the other hand, was born in Bremen, Germany, of a musical family and had studied engineering and architecture at Karlsruhe and Berlin. By 1850 he had migrated to Philadelphia, where he remained until approximately 1861 before returning to Germany. There is evidence to suggest that Runge—who probably contributed more to the Academy design and its acoustics than his American partner—was the more academically trained of the two.

Runge and Le Brun's rich Venetian design was awarded first prize in February 1855. It featured a main façade with a colonnade of Corinthian columns and pilasters at the *piano nobile* level above an arcade of ground floor entrances. Between the Corinthian columns were pairs of smaller Ionic columns supporting arches that formed a loggia with balconies opening from the grand saloon overlooking Broad Street. Unfortunately, this elegant design was simplified by the committee for economic reasons by removing the applied columns and the rusticated ground floor treatment. This gave Runge the opportunity to create a round-arch, or *Rundbogenstil*, façade in the latest German academic taste, with articulated brickwork, in the architect's words, "executed in the best style, with spirit, boldness and sharpness." The committee described the result as "massive and imposing, although exceedingly plain, with window frames shaped in a manner approaching the Gothic [sic], which is peculiarly calculated to produce a pretty effect in the evenings when the interior of the building is illuminated."

The cornerstone was laid on July 26, 1855, and the first performance (Giuseppe Verdi's four-year-old *Il Trovatore*) opened on February 25, 1857. Sidney George Fisher, whose diary gives us so many trenchant assessments of mid-century Philadelphia buildings, recorded on that day,

> Dressed & went at 8 to the opera. . . . First opera in the new house. . . .The building is very large and admirably arranged—4 tiers of boxes, an immense parquette, wide corridors, with saloons, dressing rooms for ladies, &c, all richly decorated & furnished. The woodwork is white & gold, the seats all covered with crimson velvet and the walls with crimson paper. It is thoroughly

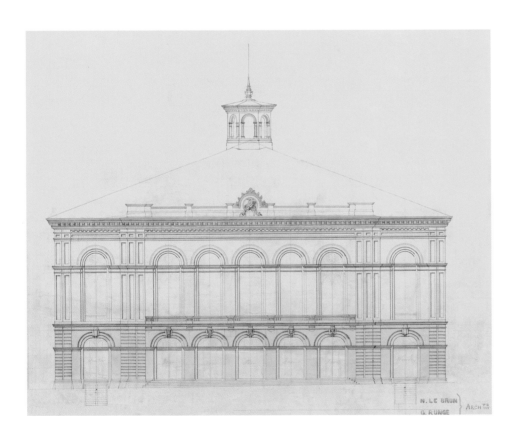

Le Brun and Runge's revised design (1855) in the German *Rundbogenstil* round-arched style. The Academy opened on February 25, 1857, with a performance of *Il Trovatore*. Historical Society of Pennsylvania.

> heated & brilliantly lighted. The central chandelier is very beautiful of gleaming crystal & diamonds.

Fisher concluded, "The whole thing is an ornament to the city & very creditable to the liberality of the gentlemen who got it up. It remains to be seen whether it can be supported."

Built in the nineteenth century as an opera house, the Academy has nonetheless had to support itself as a rental hall, hosting hundreds of programs annually, including rock concerts, political carnivals, and graduation rituals, in addition to dance and opera performances. Throughout the twentieth century, it was most associated in the public's mind with the Philadelphia Orchestra. Founded in 1900 under the baton of Fritz Scheel, the Orchestra rapidly became a world-renowned institution and the Academy's most enduring tenant. Through the reigns of Leopold Stokowski, Arturo Toscanini, Eugene Ormandy, and their

As Sidney George Fisher described the auditorium in 1855, "The woodwork is white & gold, the seats all covered with crimson velvet and the walls with crimson paper. . . . The central chandelier is very beautiful of gleaming crystal & diamonds."

successors, various proposals were advanced to find a more appropriate venue for the Orchestra than the aging opera house. Despite two successful restoration campaigns in the second half of the twentieth century by Martin, Stewart, Noble & Class (1957–1966) and Hyman Myers for the Vitetta Group (1982–2000), the Orchestra relocated to the $235-million Kimmel Center designed by Rafael Viñoly, which opened in 2001. Fortunately the expanding public support for the Philadelphia Opera Company continues to offer that brilliant blend of theater, voice, instrumental music, and architecture that is the Academy's special gift to Philadelphia.

The foyer with the original 1850s gasoliers.

WAGNER FREE INSTITUTE OF SCIENCE OF PHILADELPHIA

1700 West Montgomery Avenue
Philadelphia, PA 19121

John McArthur, architect, 1859–1865
Collins & Autenrieth, renovations, c. 1885–1895
G.W. & W. D. Hewitt, library wing addition, 1901
National Historic Landmark, 1990

Telephone for visitor information: 215.763.6529
www.wagnerfreeinstitute.org

⚘ The Civil War-era Wagner Free Institute of Science building, designed by John McArthur, Jr., in the "Greco-Roman" style (1859–1865), retains much of its original architectural integrity.

The commercial and industrial colossus that Philadelphia became in the nineteenth century poured forth riches on a scale unimaginable in previous eras, and occasionally the accumulators of this wealth were motivated to found philanthropic institutions. Just as Quaker good works of the colonial era inspired Stephen Girard to bequeath his fortune to found a college for orphaned children (pages 110–115), his charitable example deeply impressed William Wagner (1796–1885), son of a Philadelphia cloth merchant who entered Girard's counting house as an apprentice. Ultimately Wagner flourished in a variety of enterprises that allowed him to retire at the age of forty-four to devote his resources (and those of his second wife, Louisa Binney Wagner) to the pursuit of a lifelong passion for science in general and natural history in particular.

In 1841 Wagner purchased a North Philadelphia country estate known as Elm Grove, near what is now Seventeenth Street above Montgomery Lane. Here he began to offer free public lectures on mineralogy, geology, and conchology, illustrated with specimens from the *Wunderkammer* that housed his extensive personal collection. As these free programs in science education gained in popularity, and both the volunteer faculty and the curriculum expanded, Wagner moved

his informal institute to the second floor of Spring Garden Hall at Thirteenth and Spring Garden Streets. In March 1855 the Commonwealth granted the Wagner Free Institute of Science a charter, and in May that same year the first formal program schedule was announced.

The Wagner Free Institute of Science—and similar natural history museums and educational institutions founded by wealthy amateur scientists across America—occupy an important place in the evolution of American public education. Like the hundreds of privately supported libraries that were replaced once tax-supported free public libraries were established, most of these scientific societies have disappeared as natural history research and education has become common in public schools and university programs. The few that have survived—the Wagner Free Institute in Philadelphia and the Fairbanks Museum and Planetarium in St. Johnsbury, Vermont, being notable examples—remain independent and active in the twenty-first century because they continue to provide useful services and educational programs for their communities. Not incidentally, both are housed in historic buildings displaying their founders' collections assembled and arranged largely as they were in the Victorian era.

In the eighteenth and early nineteenth centuries, learned societies dedicated to literature and scholarship (in Philadelphia the American Philosophical Society, Library Company, and Athenæum, to mention three already discussed) attracted local persons with inquiring minds who were invited to participate as members. While these institutions included an interest in science and research in their early founding documents, more specialized institutions were soon established, most notably the Academy of Natural Sciences and the Franklin Institute, which were founded with a narrower focus on science and technology. Wagner was active in these organizations, but he recognized that their programs and membership remained open largely to an elite group of upper-class men. Following in the steps of his mentor, Stephen Girard, Wagner envisioned an institution committed to public education through free evening classes open to all.

In 1859 Wagner lost Spring Garden Hall as a venue for his lectures and decided to commission a new building at his own expense to be erected near his home at Elm Grove. Here he could combine his private museum and provide a lecture hall for the Institute. For his architect Wagner turned to John McArthur, Jr. (1823–1890), who is today primarily remembered for his chef-d'œuvre, Philadelphia City Hall, the tallest and largest public building in the United States at the time of its completion (pages 180–185). Born in the western lowlands of Scotland, he came to Philadelphia as a child and served an apprenticeship as a house carpenter while attending classes in architecture at Carpenters' Hall and lectures on the history of architecture by Thomas Ustick Walter at the Franklin

The second floor is occupied by a natural history museum containing Wagner's collection as expanded by Joseph Leidy in the late nineteenth century. The present layout was designed in the 1880s by Philadelphia architects Collins & Autenrieth. It is a remarkable survival of a Victorian-era museum collection.

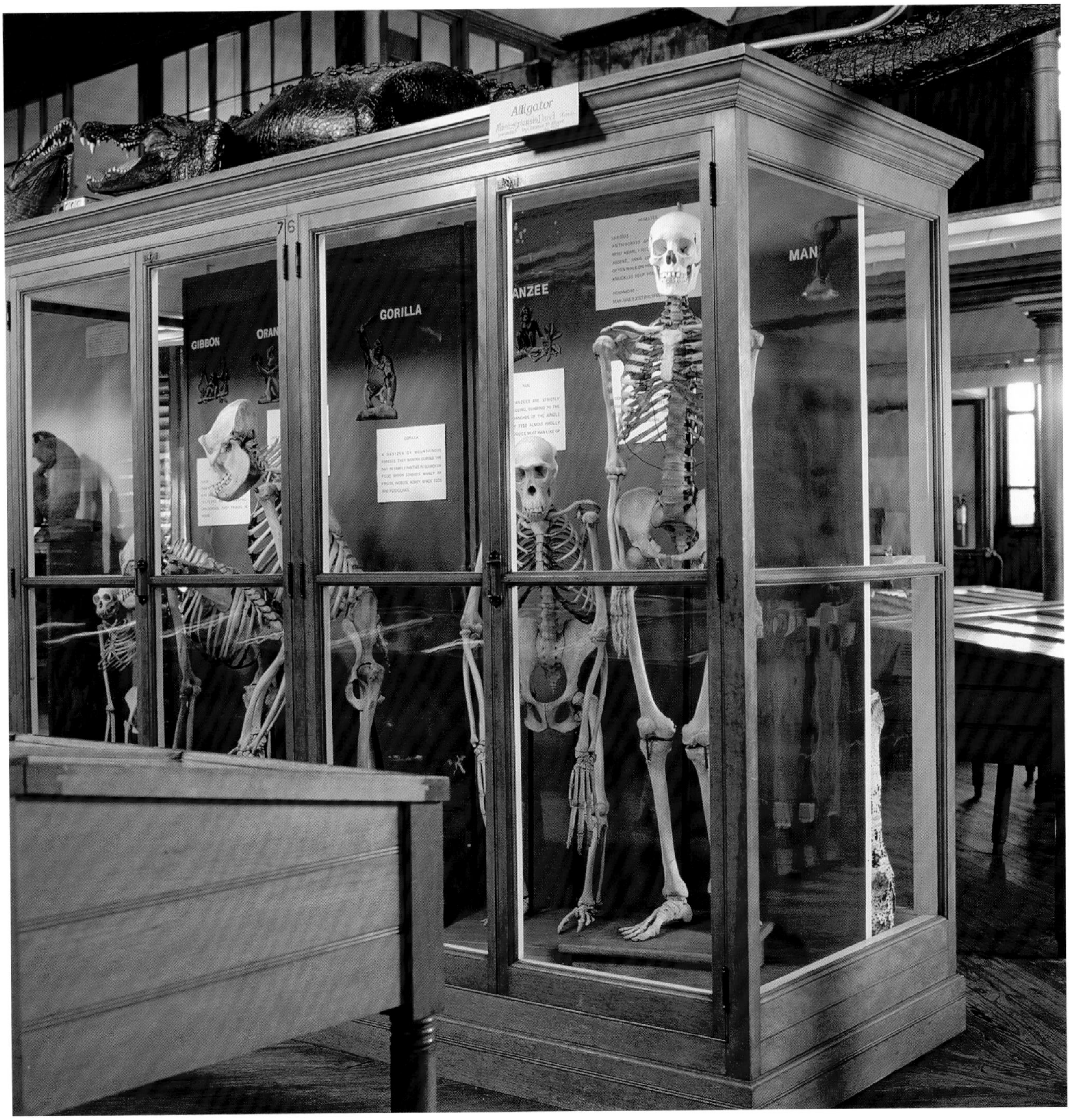

Not only did the famous naturalist Joseph Leidy (1823–1891) arrange the museum displays at the Wagner Free Institute, but he expanded the anatomical holdings, which remain particular favorites with visiting schoolchildren.

Institute. At the age of twenty-five, McArthur won his first competition, for the Philadelphia House of Refuge (1848). From that point he secured a steady stream of commissions. On the eve of being asked to design the relatively modest Wagner Free Institute building, he had just completed the last of three Philadelphia hotels: Girard House (1852), La Pierre House (1853), and Continental (1858), as well as his own large, dramatic Italianate Revival Tenth Presbyterian Church (see *Historic Sacred Places*, pages 178–83).

McArthur's building for Wagner is a two-story brick, three-bay classical temple with a street-facing pedimented gable and paired pilasters—described at the time as in the "Greco-Roman" style—that might easily be mistaken for a *retardataire* Roman Catholic parish church of the 1840s, were it not for the round-headed windows. The building opened to the public in 1865, when the Institute's lectures in mineralogy, paleontology, geology, botany, chemistry, astronomy, and engineering resumed in the new ground floor lecture hall.

The first floor lecture hall remains largely as redecorated by Collins & Autenrieth in the 1880s. Free public lectures have been given in this space since the building opened in 1865.

Following Wagner's death in 1885 the Institute trustees appointed world-renowned naturalist Joseph Leidy (1823–1891), president to lead the Institute faculty while simultaneously holding the chair of anatomy and director of the department of biology at the University of Pennsylvania and president of the Academy of Natural Sciences. During his brief tenure at the Institute he encouraged scholarly research, collecting, and publication, reorganized the collection, and expanded its anatomical holdings. Also at this time the Institute trustees engaged the architectural firm of Edward Collins (1821–1902) and Charles M. Autenrieth (1828–1906), whom we've encountered working on the Contributionship building (pages 120–123), to stucco the exterior brickwork of McArthur's building and to remodel the interior. The most dramatic impact of this campaign was the renovation of the second floor exhibition hall, which was reopened as the Museum of the Institute. The remarkable late Victorian exhibition cases, cabinets, and shelving laid out under Leidy's direction survive with little alteration.

Today the Institute continues to offer free adult science classes, it preserves and maintains the Museum Collection as a document of nineteenth-century scientific collecting that may be toured by the public, and in recent years an energetic professional staff has developed an extensive education program to provide meaningful enrichment in the sciences for disadvantaged children from local Philadelphia public schools. William Wagner would doubtless be pleased with the twenty-first-century inheritors of his legacy.

UNION LEAGUE OF PHILADELPHIA

140 South Broad Street
Philadelphia, PA 19102-3003

John Fraser, architect, Broad Street building, 1864–1865
Horace Trumbauer, architect, Fifteenth Street building, 1909–1912
National Register of Historic Places, 1979

Public tours available:
215.563.6500
www.unionleague.org

When erected at the close of the Civil War, the red brick and brownstone clubhouse of the Union League of Philadelphia was the second largest building on Broad Street, only the Academy of Music was larger (pages 154–159). Even today, surrounded by high-rise office buildings, banks, and hotels, the League's Victorian-era clubhouse holds its own architecturally. The wide sweep of stairs, snapping flags, and bronze military statues create such a presence that it would be a rare out-of-town visitor who could walk by this landmark without wondering what it was and why it was built.

The Union League was founded as a patriotic club in 1862 to support President Abraham Lincoln and his effort to preserve the Union. Early military successes by the Confederate States Army had emboldened Philadelphia's Copperheads (Democrats who strongly opposed the war and Lincoln's efforts to suppress the Southern Confederacy—so called after the venomous snake). Philadelphia had already provided large numbers of men for the Union army in response to Lincoln's call for volunteers, but among the social and economic leaders of the city—many of whom had family and business ties to the rebellious

Ceiling design by painter George Herzog (1851–1920), one of the foremost exponents of decorative painting in the United States, who also worked at the Masonic Temple, Philadelphia City Hall, and many private residences in the fourth quarter of the nineteenth century. Athenæum of Philadelphia Collection, George Herzog Collection.

region—Southern sympathy remained strong. To counter what they considered a treasonist tendency, prominent Republicans formed the League. They first published pamphlets explaining the war aims of the Lincoln administration, more than 2,000,000 copies of which were distributed throughout the country. In addition, the League supplied nine infantry regiments, equipped five companies of cavalry, and recruited eleven regiments of blacks for the Union cause.

The Broad Street façade of The Union League of Philadelphia (1864–1865) was designed in the Second Empire Style by John Fraser to house the patriotic society founded in 1862 to support President Abraham Lincoln and his effort to preserve the Union during the Civil War.

At first the Union League operated out of rented houses on Chestnut Street, but in 1864 they purchased a lot of ground between Sansom and Moravian Streets along the west side of Broad Street. To design their new building, the club engaged the Scottish-born architect John Fraser (1825–1906); the League clubhouse would be his best-known building. After the Civil War Fraser formed a partnership with Frank Furness and George W. Hewitt, but a few years later he departed for Washington, D.C., where he entered government service.

The League's lot of ground—open to streets on three sides—offered Fraser ample scope to design a building in the fashionable Second Empire Style associated

⇜ The Lincoln Memorial Room on the second floor of Trumbauer's Fifteenth Street addition focuses on the full-size bronze statue of Abraham Lincoln by Swiss-born sculptor J. Otto Schweizer (1863–1955). Carved into panels on either side is the complete text of the Gettysburg Address. Eight bronze medallion portraits of Union generals, also by Schweizer, surmount the names of the five hundred League members who fought for the Union during the Civil War.

with the imperial Bonapartist reign of Napoleon III (1852–1870) that would become popular for both residential and institutional buildings in post-Civil War America. (City Hall and the Victory Building are later Philadelphia landmarks in the Second Empire style, pages 180, 196.) The five-bay central block of Fraser's design rises three stories over a granite base, and includes a distinctive mansard roof with cast-iron cresting. This form of roof consists of two slopes—the lower nearly vertical to provide greater headroom for the attic—and is named for the French architect François Mansart (1598–1666) who used it extensively in the seventeenth century. Its great popularity in the mid-nineteenth century derived from Georges-Eugène Haussmann's rebuilding of Paris during the Second Empire.

On either side of the five-bay central block are identical one-story, one-bay pavilions, which make possible large, elegant reception rooms off the central hall, each with three tall windows looking out on Broad Street. The pavilions also heighten the grandeur of the entire composition and take full advantage of the Broad Street frontage. A tower with a mansard roof and porch projects from the façade and rises the full height of the building. Unlike many postwar Second Empire residential designs, the composition is symmetrical, excepting a four-story tower on Moravian Street. The main entrance is approached from the porch on each side of which broad flights of curved steps ascend from the pavement.

As Union League membership expanded in the post-Civil War decades, a rear annex was added, which ultimately proved inadequate. In 1905, a competition was announced to design a major addition that would extend the Fraser building on Broad Street through to Fifteenth Street. Numerous proposals were received, and Joseph M. Huston's design was chosen. Huston (1866–1940) had attended Princeton and briefly worked for Frank Furness before opening his own office in 1894. His most important nonresidential work from this period was the handsomely detailed Witherspoon Building (1895–1897) for the Presbyterian Board of Publication, which still stands at Walnut and Juniper Streets. In 1901, he won the Pennsylvania State Capitol competition. Although a high-visibility commission that would certainly have propelled his career to new heights, the Capitol proved ill-fated for Huston. He was charged with conspiracy to defraud the Commonwealth, convicted, and imprisoned. Whether Huston truly was guilty continues to be debated, but all mention of him at the League disappears and Horace Trumbauer—whose nearby Georgian Revival style Racquet Club had just been completed (pages 244–247)—was proclaimed League architect.

The grand staircase of the Victorian-era Union League building with its figural newel post gasoliers is solid walnut. Originally it was not carpeted.

Various proposals to demolish and replace the Fraser building had been rejected. The *Architectural Record* commented in 1911 that "sentiment runs high regarding the preservation of the old Broad Street building, and it will probably be many years before it will be torn down to make way for a more modern design of city-club architecture." In fact, Trumbauer's design appears to have presupposed the future demolition of the Fraser building; viewed from Broad Street the blank east wall of the twentieth-century addition looms suggestively over its Victorian predecessor. Today no member would seriously propose demolishing the original Victorian-era building.

The League acquired the balance of the land between Broad and Fifteenth Streets for which Trumbauer designed a broad-shouldered Indiana limestone, Italianate Renaissance palazzo in the manner of London Pall Mall gentlemen's clubs such as Sir Charles Barry's Reform Club. It was erected in two parts seamlessly joined, the first oriented to Fifteenth Street and the "middle building"—replacing the 1880s addition—which contained the 6,000-square-foot Lincoln Hall.

The cornerstone of the Fifteenth Street building was laid on October 9, 1909. Demolition of the 1880s addition and construction of the middle building began

The Fifteenth Street addition (1909–1912) was designed by Horace Trumbauer in the Italianate Renaissance palazzo mode.

in January 1911, and the entire complex was ready for occupancy in early 1912. While Trumbauer may have hoped to replace the Fraser building, he nonetheless successfully unified the League interior by means of a grand marble passage running from the Broad Street entrance to the Fifteenth Street entrance. Reception rooms and ample dining rooms open off both sides of this hallway. On the second level, a similar central passage runs from the Victorian-era McMichael Room overlooking Broad Street to Trumbauer's spacious library overlooking Fifteenth Street. Midway between these two, and accessible from stairs at both ends, is the Lincoln Hall assembly room.

From its earliest days on Broad Street, the Union League collected paintings and sculpture to adorn its clubhouse. After the Trumbauer addition provided greater scope for the display of fine arts, the collection expanded to the point that today the League owns one of the best private collections in Philadelphia. Paintings include such works as Thomas Sully's mammoth equestrian portrait of General George Washington at the Battle of Trenton, Peter F. Rothermel's *Reading of the Declaration of Independence*, and Xanthus Russell Smith's *The Kearsarge and the Alabama*. The sculpture collection is largely portrait busts and memorial tablets, but also includes such life-scale neoclassical idealized figures as James Henry Haseltine's *American Honoring Her Fallen Brave* and Daniel Chester French's bronze of Abraham Lincoln. The League is particularly proud of its portrait collection of presidents of the United States, albeit mostly Republicans.

Not surprisingly, the membership of the League for the first century of its existence was white, Anglo-Saxon, Protestant, male, and Republican. As residential patterns began to alter in the 1950s and 1960s, and tax laws made club dues no longer deductible, the perceived usefulness of such clubs declined. The League lost half its membership. A similar decline had spelled the end of The Rittenhouse Club, which once maintained a handsome clubhouse on the north side of Rittenhouse Square. Today only the bereft Beaux-Arts style façade remains of what was once one of the most exclusive gentlemen's club of Philadelphia. Clearly this was a wake-up call. As a consequence the Union League admitted women, blacks, Catholics, Jews, first generation Americans, and Democrats. Social historian E. Digby Baltzell commented, "the WASP male's dominance of the city, and his wife and family, is now a thing of the past; WASP males and females, Irish and Italian Catholic males and females, Jewish males and females, black males and females are all in the elitist race today; the class is irrelevant." The Union League, he concluded, "is now the most relevant club in Philadelphia." As the League has become more inclusive, membership has recovered, and once again the League is able to preserve its landmark clubhouse and the collection it contains.

MASONIC TEMPLE

1 North Broad Street
Philadelphia, PA 19107-2598

James H. Windrim, architect, 1867–1873
George Herzog, decorative painter
National Historic Landmark, 1985

Telephone for visitor information: 215.988.1900
www.pagrandlodge.org

Freemasonry has flourished in America since colonial times; the earliest Philadelphia lodge dates to 1727 when Penn's great town numbered fewer than 10,000 souls. The Grand Lodge of Pennsylvania Masons is the first lodge established in the United States and the third oldest in the English-speaking world, predated only by the Grand Lodges of England (1717) and Ireland (1727). In the eighteenth century, the Grand Lodge of Pennsylvania met at various locations, until giving young William Strickland (pages 80–85) his first known commission, to design a Gothic-style Masonic Temple to be erected on the 700 block of Chestnut Street in 1809. This temple was damaged by fire, rebuilt by Strickland without a tower, and then totally replaced in 1855 by a much grander Gothic

⇇ The Masonic Temple near City Hall was designed by James Windrim and erected in 1868–1873 to house the Right Worshipful Grand Lodge of the Most Ancient and Honorable Fraternity of Free and Accepted Masons of Pennsylvania. It survives largely as built and is open to the public for tours.

⇇ The Norman porch leads to the main entrance facing Broad Street. It is carved from blocks of Quincy granite.

J F Kennedy Bl
Broad St
BROAD ST

BEAUTY
WISDOM

NIL SINE NUMINE

(*left*) The interior halls and passages are richly embellished with painted decoration, portraits, and sculpture. This view of the second floor stair includes the allegorical figures of "Beauty" and "Wisdom" by Joseph A. Bailly (1825–1885), which were brought from the Chestnut Street Masonic Temple (1855–1873).

(*right*) The Corinthian Hall with its ivory and gold color scheme is the meeting room of the Grand Lodge of Pennsylvania and is decorated with classical architectural motifs and references to Greek mythology.

The Egyptian Hall, completed by decorative painter George Herzog in 1889, draws its stylistic inspiration from the Nile Valley. The columns surrounding the room are based on the Temples of Luxor, Karnak, and Philae.

design by Samuel Sloan (1815–1884) and John Stewart (fl. 1845–1885). The latter building soon proved inadequate for the many lodges meeting there, and the Grand Lodge resolved to erect a new Temple that would be "one of the wonders of the Masonic world" and a declaration to all of the importance of Freemasonry in Philadelphia. Grand Master Roberts Vaux exhorted all concerned: "Let us have a Temple on which the student, the scholar, and the Craftsman from all nations and of all tongues may look and learn its purpose, and understand its origin, proclaimed by every word of its architectural language, from the porch to the pinnacle."

In 1867 a building site bounded by Broad, Filbert, Juniper and Cuthbert Streets was acquired adjacent to Center Square on which the new City Hall would soon rise (pages 180–185). Arch Street Methodist Church by Addison Hutton had just been completed at Broad and Arch Streets, and across Broad Street the First Baptist Church and the Lutheran Church of the Holy Communion were already ensconced in handsome buildings by Stephen Decatur Button and Frank Furness respectively (see *Historic Sacred Places,* pages 140–43). The new Masonic Temple would make an extravagant contribution to the realization of William Penn's seventeenth-century dream of a city centered between its two rivers at the crossing of Market and Broad Streets.

After a fractious architectural competition that drew protests from the American Institute of Architects, a youthful James Hamilton Windrim won the Masonic Temple commission with a "Norman Romanesque" design over the Gothic Revival submissions of John McArthur, Jr., and the firm of Fraser, Furness & Hewitt. Windrim (1840–1919) graduated from the first Girard College class in 1856 and entered the office of John Notman who designed the Athenæum on Washington Square (pages 132–137) and several Center City churches, including the Norman Romanesque Holy Trinity on Rittenhouse Square (see "Notman Churches," *Historic Sacred Places*, 158–77). Following his employment by the Pennsylvania Railroad at the Union Depot in Pittsburgh, Windrim returned to Philadelphia, opened his own office, and promptly secured the Masonic Temple commission at the age of twenty-seven. The cornerstone was laid on June 24, 1868, and the completed building dedicated on September 26, 1873.

One breathless account of the new Masonic Temple is worth quoting. "Consider its magnitude—a granite structure 250 feet long, 150 feet wide and three lofty stories in height . . . divided into spacious Halls with their appropriate adjacent apartments." As for the exterior, "its facade, or front, is a perfect specimen of Norman architecture—notably bold, sharp, and elaborate, with not a trace of flatness or inexpression anywhere on its profile. Its most striking features

are the two Towers, which flank it, one of them piercing with its turrets the air to the height of 250 feet; and the wonderfully beautiful Norman Porch, or doorway . . . built of the hardest stone we have, the Quincy granite."

While the entire interior is richly embellished, most visitors are especially dazzled by the seven Lodge Halls named for their decorative styles: Oriental Hall (Moorish style), Corinthian Hall, Renaissance Hall, Ionic Hall, Egyptian Hall, Gothic Hall, and Norman Hall. The survival of these spaces in their original

George Herzog's preliminary watercolor studies for the decoration of the Masonic Temple survive—such as this one for the Egyptian Hall. Masonic Temple Collection.

condition makes the Masonic Temple one of the most significant Victorian-era structures in the United States and well worthy of its National Historic Landmark status. The decorative painting of the Lodge Halls is principally the work of the Munich-born decorative painter George Herzog (1851–1920), who studied with Joseph Anton Schwarzmann (1806–1890), whose son Hermann J. Schwarzmann emigrated to Philadelphia in 1868 and eventually became chief architect of the Centennial Exposition (pages 200–205). By 1874 Herzog had also arrived in Philadelphia and promptly achieved a reputation for artistic craftsmanship. It is assumed that Windrim, who chaired the Masonic Art Association, engaged Herzog to execute the Masonic Temple decoration, where he would be engaged for several years. Herzog is also known to have worked at the Union League (pages 166–171), Philadelphia City Hall, and the private residences of P. A. B. Widener, William Kemble, and William Elkins. The survival of the Masonic Temple decorative painting is all the more significant because most of Herzog's work has been lost and can only be appreciated by published accounts and the many watercolors of his designs that survive.

In addition to regularly scheduled tours of the Masonic Temple building and its art collection, there are displays of such treasures as Brother George Washington's Masonic apron and Brother Benjamin Franklin's Masonic sash in the Masonic Museum, well worth a visit in itself.

PHILADELPHIA CITY HALL

Penn Square
Philadelphia, PA 19107

John McArthur, Jr., architect, 1872–1901
National Historic Landmark, 1976

Telephone for visitor information: 215.686.2840
www.philagov.org/property/up_cityhall_tour.htm

Philadelphians rarely miss an opportunity to launch civic projects on the 4th of July, and on that date in 1874 they laid the cornerstone for a new city hall at the crossing of Broad and Market streets. But the Quaker city rarely does anything precipitously. It had required nearly a quarter century of political wrangling and often acrimonious debate to launch the project. It would take another quarter century to finish it. "We are erecting a structure that will in the ages to come speak for us with the tongues of men and angels," one orator at the time proclaimed. "This work which we now do . . . [may someday] be all that remains to tell the story of our civilization." Yet less than seventy-five years later, Lewis Mumford, historian and pessimistic observer of American urbanism, remarked that City Hall, "is an architectural nightmare, a mishmash of uglified French Renaissance styles welded into a structure rugged enough to resist an atomic bomb."

Whether champion or critic, everyone agreed the Babylonian scale of Philadelphia's City Hall was overwhelming. Topped out by Alexander Milne Calder's monumental 37-foot bronze statue of William Penn, it would briefly be the tallest occupied structure in the United States and may to this day be the tallest masonry building without a steel skeleton. Erected at a cost in excess of $24,000,000 (1901), some of the granite blocks in its foundations are 22 feet thick; its very size would protect it from repeated threats of demolition until the 1950s, when a committee of the American Institute of Architects declared City Hall "perhaps the greatest single effort of late nineteenth-century American architecture"; its being demolished "would weaken the continuity of architectural tradition of the whole country." Not only should the building be preserved, the committee declared, but it should be restored to recapture its original exuberant glory as the focal point for the city. That restoration would require another half-century to accomplish.

Our story begins with the consolidation of the City and the County of Philadelphia in 1854. With a combined population over 500,000, the city required larger administrative facilities than could be provided by the already overcrowded eighteenth-century City Hall and Congress Hall on Independence Square (pages 32–41). In 1860 the first prize in a competition to design two buildings—a city hall and a courthouse—on Center [Penn] Square was awarded to John McArthur, Jr. (1823–1890), whom we've already met as the architect of the Wagner Free Institute of Science (pages 160–165). The second premium went to Samuel Sloan, whom we've also met as architect of the Institute of the Pennsylvania Hospital (pages 148–153). The Civil War intervened before contracts could be awarded. A second competition in 1869 called for the design of a *single* building to be erected on Independence Square rather than Center Square.

← Philadelphia City Hall is presently undergoing a decades-long restoration. In this view from the Benjamin Franklin Parkway, the scaffolding around the tower has just been removed after the bronze figures were cleaned of a century of grime.

NO
TURNS
Philadelphia
TROLLEY WORKS
DO NOT
ENTER

With Thomas Ustick Walter, now dean of Philadelphia architects (pages 110–115), sitting in judgment, a McArthur design was again selected over Sloan's submission. While McArthur's 1860 proposal for Center Square had featured two Greek Revival temples that owed much to Walter's expanded United States Capitol then under construction, his 1869 submission for Independence Square took its inspiration from the new Second Empire style Louvre in Paris (1852–1857) with mansard-roofed pavilions and a sculpture-embellished tower. Unfortunately for McArthur—but happily for Independence Hall—the publication of his design, which would have surrounded and overwhelmed the revered shrine of the Revolution, unleashed a storm of protest, causing the Commonwealth to step in and nullify the completion.

The debate really revolved around whether to erect the new City Hall in the traditional business and financial center of the city near Independence Square or at the emerging hub of the enlarged metropolis at Broad and Market Streets. In an attempt to settle the issue, a referendum was called. Voters were asked to choose a site for the new public buildings between Center Square and Washington Square adjoining Independence Square—thereby removing from

↑ In 1955 the city walled off Conversation Hall—one of several grand ceremonial spaces—to create additional offices. Panels were erected to protect the carved marble, decorative plasterwork, and massive chandelier, which had been boxed and left in place. In 1983 the room was restored and is now part of the popular public tours of the building.

the equation the potential impact on Independence Hall. By an overwhelming majority, the voters favored Center Square, and John McArthur finally received his appointment as architect. He submitted the final design in April 1872 (an enlarged version of his 1869 Second Empire design for Independence Square) and began assembling his team, which ultimately would include Thomas Ustick Walter; as McArthur's chief assistant, he would have major influence on the final detail of the new building, where he labored until his death in 1887. McArthur died shortly thereafter, leaving to his fellow Scot John Ord (fl. 1871–1910) and then W. Bleddyn Powell (1854–1910) the role of chief architect.

The official description of City Hall (1872) tells us:

> It is essentially modern in its leading features, and presents a rich example of what is known by the generic term of "Renaissance," modified and adapted to the varied and extensive requirements of a great American municipality. It is designed in the spirit of French art, admirable in its ornamentation, while the whole effect is one of massive dignity, worthy of us and our posterity. . . . The whole exterior is bold and effective in outline, and rich in detail being elaborated with highly ornate columns, pilasters, pediments, cornices, enriched windows, and other appropriate adornment. . . . From the north side rises a grand tower which will gracefully adorn the public buildings, and at the same time will be a crowning feature of the city, as St Peter's is of Rome, and St Paul's of London.

The completed building houses all three branches of the city government (mayor, city council, courts) in hundreds of rooms spread over seven floors and more than one million square feet of space. Particularly for its time, the plan could hardly be more efficient. The square building encloses a central court linked to the surrounding streets by four arched openings. Fourteen entrances at street level give access to wide corridors running entirely around all seven floors (see plan). At the corners there are octagonal staircases and four banks of elevators. Originally designed for gas lighting and elevators, the development of practical electric lighting (and the invention of the electric elevator in 1880) would make City Hall an early example of the latest technology at the dawn of the twentieth century, even though it was stylistically dated by the time of its completion.

The interior finishes of City Hall are lavish and finely detailed; the polished marbles, carved wood, metalwork grills, ornamental plasterwork, mosaic floors, and decorative painting reflect the best Late Victorian craftsmanship available in Philadelphia. Perhaps the greatest decorative glory of McArthur's City Hall

is the sculpture intended "to express American ideas and develop American genius." Alexander Milne Calder (1846–1923), son of a Scottish stonecutter, is chiefly remembered for his statue of William Penn atop City Hall tower, but he also contributed hundreds of allegorical figures, keystones, spandrels, and masks that encrust the building, many unfortunately too high above the ground to be appreciated, such as the 24-foot bronze figures of a Swedish man and woman, a Native American man and woman, and the four giant eagles on the tower below the larger William Penn figure.

Encouraged by the post-World War II preservation movement, and a rising interest in the monuments of American Victorian-era architecture, even architects identified with the modern school, such as Philadelphia's Louis I. Kahn and Vincent G. Kling, called for the restoration of City Hall. In the 1960s the building was cleaned of accumulated pollution stains and encrusted pigeon droppings, and in the 1990s the first detailed historic structure report by architects, engineers, a design historian, and materials conservators—assembled by the Vitetta Group—led to the preparation of a master plan for the restoration, modernization, and rehabilitation of the interior and exterior of the building, a process that will take nearly as long as the original construction but has already returned Philadelphia City Hall to the prominence intended by its creators.

One of the four entrance pavilion passages leading to the central court gives some idea of the "Piranesian grandeur" and rich architectural detail to be found throughout City Hall.

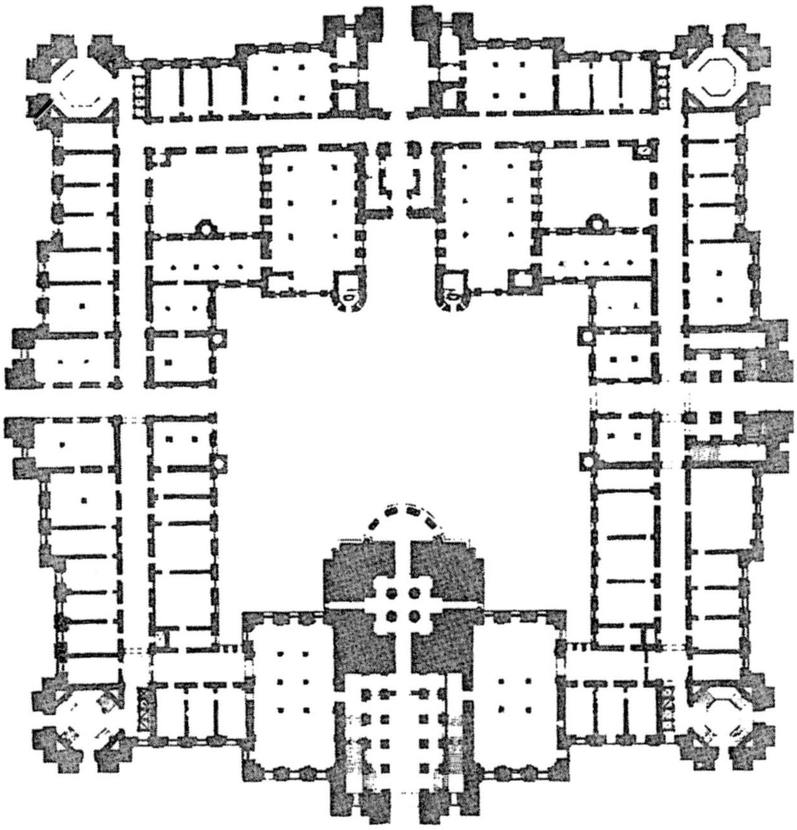

The street level plan shows the four entrance pavilions leading from Market and Broad Streets to the central court, through which thousands of Philadelphians and visitors pass every day. Notice the wide interior corridors that give the building excellent circulation on every floor. The octagonal stairs and elevators located in the corners are accessible from both corridor and street entrances. Athenæum of Philadelphia Collection.

PENNSYLVANIA ACADEMY OF THE FINE ARTS

118 North Broad Street
Philadelphia, PA 19102

Furness & Hewitt, architects, 1872–1876
National Historic Landmark, 1975

Telephone for visitor information: 215.972.7600
www.pafa.org

As Philadelphia expanded in both population and prosperity and residential neighborhoods inched westward in the nineteenth century, the city's social, cultural, and political institutions followed. (The erection of so many broad-shouldered brownstone Victorian-era churches at this time has been discussed in *Historic Sacred Places.*) In the decades bracketing the Civil War, the Academy of Music, Union League, City Hall, the Ridgway Library, and Masonic Temple all settled on Broad Street. One of these Victorian-era landmarks remains to be mentioned: The Pennsylvania Academy of the Fine Arts at Broad and Cherry Streets.

Founded in 1805 "to promote the cultivation of the fine arts," the Academy became the first art museum in the United States as well as a school for "assisting the studies and exciting the efforts of the artist gradually to unfold, enlighten

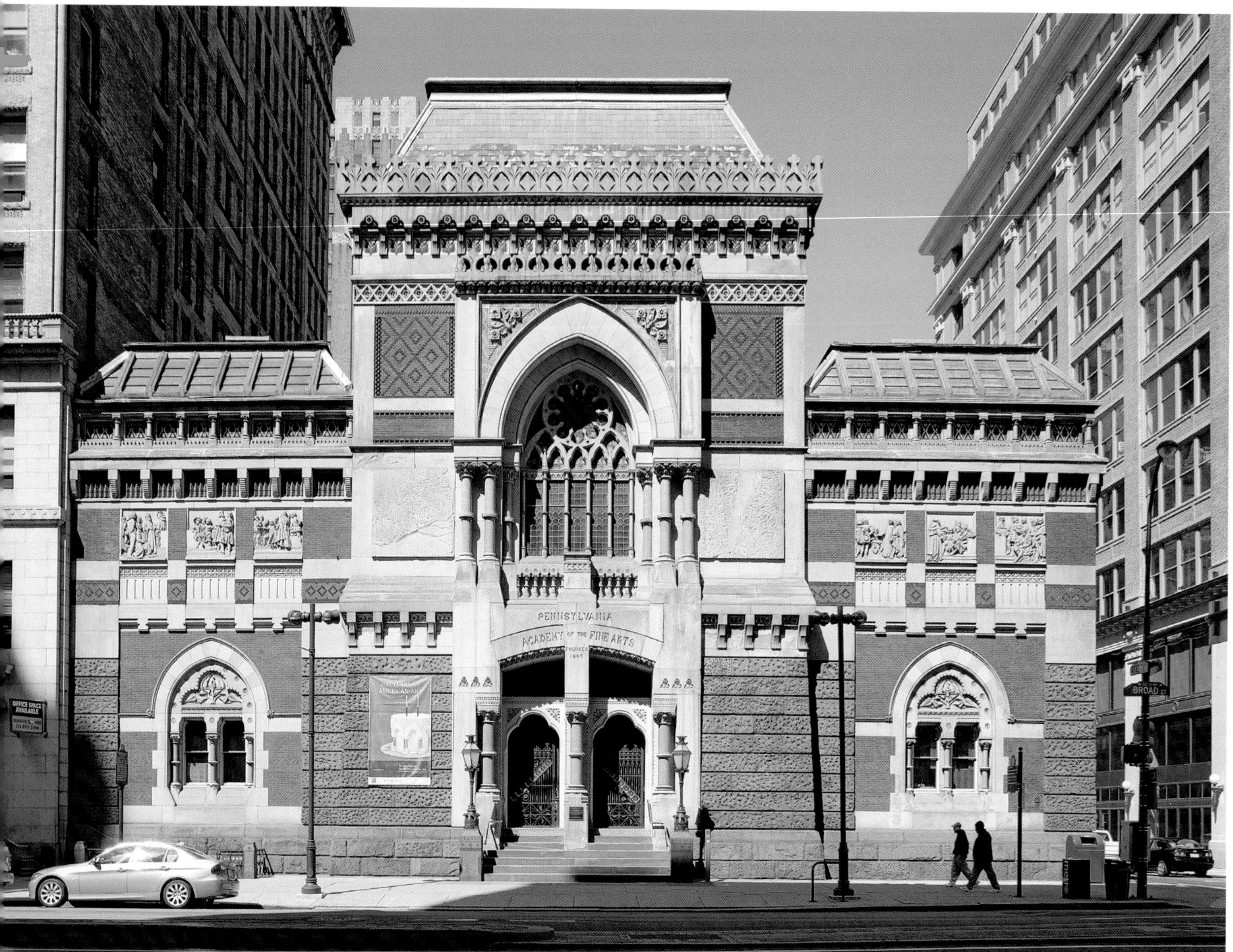

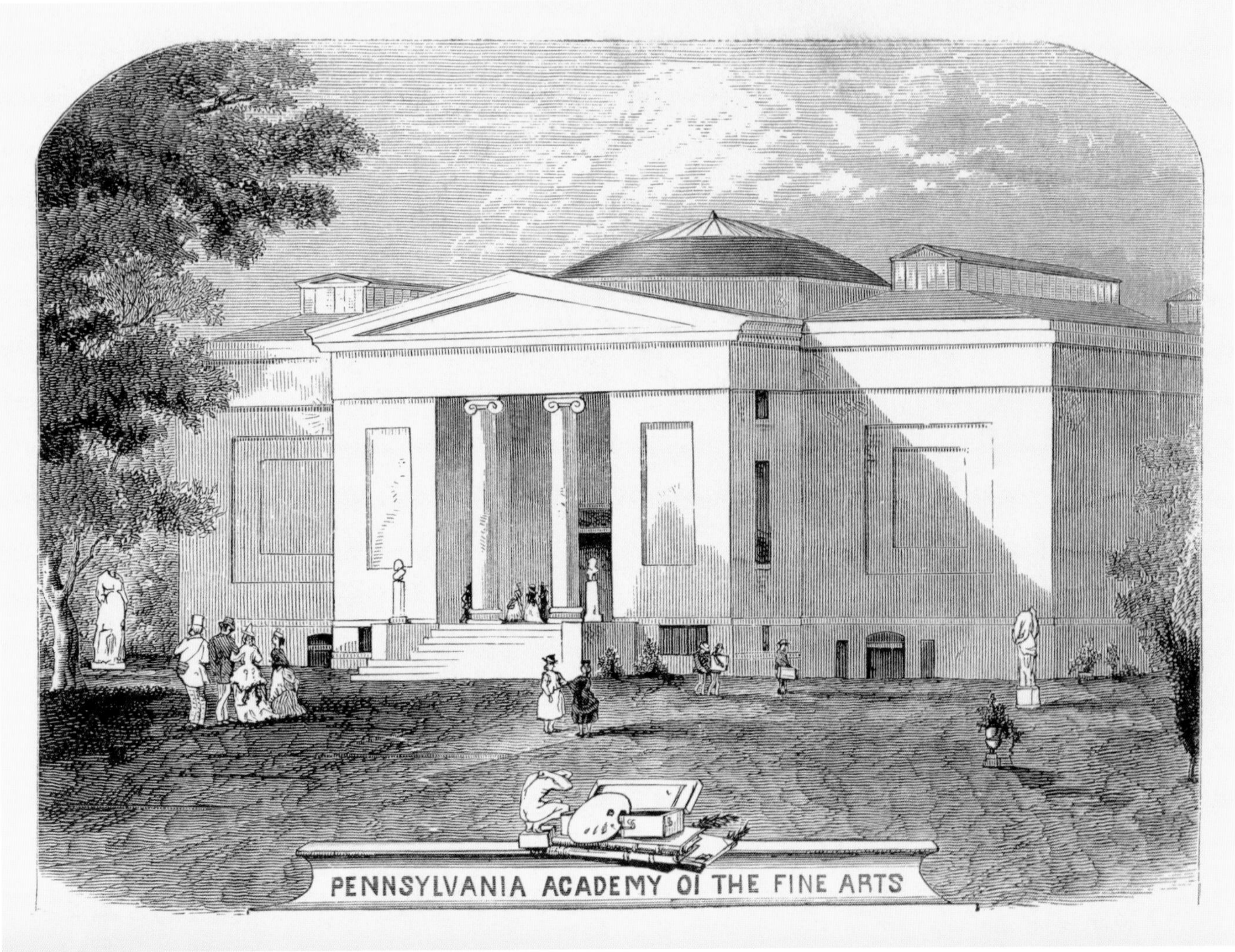

This idealized engraving of Richard A. Gilpin's Academy of Fine Arts building on Chestnut Street (1845–1846) appeared in *Lippincott's Magazine*, February 1872. Athenæum of Philadelphia Collection.

and invigorate the talents of our countrymen." Shortly thereafter, Charles Willson Peale wrote to Thomas Jefferson, "We hope soon to begin a building for the reception of casts of statues, also for a display of paintings, by the exhibition of which a revenue may be had to defray the expense of a keeper who shall be capable of giving instruction to the Pupils." Toward that end, the amateur architect John Dorsey (1759–1821) provided the design for a handsome neoclassical building to be erected on Chestnut Street between Tenth and Eleventh Streets. (It was his dabbling in architecture that prompted Benjamin Latrobe to grouse, Dorsey has "no less than 15 plans now in progress of execution, because he charges nothing for them.") After fire gutted Dorsey's building in 1845, it was rebuilt and expanded by engineer and Academy board member Richard A. Gilpin (1812–1887). As has been noted in the discussion of so many Philadelphia institutions, these early buildings of relatively modest—almost residential—scale were quickly outgrown. Certainly that was true of the

The Broad Street façade of the Pennsylvania Academy of the Fine Arts building by Furness & Hewitt, 1872–1876.

On the Cherry Street façade the richly polychrome composition of the Furness & Hewitt design can be fully appreciated.

Academy. Consequently, the directors decided to abandon Chestnut Street, which was rapidly becoming a center of commerce, for a site on more fashionable Broad Street, two blocks north of the new Masonic Temple and the future site of City Hall.

An invitation to prominent Philadelphia architects to submit designs was issued in June 1871, and the newly formed firm of Frank Furness (1839–1912) and George W. Hewitt (1841–1916) carried the day. The cornerstone of the new building was laid in December of 1872 and the completed building dedicated in April 1876 in time for the Centennial celebration. Both partners were native Philadelphians. Furness had served his apprenticeship in the office of John Fraser (best remembered for the Union League building) before joining the atelier of Richard Morris Hunt in New York. These studies were interrupted by military service during the Civil War, and then resumed. While with Hunt, Furness adopted the picturesque eclecticism that would typify his later work. Returning to Philadelphia, he joined Fraser in a new partnership with George Hewitt, who had worked with Joseph C. Hoxie and John Notman before entering Fraser's office. When Fraser left for Washington, D.C., the two younger partners formed a firm and entered the Academy competition.

The first publication of the Furness & Hewitt perspective of the Academy of the Fine Arts building appeared in *Lippincott's Magazine*, March 1872. Athenæum of Philadelphia Collection.

The original color scheme of the top-lighted stair hall was restored in the 1970s. On the far wall hangs Benjamin West's *Death on a Pale Horse* (1817).

The building as designed by Furness & Hewitt follows closely the Academy's specifications: "a two story, fireproof building with top lighted galleries of varying sizes on the upper floor, all accessible from the main stair; and a lower floor containing library, lecture room, galleries for casts, and a painting room well lighted from a window close to the ceiling." In a faint echo of the Chestnut Street Academy building, the Broad Street façade is tripartite, the central pavilion with a mansard roof projects forward and above the symmetrical wings. The eclectic polychrome surface decoration composed of varied types and colors of stone, brick, and highly colored tiles strongly reflects the Venetian neo-Gothic influence of John Ruskin and William Butterfield. When completed the building was described as being in the "Byzantine or Venetian style of architecture."

While praised as something quite new in the 1870s, by the early twentieth century the Academy building was condemned in the *Architectural Record* (1908) as "grotesque" and "the low watermark in American architecture." Only as the Victorian era came to be appreciated on its own merits after World War II did the tide begin to turn. Writing in 1951, University of Pennsylvania art historian Robert C. Smith declared that Frank Furness was "Philadelphia's greatest architect of the late 19th Century and one of the pioneers of the modern movement in America." By the 1960s the historic preservation movement had taken up the cause of Victorian-era architecture, ultimately leading a call for the restoration of such Philadelphia landmark examples as the Academy of Music, Athenæum, and Academy of the Fine Arts. Motivated by the centennial of the Academy of Fine Arts building, an extensive and highly publicized restoration was undertaken in 1973, directed by Hyman Myers for Day & Zimmermann Associates.

PHILADELPHIA HIGH SCHOOL FOR CREATIVE AND PERFORMING ARTS

(Library Company of Philadelphia, Ridgway Branch)
901 South Broad Street
Philadelphia, PA 19147

Addison Hutton, architect, 1873–1878
Philadelphia Register for Historic Places, 1972

Telephone for visitor information: 215.952.2462
www.philsch.k12.pa.us/schools/capa

The imposing classical building at the corner of South Broad and Christian Streets, which houses the Philadelphia High School for Creative and Performing Arts, was originally erected for The Library Company of Philadelphia and occupied by that august institution from 1878 until 1966. The saga of its design and construction could have been plotted by Charles Dickens.

Our tale begins with the death of Dr. James Rush (1786–1869) and his testamentary bequest of nearly $1,000,000—a prodigious sum at the time—to The Library Company. Founded by Benjamin Franklin and his friends in 1731, this "Mother of all American Subscription Libraries" provided a means for the members to pool their resources to purchase books, hire a librarian, and eventually erect a building. In an age before tax-supported free public libraries (see pages 288–291), such member-supported associations existed in nearly every large town in America. According to Franklin, "these Libraries have improved the general Conversation of Americans, made the common Tradesmen and Farmers as intelligent as most Gentleman from other Countries, and perhaps have contributed to some Degree to the Stand so generally made throughout the Colonies in Defense of their Privileges." The Library Company enjoyed steady growth and by 1773 the collection had "become large & valuable, a Source of Instruction to Individuals and conducive of Reputation to the Public." As a consequence, the second floor of Carpenters' Hall (pages 42–47) was rented where the library would remain through the Revolution and Constitution-forming period until commissioning its own building on Fifth Street opposite Philosophical Hall in 1789.

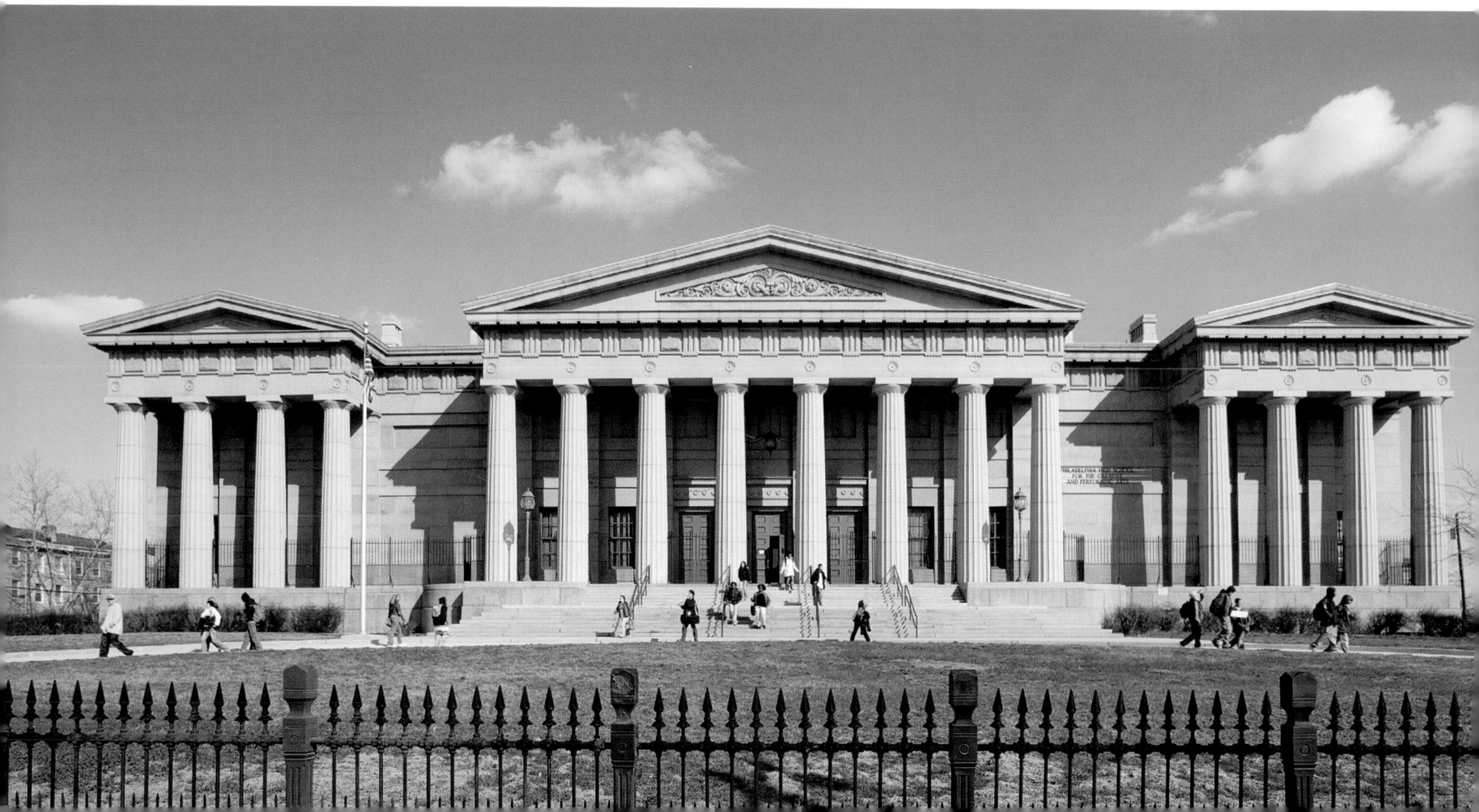

↑ The Philadelphia High School for Creative and Performing Arts is housed in a building designed by Addison Hutton for The Library Company of Philadelphia. The library occupied the Greek Revival structure from 1878 to 1966.

By the mid-nineteenth century, the collection exceeded available space in Library Hall, and it was to assist the Library Company to acquire new quarters that Dr. Rush made his generous bequest to acquire land, as he stipulated, "between Fourth and Fifteenth and Spruce and Race Streets" on which to erect a "fire-proof building sufficiently large to accommodate and contain all the books of the Library Company of Philadelphia." A man of strong opinions, he also directed that the building should be substantial, but "without any large, lofty, or merely ornamental halls or lecture-rooms." He warned against lectures and exhibitions, which he considered "foreign and inconsistent with the legitimate purposes of a public library." However, as in the case of Stephen Girard a generation earlier, Dr. Rush could not leave well enough alone; he kept adding codicils about the nature of the books the library could acquire (no "ephemeral biographies, novels, and works of fiction or amusements") and how the building should be appointed ("let it not keep cushioned seats for time-wasting and lounging readers, nor place for every-day novels, mind-tainting reviews, controversial politics, scribblings of poetry and prose, biographies of unknown names, nor for those teachers of disjointed thinking"). Finally, lest he and his wife be forgotten, their bodies were to be interred in the building.

As whimsical as some of Dr. Rush's conditions seem today, the one that would cause the most trouble removed the instructions on the *location* and *design* of the building in favor of assigning his executor complete discretion over such matters. The executor, Henry J. Williams, Dr. Rush's brother-in-law, announced that it had been Dr. Rush's deathbed wish that the library be erected at Broad and Christian Streets, and pursuant to those instructions, he had purchased a lot of ground at that location. Not surprisingly, the members of the Library Company were ambivalent, given the conditions of the gift. All protests to the contrary, Mr. Williams remained adamant.

While the Library Company argued, the executor proceeded to construct the building. He also announced it was to be named for Jacob Ridgway, father of Dr. Rush's late wife, whence the money had originally come. Mr. Williams also selected an architect. Within months of Dr. Rush's death, Addison Hutton (pages 238–243) reported to his brother, "I am ordered to make plans and specifications in full for the Rush Library (without, however, the comfort of knowing certainly that they will be adopted)!" It later came out that Mr. Williams had made a similar demand of John McArthur, who had been awarded the City Hall commission. Nonetheless, Hutton prepared the drawings and on January 26, 1871, reported that his design had been accepted. It would take seven years for the building to be completed and occupied. The delay in part was caused by the Library Company's attempt to have Williams removed as executor of the estate—an effort that ultimately failed. Hutton's contract was finally signed, the drawings approved, and the cornerstone laid on June 29, 1874.

Based on the Parthenon in Athens, the resulting three-Doric-portico façade of gray granite stretches over 100 feet parallel to Broad Street, set back in its own park. According to his biographer, Elizabeth Biddle Yarnall, it was one of Hutton's favorite buildings and quite unlike any of his other major commissions, owing more to early nineteenth-century Greek Revival buildings like William Strickland's Second Bank of the United States (pages 80–85) than to the Italianate and mansard styles popular at the time. Architectural historian George B. Tatum has speculated, "Hutton's Ridgway Library may fairly be regarded as the last major expression of a [Greek Revival] style that in its distinctive and widespread application has often been regarded as one of the earliest architectural expressions of the new American nation." Unfortunately, it was not a good library.

Reluctantly the Library Company accepted the Ridgway Branch, to which its extraordinary historic collections were moved from Library Hall on South Fifth Street, which was sold and demolished. Simultaneously the directors commissioned Frank Furness to design another fireproof building at Locust and Juniper Streets, which was closer to the homes of the Company's members and from which it could provide a circulating collection free of Dr. Rush's restrictions. This building was also demolished (1940) when the Library Company combined all its operations on Broad Street. While the move reduced operating

The Library Company was founded by Benjamin Franklin and his friends in 1731 as a subscription library. After half a century in rented rooms, in 1790 it moved into its own building, designed by the amateur architect William Thornton (1759–1828). Having outgrown this building, it moved to new quarters and the building was sold and demolished. The American Philosophical Society patterned its 1954 library building on the Thornton design. William Birch, *City of Philadelphia* (1800). Athenæum of Philadelphia Collection.

The cavernous interior of the Ridgway Branch as it now appears.

overhead, it did nothing to improve the impractical floor plan of Hutton's building or the declining neighborhood.

By the 1950s it had become clear to the Library Company directors that the only practical future was to become a special collections research library focused on what scholars had come to recognize as one of the finest existing collections of Americana. In 1966 the library—and the remains of James and Phoebe Ann Rush—moved from the "totally inadequate and unsuitable" building on Broad Street to a modern facility on Locust Street next to Addison Hutton's Historical Society of Pennsylvania.

Fortunately the City of Philadelphia agreed to purchase the Ridgway building and its block-long site. Various proposals—neighborhood recreational center, arts center, sports museum—were advanced over the next two decades as the building moldered. In 1998, however, the Ridgway Library building was transformed by the architectural firm Kise Straw & Kolodner into the Philadelphia High School for Creative and Performing Arts, which now anchors the south end of the Avenue of the Arts and offers majors in creative writing, visual arts, dance, theater, and instrumental and vocal music.

VICTORY BUILDING

(Mutual Life Insurance Company of New York)
1001–1009 Chestnut Street
Philadelphia, PA 19107

Henry Fernbach, architect, 1873–1875
Phillip W. Roos, architect, 1890–1891
National Register of Historic Places, 1980

Redeveloped as condominium; not open to the public

While not a National Historic Landmark, the seven-story Victory Building at Tenth and Chestnut Streets is included here because it has been declared by the National Register of Historic Places to be "one of the finest examples of the Second Empire mode in the United States . . . richer in sculptural decoration and more sensitive in its composition than its two best-known and larger contemporaries, the extant State, War and Navy Building in Washington and the Western Union Building in New York." If this were not enough, it may also be the earliest Second Empire style office building erected in Philadelphia and one of the few examples in that once popular "modern" style for commercial structures to survive successive waves of urban development. With the Victory Building, City Hall (pages 180–185) and the Union League Club (pages 166–171), Center City is fortunate to have three celebrated—yet vastly different—examples of this style within a short stroll of each other.

Detail of the richly modeled Chestnut Street façade of the lower floors of the Victory Building, designed in 1873–1875 by New York architect Henry Fernbach as the Philadelphia headquarters of the Mutual Life Insurance Company of New York.

This 1880 view of the Mutual Life Insurance Company building illustrates the original appearance of Fernbach's Second Empire style design. This image is reproduced from *Baxter's Panoramic Business Directory*. Athenæum of Philadelphia Collection.

The first three-story-on-raised-basement stage of the present Victory Building was designed and erected in 1873–1875 by New York architect Henry Fernbach as the Philadelphia headquarters of the Mutual Life Insurance Company of New York, one of the most successful competitors in the rough-and-tumble (and largely unregulated) nineteenth-century world of marketing life insurance. The American life insurance industry had its origins in the eighteenth century when the Presbyterian Synods in Philadelphia and New York established the Corporation for Relief of Poor and Distressed Widows and Children of Presbyterian Ministers in 1759, followed in 1769 by a similar corporation for the families of American clergymen in the Communion of the Church of England. Several companies selling life insurance to the general public existed in the late eighteenth and early nineteenth centuries, but they all failed until the 1812 founding of the Pennsylvania Company for Insurances on Lives and Granting of Annuities (which would cease issuing life insurance policies in 1872). In the 1840s there was an explosion in the number of life insurance policies being written, with a few major companies enjoying the lion's share of the feast. One of these was the

The Victory
Jefferson

Mutual Life Insurance Company of New York, founded in 1843. This rapid expansion was due first to new state laws granting women the right to protection by insurance and, second, to the emergence of mutual life insurance companies.

Until the 1840s a married woman often could not benefit directly from an insurance policy on her husband, nor could she enter into a contract to insure herself or her children. New York was the first to grant these rights, followed quickly by other states. The second development was the founding of mutual life insurance companies in which profits were to be returned to the policyholder—usually in the form of reduced premiums—rather than a group of stockholders. (These companies were a response to the Panic of 1837 which caused widespread suspicion of any enterprises organized as stock companies—be they banks, insurance companies, canals, or railroads.)

Moving into what would prove to be a lucrative Philadelphia market, the Mutual Life Insurance Company also imported its architect. Henry Fernbach (1829–1883) had been born in Prussian Silesia and educated at the Berlin Building Academy before emigrating to New York City on the eve of the American Civil War. He is known to have designed several commercial buildings, including the Stern Brothers Store of 1878, one of the largest cast-iron buildings in New York. Fernbach's Mutual Life Insurance building on Chestnut Street consisted of three stories of Rhode Island granite on a raised basement with a complex five-bay façade exhibiting classical engaged columns, pilasters, balustrades, and balconies, each floor treated differently and continuing with a rounded corner onto Tenth Street. Declaring its French Renaissance heritage influenced by the Haussmannization of Paris during the imperial Bonapartist reign of Napoleon III, the entire building was capped by a high mansard roof. When the building was completed in the summer of 1875, the *Public Ledger*'s architectural critic unequivocally declared that, for beauty and convenience, "it is not equaled by any building in America, and is unsurpassed by any in Europe."

Within a few years (1890–1891) Mutual Life commissioned another New York architect, Phillip W. Roos, temporarily to remove, simplify, and clean Fernbach's mansard roof, add three relatively restrained stories to the building, and replace the roof. In 1901–1902, the New York firm of Roos and Brosam designed a ten-story addition at 1007–1013 Chestnut Street. Following the departure of the insurance company in the 1920s, the building passed through several hands as the neighborhood changed. For many years it stood empty until eventually redeveloped as residential condominiums.

In 1890–1892 three floors were added to the Mutual Life Insurance Company building, but the original mansard roof form was retained.

MEMORIAL HALL

(Centennial Exhibition Art Gallery)
North Concourse Drive at Forty-Second Street
West Fairmount Park
Philadelphia, PA 19131

Hermann J. Schwarzmann, architect, 1875–1876
National Historic Landmark, 1976

Telephone for visitor information: 215.685.0047
www.phila.gov/fairpark/arch1.htm

On March 3, 1871, the United States Congress authorized a national celebration to commemorate the hundredth anniversary of American independence to be held in Philadelphia. Popularly known as the Centennial Exhibition, the jaw-breaking official title was the International Exhibition of Arts, Manufactures, and Products of the Soil and Mine. As a site for the celebration, the City of Philadelphia temporarily transferred 450 acres of West Fairmount Park to the newly appointed United States Centennial Commission, composed of representatives from every state and territory. A widely advertised architectural competition to design the exhibition buildings was announced in 1873. The request for designs specified a temporary main building covering twenty-five acres (to include a five-acre Memorial Hall) and a separate two-acre Art Gallery building. Forty-three submissions were received from eleven states and the District of Columbia; ten finalists were selected, and from these four were awarded prizes, with first premium going to the Philadelphia firm of Collins & Autenrieth (pages 120–123). But all the winning proposals were expensive, and the country was in the grip of a financial panic triggered by the collapse of Jay Cooke's Philadelphia banking house. While the commissioners dithered, Herman J. Schwarzmann,

the youthful chief engineer of Fairmount Park, quietly planned the water and drainage infrastructure that such a massive undertaking would require.

Schwarzmann (1846–1891) was the son of a Bavarian decorative painter and a former army officer who had immigrated to United States in 1868. The following year he secured appointment as one of the assistant engineers working for the Fairmount Park Commission, where he quickly proved to be exceptionally talented, industrious, and ambitious. In anticipation of the Centennial, the Fairmount Park Commissioners appointed Schwarzmann chief engineer of Fairmount Park and dispatched him to study the International Exposition of 1873 being held in Vienna. Returning to Philadelphia, and working entirely on his own recognizance, Schwarzmann, he later reported, "commenced to prepare plans for Memorial and Horticultural Halls, outside of the competitive designs, no decision having been reached at the time." His designs were submitted to the Centennial Board of Finance and promptly adopted over all the previous submissions. The board also appointed him "Chief Engineer of the Exhibition Grounds and Architect of the Permanent Buildings and of Other Structures of the Centennial Board of Finance."

(*left*) The "Great Hall" of Memorial Hall.

(*right*) Stucco detail in the "Great Hall" of Memorial Hall.

As summarized by his chief biographer, John Maass, Schwarzmann's accomplishments in the subsequent months were prodigious.

> In just under two years Schwarzmann had transformed 285 acres of fields, swamps and ravines into building lots, gardens and landscaped grounds. The work force under his command had moved over 500,000 cubic yards of earth; graded and surfaced 3 miles of avenues and 17 miles of walks; built a railroad with 5½ miles of double track; erected 16 bridges; put up 3 miles of fence with 179 stiles and gates; constructed 7 miles of drains, 9 miles of water pipes, 16 fountains, and 8 miles of gas pipes; installed three separate telegraph systems with underground cables; planted 153 acres of lawns and flower beds, and over 20,000 trees and shrubs. Every one of the 249 large and small structures was completed; Schwarzmann had designed 34 of these himself, including the two permanent buildings.

Of all the buildings Schwarzmann designed, Memorial Hall is, in the words of one Centennial guidebook, "the most imposing and ornate of all the structures . . ., built at a cost of $1,500,000 . . ., to be used during the Exhibition as an Art Gallery, after which it is designed to make it the receptacle of an industrial and art collection similar to the famous South Kensington Museum, at London." (The latter institution—renamed the Victoria and Albert Museum in 1899—had been founded following the Great Exhibition of 1851 in London.)

According to the official description of Memorial Hall, "the entire structure is in the modern Renaissance" style. "The materials are granite, glass, and iron. No wood is used in the construction, and the building is thoroughly fire-proof. The structure is 365 feet in length, 210 feet in width, and 59 feet in height . . . surmounted by a dome." Athenæum of Philadelphia Collection.

The cornerstone of Memorial Hall was laid on July 4, 1874, the same day city dignitaries dedicated the cornerstone of City Hall (pages 180–185) and opened a new bridge across the Schuylkill River leading to the Exhibition site. Schwarzmann had prepared the drawings, written the specifications, obtained bids, and awarded building contracts for Memorial Hall in just twenty days. The prototype for his design was a monumental Prix de Rome project at the École des Beaux-Arts for "Un Palais pour l'Exposition des Beaux-Arts" by Nicolas Félix Escalier which had been published in the *Croquis d'Architecture* in 1867. Schwarzmann's adaptation of the design is sometimes cited as the first of the academic classical Beaux-Arts Style buildings in America that would become popular in later decades, especially after our architects began to attend the École des Beaux-Arts in Paris. When Americans flocked to the World's Columbian Exposition in

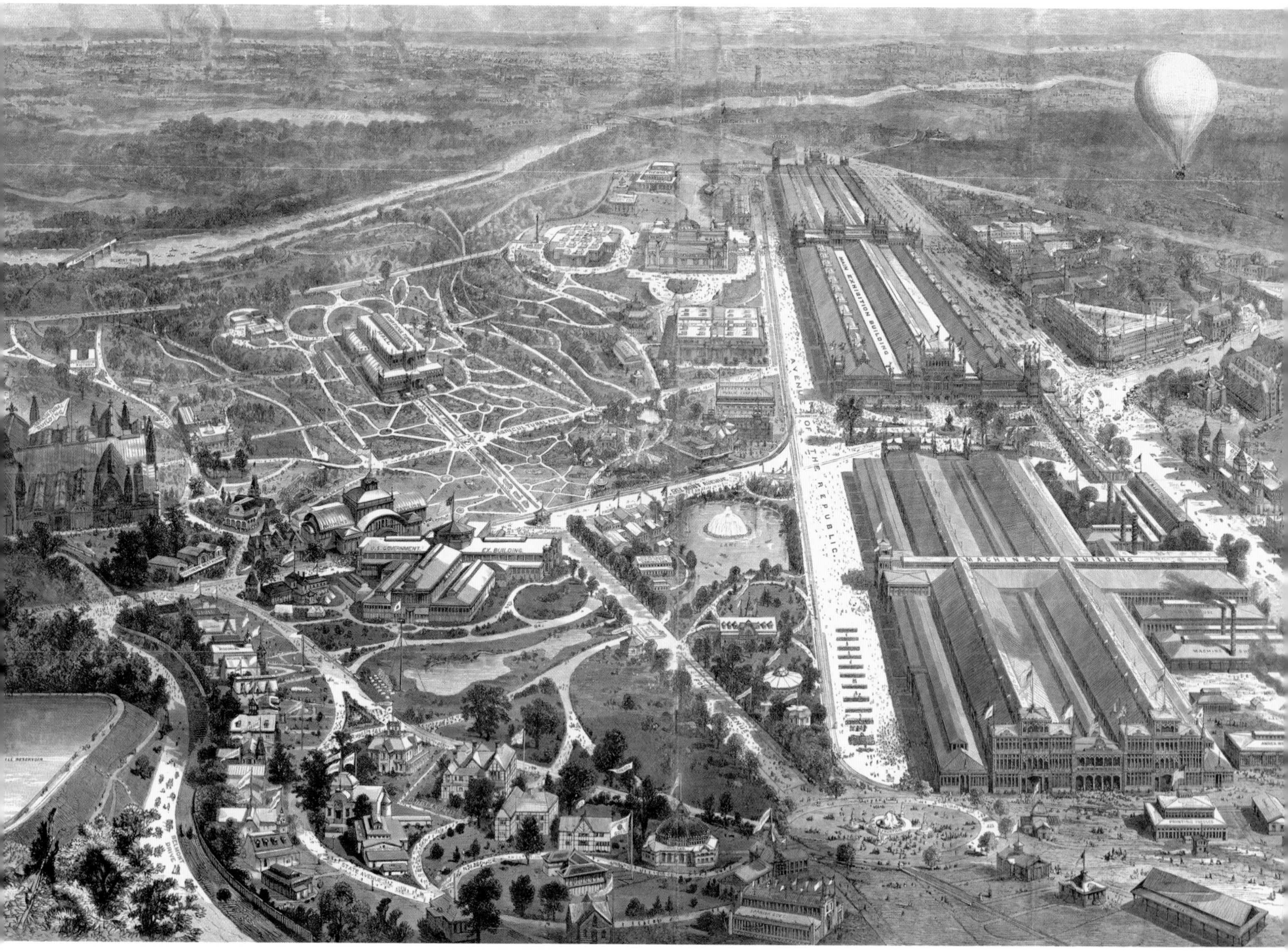

↟ Balloon view of the Centennial Exhibition, Philadelphia, 1876. Athenæum of Philadelphia Collection.

Chicago (1893), the entire "White City" reflected the monumental Beaux-Arts tradition that would so influence the City Beautiful movement (pages 268–277). It may also be the first American art museum in the Beaux-Arts style; it would to be followed by the Art Institute of Chicago, Milwaukee Public Museum, Brooklyn Museum, and Detroit Institute of Arts.

When the Centennial Exhibition closed, Memorial Hall became the Pennsylvania Museum and School of Industrial Art, later renamed the Philadelphia Museum of Art. After the Museum of Art building on Fairmount opened in 1928 (pages 278–283), Memorial Hall functioned as an occasional exhibition space until returned to the Fairmount Park Commission in the 1950s. After standing empty for several years, the building reopened as offices for the Park Commission staff and as a community recreational center, with a basketball court inserted in the West Gallery and a swimming pool embedded in the East Gallery. In 2004 the Park Commission approved plans to allow the Please Touch Museum to relocate from North Twenty-First Street to the Hall, which is being renovated for that purpose as this entry is written.

BOATHOUSE ROW

Kelly Drive (formerly East River Drive)
Fairmount Park
Philadelphia, PA 19130

National Historic Landmark, 1987

www.boathouserow.org

As Martin Luther King Drive snakes into its last turn toward the city, a marvelous panorama of historic landmarks is revealed.

The most appealing approach to Philadelphia is provided by the Martin Luther King Drive (formerly West River Drive), where the stressful crush of Schuylkill Expressway traffic is exchanged for a leisurely sweep through the seasonal delights of the riverbank landscape. But the best is yet to come. As the Drive snakes into its last turn toward the city, a marvelous panorama of historic landmarks is revealed. Clinging to the far bank, upriver from the Schuylkill River dam and the Fairmount Water Works complex (pages 74–79), are fifteen boathouses. Looming over this scene from its rock-faced acropolis is the Philadelphia Museum of Art (pages 278–283). Behind these landmarks rise the skyscrapers of the twenty-first-century city. One wonders if there could there be another such composition in America. (The same view is even more startling when suddenly revealed from a southbound Amtrak train, after emerging from the industrial wasteland of North Philadelphia.)

Thomas Eakins, *Max Schmitt in a Single Scull* (1871). Oil on canvas, 32½″×46¼.″ Eakins (1844–1916) was himself a skilled oarsman. Metropolitan Museum of Art, Purchase, The Alfred N. Punnett Endowment Fund and George D. Pratt Gift, 1934. Image © The Metropolitan Museum of Art.

Boathouse Row is the home of the Schuylkill Navy, which styles itself "the oldest amateur athletic governing body in the United States." The number of rowing clubs included in the Navy has varied since its founding in 1858, but there are currently ten clubs joined under a charter "to secure united action among the several Clubs and to promote amateurism on the Schuylkill River." The immediate antecedents of the current association were private clubs such as the Bachelor and Undine formed in the 1850s to encourage, in the words of the Undine founders, "healthful exercise, relaxation from business, friendly intercourse and pleasure, having in view to this end the possession of a pleasure barge on the River Schuylkill."

Vessels propelled by oars have been used since ancient times for transport, fishing, commerce, war, and lifesaving. Rowing for exercise, recreation, or competition, however, is largely a nineteenth-century phenomenon, spawned in part by the founding of collegiate rowing clubs at Cambridge and Oxford in the 1820s and then Yale and Harvard in the 1840s. General audiences were also

reached through publications such as Donald Walker's *Manly Exercises* (Philadelphia, 1837)—that extolled the virtues of rowing for health and fitness—and the widely popular novels of William Taylor Adams (1822–1897). Writing in the 1850s under the pseudonym "Oliver Optic," Adams influenced thousands of young men to become aware of the new sport of rowing from reading his books.

The Philadelphia boating and skating clubs exploited the long, relatively calm, freshwater lake created when the Schuylkill waters, restrained by the Fairmount dam, inundated what previously had been a rock-filled tidal stream (pp. 74–79). The first boathouses were unpretentious, utilitarian affairs, hardly more than frame sheds to protect the boats. However, once the City of Philadelphia gained control of the Lemon Hill and Sedgeley estates (see *Historic Houses*, pages 8–12) and, under the Act of Consolidation, was granted the power to create public parks, the temporary sheds were ordered demolished. Substantial new boathouses began to appear in the 1860s, especially after the Fairmount Park Commission began reviewing plans "for all houses and buildings now built in or to be built in any part of the Park grounds, by or for boat or skating clubs, or zoological or other purposes." The Park Commission initially favored stone buildings in the popular Victorian Gothic style associated with the Centennial

The Undine Barge Club boathouse, 13 Boathouse Row, by Furness & Evans, architects, 1882–1883, is one of the best preserved of the historic boathouses belonging to the clubs constituting the Schuylkill Navy.

Boathouse Row is clustered along the east bank of the Schuylkill River below Lemon Hill, the elegant Federal villa erected in 1799–1800 for the Philadelphia merchant Henry Pratt. The surrounding estate was the first land acquired for what would ultimately become Fairmount Park, the largest urban park system in America, encompassing 9,200 acres.

Exhibition. But gradually it relaxed this rule, permitting the Italianate, Mediterranean, Eastlake, Shingle, and Colonial Revival styles that give Boathouse Row its rich architectural diversity.

The larger clubhouses erected in the late decades of the nineteenth and early decades of the twentieth centuries provided commodious facilities for the boats and rooms for the increasingly popular club social events, especially as membership expanded and rowing became an Olympic event. By the twentieth

↑ The Fairmount Water Works and the Philadelphia Museum of Art as seen with the Undine Barge Club boathouse in the foreground.

century, Philadelphia had become recognized worldwide as a major center for rowing with many Schuylkill Navy oarsmen winning national and international championships.

Space here does not allow discussion of all fifteen boathouses, so one will have to stand as proxy for all. Many of the boathouses were erected by architects who are little known today. The Undine, however, at 13 Boathouse Row, is a notable exception. Founded in 1856, the Undine Barge Club takes its name from the female water spirit of Teutonic folklore popularized by Friedrich de la Motte Fouqué in his *Undine*, published in 1811. The Undine Club first engaged the firm of Frank Furness & George W. Hewitt to design Castle Ringstetten (1875) as an "up-river" clubhouse, and in 1882 turned again to Frank Furness and his new partner, Allen Evans, for a structure on Boathouse Row. In the latter case, Furness & Evans created a two-and-one half-story building of undressed stone, the main floor serving functionally as a boat storage room with two large "barn" doors opening directly onto the river ramp and floats. Access to the dressing rooms and lounge space is by a stair rising within a picturesque tower. At the west end of the second floor a wide porch overlooks the river. In addition to being one of the best preserved examples of Furness & Evans's work, the Undine clubhouse was extensively restored in the late 1990s under the direction of George Skarmeas, AIA, for The Hillier Group.

PHILADELPHIA ZOOLOGICAL GARDENS GATEHOUSES

3400 West Girard Avenue
Philadelphia, PA 19104-1196

Furness & Hewitt, architects, 1875–1876
National Register of Historic Places, 1956

Telephone for visitor information: 215.243.1100
www.philadelphiazoo.org

It might not occur to the casual observer to look for noteworthy architecture at the Zoological Society of Philadelphia. But when the Zoo opened its gates in West Fairmount Park in 1874, it came into possession of the extraordinary Philadelphia Schuylkill River villa called The Solitude, erected by John Penn (1784–1785). Now used by Zoo administrators as offices, the house is occasionally open to the public (see *Historic Houses*, pages 61–70).

In its own right, America's first zoo has throughout its history commissioned buildings and pavilions for its charges from such architects as Frank Furness, George W. Hewitt and William D. Hewitt, Theophilus Parsons Chandler, Jr., Walter Mellor and Arthur I. Meigs, and Paul P. Cret, among others. One Zoo official commented in the 1980s, "there is no zoo that I know of that has paid as much attention to the quality of its buildings or its art collection as we

have in Philadelphia, or whose grounds present a more pleasing blend of art and nature."

Initially laid out as a picturesque Victorian garden by Herman J. Schwarzmann, chief engineer of Fairmount Park (pages 200–205), the Zoo occupies forty-two acres. Most of the original Victorian structures have been replaced by more modern facilities for its 1,500 specimens, with the notable exception of the entrance pavilions designed by the firm of Furness & Hewitt and erected in 1875–1876.

The granite rubble and brick two-story gatehouses, with their steep hipped roofs with cross gables and jerkinhead roofs supported by bold brackets, are the signature buildings of the Zoo through which thousands of visitors daily pass to enter the gardens. Popularly attributed to Frank Furness (1839–1912), the architects of record are the firm of Furness and George W. Hewitt (1841–1916), who were partners from 1871 through 1875, which puts their Zoo commission at the point the partnership was breaking up. Most scholars of the partnership attribute the antelope house and aviary to Hewitt and the elephant house and restaurant to Furness—all buildings that have been demolished. The gatehouse pavilions may actually have been Hewitt's project, although some scholars suggest Furness had a hand in the design.

In the twentieth century various changes and additions were grafted onto the original pavilions and the Victorian iron gates and signage removed. In 1988 the pavilions were adaptively reused as ticket booths with the fences and gates recreated by the Philadelphia firm of Agoos/Lovera Architects.

The Victorian entrance pavilions at the Philadelphia Zoo were designed by the architectural firm of Furness & Hewitt (1875) and are shown here as they appeared in the nineteenth and early twentieth centuries, before modifications. Athenæum of Philadelphia Collection.

When Herman J. Schwarzmann was in Vienna studying the International Exhibition of 1873, the Philadelphia Zoological Society asked him to look into European zoological gardens. He also recommended to the Fairmount Park Art Association a new bronze figural group by the German artist Wilhelm Wolff (1816–1887) entitled *The Dying Lioness*, a cast of which was subsequently erected at the main entrance of the Zoological Gardens.

ANNE AND JEROME FISHER FINE ARTS LIBRARY, UNIVERSITY OF PENNSYLVANIA

(University Library and Museum; Furness Library)
220 South Thirty-Fourth Street
University of Pennsylvania
Philadelphia, PA 19104

Frank Furness of Furness, Evans & Company, architect, 1888–1891
National Historic Landmark, 1985

Telephone for visitor information: 215.898.8323
www.upenn.edu

When the Philadelphia architects Venturi, Rauch and Scott Brown completed their restoration of Frank Furness's great library in the heart of the University of Pennsylvania campus (1991), a *New York Times* architecture critic ruminated, "it is precisely the kind of building that everyone used to hate, and that it is now nearly impossible not to love: a Victorian monster, its deep, flaming rust brick and terra cotta arches and gables and towers and crenellations and dormers piled into a mass that is at once hysterical and serene." The generational shift in attitude toward nineteenth-century architecture that occurred between 1960 and 1990 came just in time to save several such Philadelphia Victorian-era landmarks, including the Academy of Music, Philadelphia City Hall, the Pennsylvania Academy of the Fine Arts, and the Reading Terminal train shed, to name only the most obvious examples discussed in this book.

In most libraries prior to the late nineteenth century, books and their readers shared the same space—as in the members' reading room at the Athenæum (pages 132–137)—with books assigned a fixed location on the shelves. These circumstances reflected the relatively small and static collection of books owned by most institutions, including colleges, and the heavy reliance on classroom lectures rather than assigned reading and original research. At the University of Pennsylvania in 1885 the library that served a faculty of nearly 150 and a student body of more than one thousand was housed in a single room at College Hall.

West façade of Frank Furness's University of Pennsylvania Library (now Anne and Jerome Fisher Fine Arts Library). To the right of the porch is the Arthur Ross Gallery, originally designed by Robert Rodes McGoodwin (1931) to house the Horace Howard Furness Shakespeare Library.

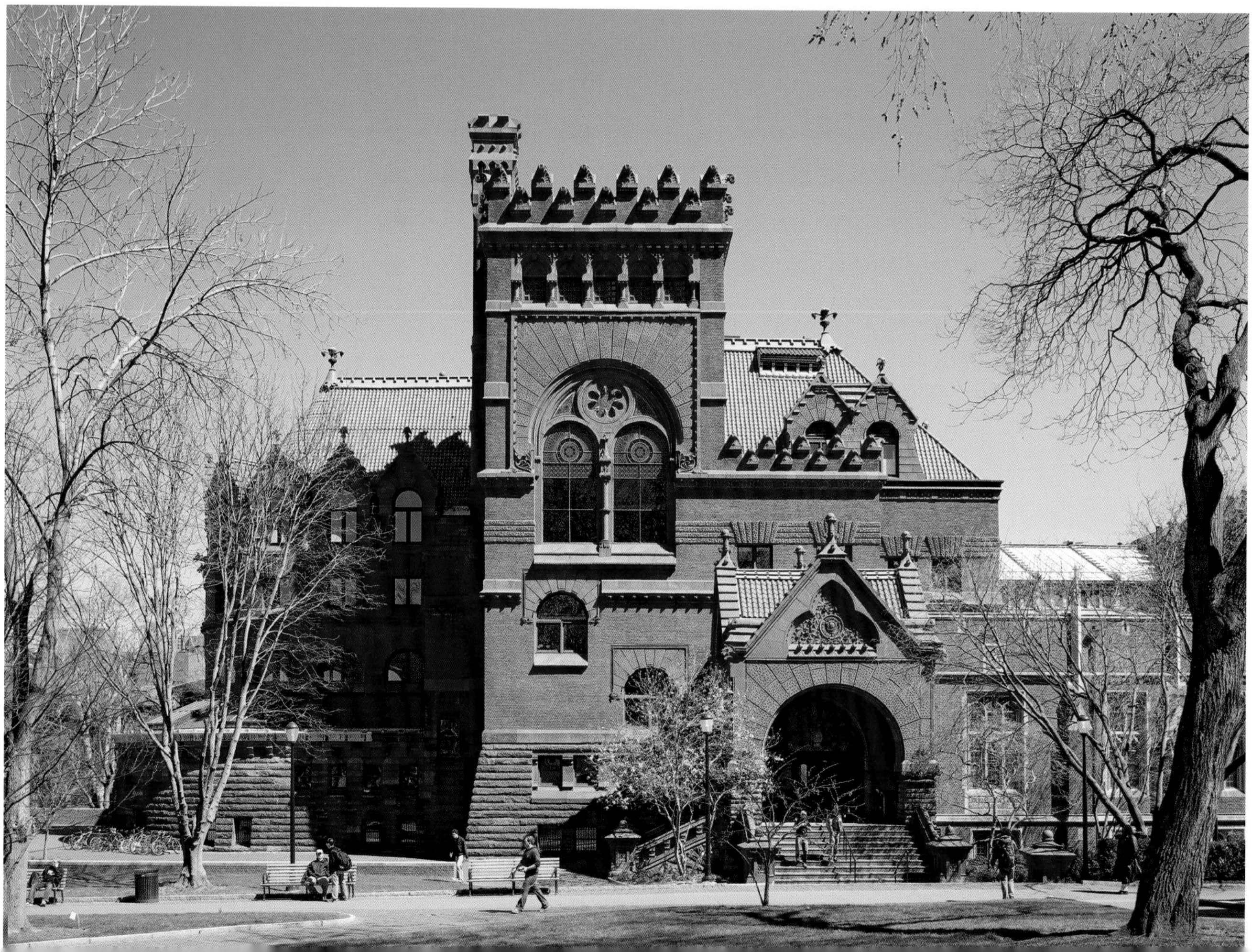

The soaring main reading room was divided in 1922 and restored to its original glory during the restoration of the late 1980s.

To expand the size and use of the library, provost William Pepper hired a new librarian and announced, "the time has now come when a separate fire-proof library building is imperatively demanded."

To plan the new library, Pepper assembled a committee headed by the eminent scholar Horace Howard Furness (1833–1912), who promptly recommended the appointment of his brother, the architect Frank Furness (pages 186–191), who had designed the new building for the Library Company (pages 192–195) and retrofitted another for the Mercantile Library. The architect in turn consulted Melvil Dewey (1851–1931), librarian of Columbia College, founder of the first training program for librarians, and developer of the Dewey decimal system of book classification. Furness also sought advice from Justin Winsor (1831–1897), librarian of Harvard College and a founder with Dewey of the American Library Association. Winsor was a scholar-librarian and an outspoken advocate for the library as the center of a modern university. Such men would reinvent the academic library, arguing for buildings with clearly delineated reading rooms, reference rooms, and staff offices separated from expandable book stacks of metal shelves and narrow aisles to which general readers did not have access. All these functional features—familiar to patrons of academic libraries today—would be incorporated into the new University of Pennsylvania Library, making it a landmark in the evolution of modern library design.

The library cornerstone was laid in 1888 and the completed building dedicated on February 7, 1891. Furness scholar George Thomas summarized the result: "though there are hints of history in its gargoyles, Penn's new library was a conflation of towers, chimneys, sky-lighted rooms and foundry-like clerestoried halls whose closest [architectural] sources were the factories of Philadelphia." While Furness enjoyed a highly successful career in Philadelphia—he was responsible for more than seven hundred commissions—some critics referred to his work as "the Furnessic reign of architectural terror," which, for its eccentricity, fell into disrepute as the taste for Beaux-Arts principles of European classicism gained ascendancy in the decades after the Columbian Exposition in Chicago (1893). Even the trustees of the University of Pennsylvania later turned away from Furness in favor of the Collegiate Gothic historicism of Walter Cope and John Stewardson, who became the campus architects.

After Furness's death in 1912 his office did return to the campus for several additions to the library. In 1914–1915 they designed the Duhring Wing to extend the bookstacks to the south; the main reading room was cut in half in 1922 to insert an additional floor; and in 1923–1924 a reading room to house

↑ This view of the semicircular north end of Fisher Library demonstrates the exotic detail and varied textures of Furness's design.

A detail of Furness's idiosyncratic architecture (1888–1891).

the library of Henry C. Lea was added on the Thirty-Fourth Street side. Finally, in 1931, Robert Rodes McGoodwin (1886–1967), a graduate architect of the University of Pennsylvania, instructor in architecture, and trustee of the School of Fine Arts, designed the Horace Howard Furness Shakespeare Reading Room on the west side. Both the Lea and Furness rooms were moved, together with the most of the University's book collection, when the Van Pelt Library was constructed (1962). At that time the building was turned over to the Graduate School of Fine Arts and renamed the Furness Library (1963). Following the restoration in the 1980s, the library was renamed the Anne and Jerome Fisher Fine Arts Library in recognition of their support of the successful effort.

PHILADELPHIA AND READING RAILROAD TERMINAL HEAD HOUSE AND SHED

(Pennsylvania Convention Center)
1115–1141 Market Street
Philadelphia, PA 19107

Francis H. Kimball, head house architect, 1891–1893
Wilson Brothers and Company, train shed engineers
National Historic Landmark, 1976

Telephone for visitor information: 215.418.4700
www.paconvention.com

On the evening of November 6, 1984, the last train pulled out of the Philadelphia and Reading Railroad shed in Center City. It was both a symbolic and a sentimental departure. A few minutes later a crew began tearing up the tracks. The largest single-span, arched-roof train shed in the world had ceased to serve its intended purpose.

Train shed is a prosaic term for those awe-inspiring creations of our Victorian forebears that enclosed vast spaces over multiple railroad tracks filled with intimidating locomotives arriving and departing in belching clouds of smoke and steam. A bustling train shed could make the most mundane trip into an adventure, even after Art Moderne electric or diesel streamliners replaced steam. But these are fading memories. The train sheds of Philadelphia, like the mighty

corporations that commissioned them, are gone. All save one, and it echoes the babble of partying conventioneers rather than the rumble of locomotives.

In the decades following the Civil War, the rapidly expanding railroad system crossed the North American continent and launched a frenzy of consolidation that spawned competitive rivalries among tycoons of the major trunk lines. Grand terminals in metropolitan areas (a form of architectural braggadocio) were one result. In Philadelphia, three competing corporations—the Pennsylvania, the Baltimore and Ohio, and the Reading—each erected a large Victorian terminal. The grandest of these, the Pennsylvania Railroad's Broad Street Station next to City Hall—constructed in stages between 1880 and 1892—included a 300-foot single-span train shed, then the largest in the world. (The Galérie des Machines designed and built for the Exposition de Paris in 1889 and demolished in 1909 spanned 364 feet. It was the largest wide-span, iron-framed structure erected for any purpose in the nineteenth century.) The Broad Street train shed came down after a fire in 1923 and the station itself was closed and demolished in 1952. The Baltimore and Ohio erected its picturesque station designed by Frank Furness at Twenty-Fourth and Chestnut Streets in 1886. Following a fire it too was demolished in 1963.

The Philadelphia and Reading Rail Road (usually called simply the Reading Railroad) was chartered in 1833 to lay a line between its namesake cities following the Schuylkill River; over subsequent decades it rapidly expanded into the rich coal regions of northern and western Pennsylvania and into New Jersey by leasing or acquiring smaller regional railroads. It was to consolidate the Reading's passenger facilities and to exploit the growing commuter-rail business in competition with the Pennsylvania Railroad (which was building its Broad Street Station) that the Reading decided in 1891 to erect a grand head house terminal for passenger facilities and corporate offices adjoining a new train shed. To avoid street-level crossings, the shed would be accessed at the second floor level from a system of elevated viaducts. The site coveted by the Reading Railroad for its flagship terminal was the intersection of Market and Twelfth Streets in the heart of Philadelphia's retail food marketing district near the new City Hall.

As early as the seventeenth century, Philadelphia's major food markets had been confined primarily to High Street, ultimately prompting its renaming as Market Street (see pages 66–68). Following the condemnation and demolition of the market sheds in the mid-nineteenth century, two substantial brick market houses, the Farmers' Market and the Franklin Market—the latter claiming to be the largest market house in the world—were erected at Twelfth and Market Streets. The market owners agreed to sell their land to the Reading for one million dollars and the construction of a new market to be located below the

→ The richly modeled Italianate Renaissance Revival Philadelphia and Reading Railroad Head House facing Market Street at Twelfth Street was designed by Francis H. Kimball and erected in 1891–1893. A century later, after a restoration recaptured its former glory, the terminal building became the grand entrance to the Pennsylvania Convention Center.

proposed train shed. The new Reading Terminal Market opened in 1892 with 795 stands occupying 78,000 square feet. This symbiotic relationship between the victualers and the railroad allowed suburban households to have grocery orders placed on outward bound trains, which would be held at the local station until collected. The Farmers' Market rapidly became a much beloved Philadelphia institution that has successfully weathered the decline of its host railroad, years of neglect, and the rebirth of the train shed as part of the Pennsylvania Convention Center.

The 256-foot-wide single-span roof of the train shed designed by Philadelphia architect and engineer Joseph M. Wilson is clearly shown in this construction photograph dating from c. 1892. Historic American Building Survey. Library of Congress, HABS PA, 51-PHILA, 521-8.

Let's return to 1891. To design the new train shed the Reading selected architect and engineer Joseph M. Wilson (1838–1902), a native of Phoenixville, Pennsylvania, who received his education as a civil engineer from the Rensselaer Polytechnic Institute and immediately found employment with the Pennsylvania Railroad. After working with Hermann J. Schwarzmann at Memorial Hall (pages 200–205), Wilson founded Wilson Brothers & Company, which rapidly became one of the most successful Philadelphia engineering firms, responsible not only for the 256-foot-wide Reading train shed (1891–1893) but the larger and now demolished Broad Street shed for the Pennsylvania Railroad (1892–1893). Wilson would declare,

> It has come to be recognized that this is the proper form of roof for a large railway station, reducing to a minimum the destructive action to the iron or steel construction from the sulphurous vapors emitted by the locomotives, and adding improved aesthetic effect. In designing such a roof, it is an object to mass the material together as much as possible, avoiding a great number of small pieces and leaving wide open spaces; also to provide ample light and ventilation.

To design the nine-story pink brick, granite, and cream-colored terra cotta head house terminal to stand in front of Wilson's train shed, the Reading selected New York architect Francis H. Kimball (1845–1919). He had served an apprenticeship in the London office of Gothic revivalist architect William Burges (1827–1881), whose vigorous polychrome effects may have influenced the richly modeled façade of Kimball's head house. After World War II, however, in an unfortunate effort to "streamline" the Italianate terminal, Kimball's handsome design was neutered by removing many of its distinctive stylistic elements. The two-story loggia with six arched openings overlooking Market Street was bricked shut (the same fate suffered by Schwarzmann's Memorial Hall). The boldly projecting decorative cornice, an important element of any Italianate Renaissance Revival building, was stripped off, and the ground floor rusticated entrances were obliterated by the installation of featureless steel shop fronts and neon signs. To compound the offense, these architectural modifications failed to arrest the plummeting decline in train ridership in the face of increasing suburbanization and government subsidized highways, which encouraged commuting by private automobile.

The northeast extension of the Pennsylvania Turnpike and the completion of the New Jersey Turnpike proved to be the fatal thrusts into the Reading's suburban market. The formation of the Southeastern Pennsylvania Transportation

The train shed now provides a Grand Hall and ballroom for the Pennsylvania Convention Center.

Authority (SEPTA) to take over the region's bus, streetcar, and commuter rail system attempted to help, but in 1971 the Reading declared bankruptcy, and in 1976 it sold its railroad interests to the Consolidated Railroad Corporation (Conrail).

For years city planners had recommended an underground connection of the Pennsylvania and Reading commuter lines to provide "run-through" operations from the west and south to the northeast. Once the commuter tunnel had been completed and the Market Street East Station opened, there no longer seemed any practical use for the old Reading train shed and head house terminal. Architectural historians and preservationists feared the structures would soon join the dreary list of demolished landmarks. That is, until the long-discussed plans for a modern convention center in Center City finally resulted in the formation of the Pennsylvania Convention Center Authority, which engaged the Atlanta architectural firm of Thompson, Ventulett, Stainback & Associates to work with the Vitetta Group, Kelly/Maiello, and Saxon/Capers—all from Philadelphia—to design the new exhibition buildings facing Arch Street (opened 1993), renovate the Reading Terminal Market, and adaptively reuse and restore the head house and train shed.

The renovated terminal opened in 1994 in its new guise as the Market Street gateway to the Convention Center, while Joseph Wilson's National Historic Landmark train shed was skillfully integrated with the new exhibition halls on Arch Street as a ceremonial Grand Hall and ballroom. And beneath the train shed, the renovated Reading Terminal Market continues to provide the expanding Center City residential population with fresh produce, meats, and fish—as it has done for more than a century.

PSFS

TWENTIETH-CENTURY PHILADELPHIA

The Bellevue

John Wanamaker Department Store

Historical Society of Pennsylvania

Racquet Club of Philadelphia

Benjamin Franklin Bridge

Thirtieth Street Station

United States Custom House

Philadelphia Savings Fund Society Building

Benjamin Franklin Parkway

Philadelphia Museum of Art

Insurance Company of North America Building

Free Library of Philadelphia

Rodin Museum

Board of Education Administration Building and Fidelity Mutual Life Insurance Building

The Philadelphia Savings Fund Society building (1929–1932) by architects George Howe and William Lescaze is an icon of twentieth-century modernism. It is widely considered the first International Style American skyscraper.

THE BELLEVUE

(Bellevue-Stratford Hotel)
200–216 South Broad Street
Philadelphia, PA 19102

G.W. and W. D. Hewitt,
architects, 1902–1904
Hewitt & Paist, architects,
additions to west, 1910–1911
National Register of Historic Places, 1976

Telephone (Park Hyatt):
215.893.1234
www.parkphiladelphia.hyatt.com

Once upon a time in Philadelphia, there were two modest red-brick hotels at Broad and Walnut Streets. The first of these, called the Bellevue, occupied the northwest corner; the second, called the Stratford, occupied the southwest corner. Both were acquired in the latter decades of the nineteenth century by George C. Boldt, an entrepreneurial German immigrant, who ultimately demolished the Stratford and erected on its site a massive, picturesque, French Renaissance-style hotel designed by the fashionable Philadelphia architects G. W. & W. D. Hewitt. Boldt named his new hotel the Bellevue-Stratford.

George C. Boldt (1851–1916) was a classic Horatio Alger rags-to-riches hero. He arrived in New York City not yet twenty years old and virtually penniless, and he found work as a dishwasher. After a failed effort to make his fortune in

The Bellevue on South Broad Street was designed by George W. Hewitt and William D. Hewitt and erected in 1902–1904. It was expanded by Hewitt & Paist, architects, in 1910–1911.

The Bellevue's richly modeled mansard roof is worthy of Georges-Eugène Haussmann's rebuilt Paris.

Texas, Boldt moved to Philadelphia, eventually becoming head waiter at the prestigious Philadelphia Club (pages 124–129). When he expressed the dream to someday become the proprietor of a modest hotel, several Club members offered to support him in such a venture. His successful management of the two Philadelphia Broad Street hotels led to his being invited by William W. Astor to manage his magnificent new Waldorf Hotel (1893) on Fifth Avenue in New York City. By 1902 Boldt had amassed both the personal capital and additional investors to expend $8,000,000 creating what the *Philadelphia Inquirer* proudly declared "the most magnificent hotel in this country."

To design his eighteen-story, fireproof, steel-framed luxury hotel—equipped with elevators and rooms with private baths and telephones—Boldt turned to the brothers George W. Hewitt (1841–1916) and William D. Hewitt (1847–1924), who had formed an architectural firm in 1878 and rapidly established a reputation as outstanding designers of both ecclesiastic and residential properties for socially prominent patrons such as Henry Howard Houston in Chestnut Hill. For Houston they designed Druim Moir, the Wissahickon Inn (now Chestnut Hill Academy), and St. Martin-in-the Fields Episcopal Church (see *Historic Sacred Places*, pages 282–87). They would also contribute to the look of early twentieth-century Philadelphia with commercial buildings like the Bourse (Fifth to Sixth Streets between Chestnut and Market) and their most important commission, the extravagant Bellevue-Stratford.

When the Bellevue-Stratford opened on September 20, 1904, its many rooms—ultimately expanded to more than 1,000—were tended by a staff of 800, including, according to one breathless account, women "whose only duty is to act as trunk packers for the women guests, and who are skilled in putting

→ With more than 1,000 rooms, the Bellevue-Stratford Hotel was served by a staff of 800. As suggested by the lobby, the architects sought to produce an impression of "overpowering and spacious magnificence."

↑ The ballroom could hold 2,000 guests.

away expensive dresses without mussing them." A reviewer for the *Architectural Record* (March 1905) remarked, "the new Bellevue-Stratford makes any hotel building, which preceded it in that vicinity, look insignificant." Previously the best hotels in Philadelphia "had a reputation for good cooking and good service; but the buildings in which they were housed were antiquated." This new "sky-scraper," the architectural critic explained, is "decorated with every intention of obtaining a good-looking, as well as a showy, effect." As for the interior, George C. Boldt and his architects sought to produce an impression of "over-powering and spacious magnificence" with a palatial, opulent lobby having "walls and columns . . . resplendent with marble and gilt" and a lavishly decorated Grand Ballroom able to hold 2,000 guests.

Overnight the Bellevue-Stratford became the place to stay or be seen in Philadelphia, and as the decades passed she became Philadelphia's "grande dame hotel." Looking back on more than seven decades, a *Philadelphia Inquirer* staff writer gushed, "royalty and presidents, opera stars and prizefight promoters, debutantes and business tycoons have stayed there. The Bellevue has played host to every president since Theodore Roosevelt, and during the Sesquicentennial in 1926 the storied Queen Marie of Rumania occupied the royal suite." But the aging hotel could not survive Legionnaires' disease, a mysterious ailment that killed 29 conventioneers and sickened 179 others in the summer of 1976. Occupancy plummeted and the doors were closed on November 18, 1976. The *Chicago Tribune* sang the requiem, "it is sad to see the Grand Old Lady of Broad Street done in by gossip. But that's a disease against which not even her finest old Main Line connections could provide immunity."

For nearly two years, the threat of demolition hung over the Bellevue-Stratford. In 1978, however, the hotel was purchased by Richard I. Rubin Associates, to be managed by the Fairmont Hotel Company from San Francisco after a $25,000,000 renovation by Day & Zimmerman Associates under the direction of Hyman Myers, FAIA, associate-in-charge. This highly acclaimed refurbishment returned the newly named Fairmont Hotel to operation in 1979; the following year management of the hotel was taken over by Western International Hotels and it was renamed the Bellevue-Stratford. After struggling for six years, the building was closed again and converted to mixed use with offices on several floors and a Park Hyatt Hotel on six floors. With the addition of a parking garage, health club, shops, and a gourmet food court, the Bellevue finally achieved a successful twenty-first-century mixed use and reasserted its prominence as one of the key Philadelphia landmarks on revitalized Broad Street south of City Hall.

According to one reviewer, the stairs from the lobby, "resplendent with marble and gilt," made any other Philadelphia hotel "look insignificant."

JOHN WANAMAKER DEPARTMENT STORE

(Macy's)
1300–1324 Market Street
Philadelphia, PA 19107

Daniel H. Burnham & Company, architects, 1902–1911
National Historic Landmark, 1978

Telephone for visitor information: 215.241.9000

To countless Philadelphians who remember a time before suburban malls, an invitation to "meet me at the Wanamaker's eagle" for shopping and an elegant lunch at the Crystal Tea Room promised to be a festive occasion, especially during the holiday season when the grand court became a winter wonderland and the massive organ boomed out carols. The eagle and the organ are still there, but the Wanamaker name is gone from the building, and even the "department store" concept he pioneered is an antiquated term.

In the history of retailing, the name of John Wanamaker (1838–1922) looms large. While he did not invent the American department store—a popular Philadelphia myth—he most certainly was one of its leading pioneers. Born in Philadelphia, the son of a prosperous brick maker, young Wanamaker seriously considered the ministry before entering the men's clothing business in 1861 with a store called Oak Hall at the southeast corner of Market and Sixth Streets. An innovative retailer, he ran full-page advertisements in newspapers and such popular magazines such as *Century* and *Scribner's*, and even helped to found two national periodicals to carry his message—*Everybody's Journal* and *Farm Journal*. Mid-century developments in anthropometry and sewing machines made practical the mass distribution of men's readymade clothing, and Wanamaker exploited

⚘ The present store was erected on the site of Wanamaker's Grand Depot, which opened in 1878 and boasted "the largest space in the world devoted to retail selling on a single floor." Athenæum of Philadelphia Collection.

ONE
WAY
13th St
13TH STREET
NO
TURN
ON
RED
THE ART
OF CAN
13TH

→ → The John Wanamaker Store (1902–1911) was designed by D. H. Burnham & Company as the first modern "department store" in Philadelphia.

← The grand court measures 112 by 66 feet and rises to a height of 150 feet. The famous organ designed by George Ashdown Audsley for the St. Louis Exposition of 1904 was installed in 1911.

the marketing potential. He offered tailors at the store to alter the readymade clothing and advertised "Full Guarantee, One Price, Cash Payment, and Cash Returns"—and his business flourished.

In 1874 Wanamaker purchased and renovated the Pennsylvania Railroad freight depot at Market and Thirteenth Streets and opened a dry goods store called The New Establishment, offering men's and women's clothing, fabrics, and household linens. After enjoying success during the Centennial Exhibition in 1876, and failing to attract other retailers to open specialty shops in the depot, he expanded the building to cover two acres and reopened in 1877 as the departmentalized Wanamaker Composite Store, known popularly as the Grand Depot or Wanamaker's New Kind of Store. The following year he installed arc lights in his show windows, and in 1880 the store became the first to adopt Thomas Edison's incandescent electric lamps to light the interior. Concurrently the variety of "departments" increased: china (1878); carpets, sporting goods, jewelry, and refrigerators (1880); beds, antique furniture, optical goods, gas stoves, and art (1881); books and a soda fountain in 1882. By the late 1880s, according to historian Robert Sobel, the Grand Depot was "the most famous store in the nation." It was time to consider an even grander building.

In 1901 Wanamaker announced his plan to erect a new building on the city block bounded by Chestnut, Market, Juniper, and Thirteenth Streets. Respected Philadelphia architect Edward P. Hazlehurst (1853–1915), who had just returned to Philadelphia from his remodeling of Grand Central Station in New York City, and the politically well connected firm of James Windrim (1840–1919) and John T. Windrim (1866–1934) both submitted drawings. A highly finished set of drawings was also prepared by New York theater architect Francis H. Kimball (1845–1919), best known locally for his design of the Reading Terminal head house near Wanamaker's Grand Depot on Market Street (pages 218–223). Ultimately all these submissions were rejected in favor of the Chicago architectural firm D. H. Burnham & Company.

Only the Burnham and Kimball drawings are known to survive, but it is revealing to compare them. Kimball's overly fussy Baroque pastiche looked back to the nineteenth century and may even have consciously intended to echo the Grand Depot with its towers and minarets. In contrast, the Burnham firm's design was suavely current. Like the firm's nearby Land Title Building on South Broad Street (built in two stages, 1897–1898 and 1902), it is in the "commercial classical" mode for which the firm was already famous.

At the time he designed the Wanamaker Store, Daniel H. Burnham (1846–1912) was well on his way to heading the world's largest architectural firm. Burnham and Root, organized with his first partner, John Wellborn Root (1850–1891), had rapidly become the leading "Chicago School" architects after the

The eagle in the grand court was created by German sculptor August Gaul for the German pavilion at the St. Louis Exposition of 1904. It was cast in parts—there are 5,000 individual bronze feathers—and assembled on site.

great fire of 1871. Following Root's death in 1891, Burnham carried on as D. H. Burnham and Company to design the 1893 World's Columbian Exposition in Chicago, which greatly influenced the City Beautiful movement grounded in the classical principles of the École des Beaux-Arts (see pages 268–272). Across America corporate leaders looked to Burnham for the Olympian grandeur of Greece and Rome. By 1901 his architecture was identified with America's rising industrial might and imperial optimism. Wanamaker's biographer tells us:

> Wanamaker had first admired [Burnham's] work at the World's Fair 1893, and he knew that Burnham had been retained for Marshall Field's new store. Philadelphia local pride, and the "strong representations" (as he called them) of Philadelphia and New York friends did not prevent him from going to Chicago for his architect.

To a man as conscious of his standing as America's merchant prince, the appeal of a Burnham design must have been overwhelming.

The new Wanamaker Store was built on the site of the Grand Depot in three stages beginning in 1902, and the completed whole was dedicated on December 30, 1911. The previous day, Burnham left Chicago by special train accompanied by a large party of the great and good of that city, joined in Philadelphia by President William Howard Taft, who gave a formal dedicatory address. At the close of the ceremony, Burnham presented John Wanamaker with a gold key to his building, and the party retired to the home of P. A. B. Widener to view his art collection before reboarding their train for the return to Chicago.

The new twelve-story, steel-frame Wanamaker Store in the Roman Doric style is clothed in limestone and granite and has a floor area of nearly forty-five acres. It rises in three stages: a base with giant pilasters to give a sense of support around the large ground floor display windows, a main body of seven stories in rusticated ashlar, and topped with a two-story arched-window arcade with a band of small square windows directly under the projecting cornice. The interior five-story grand court contains the famous organ designed by George Ashdown Audsley (1838–1925)—said to be the largest in the world—acquired after the Louisiana Purchase Exposition in St. Louis (1904), as was the ten-foot bronze eagle by German sculptor August Gaul (1869–1922). The Crystal Tea Room on the eighth floor covered 22,000 square feet and seated 1,000. At the time it was the largest dining room in Philadelphia. Fifty passenger elevators moved customers from floor to floor, and every effort was made to make the building fireproof and equipped with isolated exit stairs. Wanamaker was justifiably proud of his new building. At the dedication he remarked:

> This notable edifice of ours takes its place as a central commanding figure in Philadelphia city life..., but more than this, it is a national building, specifically prepared to install the home of the new kind of store that originated here, embodying the new American mercantile system of retail commerce, which has spread over the world.

But not even a far-sighted merchant like John Wanamaker could have anticipated the mid-twentieth-century decline of American cities in the face of suburban sprawl and auto-centric shopping malls and box stores. The once proud Center City landmark gradually declined in the decades following World War II. In the late 1980s the building was reconfigured for mixed use: the lower floors to continue as retail space with the commercial offices on the upper floors accessed from the former carriage drive on Juniper Street opposite City Hall.

HISTORICAL SOCIETY OF PENNSYLVANIA

1300 Locust Street
Philadelphia, PA 19107-5699

Addison Hutton, architect, 1904–1910

Telephone for visitor information: 215.732.6200
www.hsp.org

The Historical Society of Pennsylvania is one of the premier independent research libraries in America. By the time of its founding in 1824, five other states had already established similar institutions. This apparent tardiness is misleading. It was caused by the earlier founding of The American Philosophical Society (pages 48–53) and The Athenæum of Philadelphia (pages 132–137), which shared quarters on Independence Square and had expressed an intention to form libraries of historic books and manuscripts. The Athenæum in 1814 declared its interest in "collecting historical and other monuments, connected with the history and antiquities of America," and Peter S. Du Ponceau (1760–1844), who was active in both organizations, asked in 1815, "How can the Historian himself

Prior to erecting its present building, the Historical Society occupied the Powel-Patterson House, designed by William Strickland in 1832. Historical Society of Pennsylvania.

perform his task with honor and credit if the materials for his work are not collected and preserved for him, before all-devouring time has blotted from the memory of men those interesting details, which alone can give the key to the true causes of public events?"

Late in 1824, Thomas I. Wharton, a founder of the Athenæum, and several other individuals active in the existing societies met at Wharton's home to found a society for the specific "purpose of elucidating the history of Pennsylvania." A room was promptly rented in Philosophical Hall "over the Athenæum," where the new Society would remain until invited to become a tenant in the Athenæum's new building designed by John Notman on Washington Square. These rooms would house the Historical Society for the next quarter century.

The Historical Society's collections grew rapidly after the Civil War, exceeding available space at the Athenæum. In 1872 the Society leased the two-story Picture Building on the grounds of Pennsylvania Hospital, which had been erected in 1817 to display Benjamin West's *Christ Healing the Sick* (page 59). Shortly thereafter the Society acquired the first of what would be many internationally significant collections, when it purchased 20,000 documents relating to William Penn and his family. The Historical Society remained in the Picture Building until the 1880s, when the directors purchased the Powel-Patterson Mansion at the intersection of Locust and Thirteenth Streets.

Erected in 1832 by John Hare Powel (1786–1856), the Historical Society's new headquarters was a handsome Greek Revival house and one of the few examples of William Strickland's domestic architecture of which we have detailed knowledge. Powel wrote to a friend, "I am about to build a house 60 feet

The Historical Society of Pennsylvania has occupied the southwest corner of Locust and Thirteenth Streets since the 1880s. The present Georgian Revival building by Addison Hutton was erected in 1904–1910.

by 44 feet on Locust street between 13th and Juniper streets. [I therefore] . . . place myself on the frontier and . . . my friends condemn me for leaving what is termed the fashionable part of town." Perhaps he ultimately found the location too unfashionable. The paint was hardly dry when Powel auctioned the elegant contents and sold the house to wealthy cotton mill owner General Robert Patterson (1792–1881) in 1835. It passed from Patterson's heirs to the Historical Society in 1883. The purchase of an adjoining lot to the west provided space to erect a new assembly hall addition in the fashionable High Victorian taste.

The move into the Powel-Patterson House unleashed a flood of gifts and bequests from Philadelphia families with deep historical roots, particularly portraits by Benjamin West, John Singleton Copley, John Neagle, Thomas Sully, and members of the Peale family, as well as marble busts, decorative arts (especially tall case clocks), and other domestic treasures. This accumulation of material culture—in addition to manuscript, print, and rare book collections of both local and national importance—prompted the trustees to approach the Commonwealth of Pennsylvania in 1903 for funds to replace the Powel-Patterson House with a new, fireproof building of ample capacity. With a grant from the state, the fashionable Philadelphia architect Addison Hutton was engaged to design the new facility.

Hutton (1834–1916), a birthright Quaker, was a native of Westmoreland County, Pennsylvania, where he worked as a carpenter and schoolteacher before coming to the attention of Philadelphia architect Samuel Sloan, with whom he eventually entered a brief partnership. Hutton secured several hundred commissions during his long and successful career, including the Arch Street Methodist Church (*Historic Sacred Places*, pages 140–43) and the Ridgway Library for the Library Company of Philadelphia (pages 192–195).

The new Historical Society building would emerge in stages. The High Victorian style assembly hall addition to the west of the Powel-Patterson House was demolished in 1904 to make way for five bays of the new red-brick-trimmed-with-marble Georgian Revival building. Given the prejudice in favor of seventeenth- and eighteenth-century American history at the time, this style was doubtless thought an appropriate choice, although contemporary reviewers compared it unfavorably to Daniel H. Burnham's nearby Land Title Building.

Then, in 1905, the Powel-Patterson House came down and the full scope of Hutton's design was revealed. The entire four-story brick building over a high basement stretches eleven bays on Locust Street and ten bays on Thirteenth Street. At the west end, two bays are recessed and the other nine bays along Locust Street are clustered into groups of three, the middle group of which is a projecting two-story marble portico supported by clustered Ionic-style marble columns, perhaps a nod to William Strickland's Doric style portico on the Powel-Patterson House. Flanking the portico are three-bay clusters with a large Palladian window centered on the ground floor of each. The east Palladian window illuminates the ground floor stair hall and the west Palladian window the galleried assembly hall, now the Society's principal research reading room. All windows have lintels and keystones except at the second floor, where the windows are given recessed arched heads. A balcony in the middle of the Thirteenth Street façade echoes the parapet of the Locust Street portico. The three windows

Originally intended as an assembly hall, this lofty room was divided in the 1970s by dropping the ceiling to provide additional work space on the floor above. During the renovations by Venturi, Scott Brown and Associates in 1997–1999, the room was handsomely restored for use as the main reading room for the many scholars from across the nation and abroad who are attracted by the Society's unrivaled research collection of manuscripts, prints, and photographs.

NEW CENTURY GUILD
Founded 1882 by Eliza S. Turner. One of the oldest and largest organizations created to advance the interests of women in the labor force. Originally located on Girard St., the Guild moved to Arch St. in 1893 and to this location in 1906.
NO STOPPING BUS ZONE
2 HR PARKING 8 AM – 6 PM
THE HISTORICAL SOCIETY OF PENNSYLVANIA

of the third and fourth stories over the portico and the parapet are embellished with decorative keystones and rusticated surrounds.

Designed to provide a fireproof repository for the Historical Society's collections, while lending the gravitas thought at the time appropriate for the headquarters of a learned society, Hutton's building successfully served the Historical Society for several decades. The first major modifications and mechanical upgrades, in the 1970s, were prompted by the continued growth of collections, aging of mechanical systems, and expanding program needs. Not all these changes were sympathetic to the building, and by the end of the twentieth century a more extensive renovation and reconfiguration of the interior was desirable. This building campaign by the Philadelphia architects Venturi, Scott Brown and Associates gave the Historical Society of Pennsylvania a safe repository for its collection while creating a more sympathetic environment for members and the public.

The marble portico and entrance were designed as an echo of the portico of the Powel-Patterson House, which stood on the site from 1832 to 1905.

RACQUET CLUB OF PHILADELPHIA

213–225 South Sixteenth Street
Philadelphia, PA 19102

Horace Trumbauer, architect, 1906–1907
National Register of Historic Places, 1979

Members only
Telephone for information: 215.735.1525
www.rcop.com

In writing about London clubs, the late duke of Devonshire remarked that all clubs have "the same general purpose, that of providing a meeting place for like-minded men, so each has its own special flavour." While the gender reference is no longer politically correct, and many clubs in both London and Philadelphia have dropped their male exclusivity, the concept of "like-mindedness" still holds true, particularly in the case of the Racquet Club of Philadelphia.

Founded by a group of athletic gentlemen in the early 1880s, the Racquet Club incorporated in 1889, settled into a house at 923 Walnut Street, and promptly engaged the firm of Furness, Evans and Company to add two racquet courts. Club membership rapidly expanded through the 1890s to include a number of wealthy Philadelphians such as George D. Widener (son of traction magnate P. A. B. Widener). It was the younger Widener who, acting for the club, acquired an option on 213–225 South Sixteenth Street and selected the architect to design a new and substantially larger clubhouse to accommodate courts for tennis, squash, and racquets as well as a swimming pool and other recreational facilities, which prompted social critic and historian Nathaniel Burt to call it "by far the best appointed . . . of all Philadelphia's clubs."

That Widener should have chosen Horace Trumbauer to design the new clubhouse is no surprise. Trumbauer (1868–1938) had already established a relationship with P. A. B. Widener, for whom he designed Lynnewood Hall in Elkins Park (1897–1900), and over the coming decades he would be responsible for numerous buildings for the family, including the Widener Memorial Training School for Crippled Children (1902–1914) and the Harry Elkins Widener Memorial Library at Harvard University (1912–1914). (The *Titanic* disaster in 1912 proved to be particularly tragic for the Racquet Club. Members George D. Widener, Harry Elkins Widener, and John B. Thayer, Jr., were lost in the sinking.)

A native Philadelphian, Trumbauer served his apprenticeship in the office of G. W. and W. D. Hewitt during the period the firm was designing Druim Moir for Henry H. Houston in Chestnut Hill (*Historic Sacred Places*, pages 282–87). In fairly short order he established his own office and by 1893 had caught the eye of the sugar refiner William W. Harrison, for whom he created Grey Towers (now Arcadia University). This commission set him on a career that included several large country and suburban houses for newly wealthy Philadelphia industrialists. In the years just prior to the Racquet Club and his Union League annex commission, Trumbauer's office produced Chelten House in Elkins Park for George W. Elkins (1896) and The Elms for Edward J. Berwind (1899) and Chetwode for William S. Wells (1900), both in Newport, Rhode Island, in addition to Lynnewood Hall for the Wideners (1898).

↞ The focal point of the imposing Georgian Revival style façade of the Racquet Club by Horace Trumbauer (1906–1907) is a large Doric frontispiece centered on a pedimented pavilion.

The Georgian Revival style carries into the forty-foot-square main hall, where fluted pilasters support a Doric order entablature. The processional stair rises through the center arch and then splits to the left and right to rise to the second floor.

Work began on the Racquet Club of Philadelphia in spring 1906 and was completed the following year. Structurally it is reinforced concrete with brick curtain walls trimmed with marble and terra cotta. The three-story Georgian Revival-style façade on Sixteenth Street is deceptive; the full height of the L-shaped building is six stories, with the upper floors and rear wing on Sydenham Street providing private dining rooms, offices, and extensive athletic facilities (racquets, squash, court tennis, Turkish bath, gymnasium, and swimming pool). From the point of view of architectural history, the use of reinforced concrete construction is significant. Developed in the late nineteenth century, it combined the tensile strength of steel with the plasticity and compression strength of concrete. The first reinforced concrete structure in the United States was the Pacific Coast Borax Company refinery in Alameda, California (1893), and the first skyscraper to use the system was the Terminal Station in Atlanta (1904). Trumbauer began designing the clubhouse in 1905, making the Racquet Club one of the earliest uses of reinforced concrete in Philadelphia—all clothed in a suave if somewhat overblown version of Philadelphia's traditional red brick Georgian architecture.

Both members and the press were impressed with the completed building. A *Philadelphia Record* reporter exclaimed, "No where in the world is there a club house so complete with so many unique features as the new home of the Racquet Club," while the *Evening Bulletin* marveled at the "impression of richness and elegance which is not often found in a club house." There were also comments relating to the labor-saving devices and mechanical marvels of the new century. Elevators, pneumatic tube communication systems, and the use of compressed air to open and close the oversized windows all elicited comment. The swimming pool on the *third floor* did not escape notice. When filled with water the 36- by 36-foot pool weighed 1,500,000 pounds and could only have been made possible by a steel cradle supported by twelve reinforced concrete columns firmly anchored deep below the sub-basement. It is no wonder the Trumbauer office had brought in as consultants the Roebling Construction Company of bridge-building fame.

The Racquet Club building remains largely unaltered except for mechanical system upgrades. As for all social clubs, there have been changes in the membership. The admission of women, the creation of a "suburban" membership category for those who live and work at least five miles from Center City, and the introduction of golf and sailing programs have helped hold the line against the changing demographics that have proved fatal to several city clubs since the 1960s. Whether the much discussed "return to the city" movement will reverse the decline of private city clubs remains to be seen.

This drawing is for the Sixteenth Street elevation of Horace Trumbauer's Racquet Club as approved by club president James Potter on April 11, 1906. Work began on April 23, 1906, and the building officially opened on October 7, 1907. Athenæum of Philadelphia, Horace Trumbauer Collection, gift of The Racquet Club of Philadelphia.

BENJAMIN FRANKLIN BRIDGE

(Delaware River Bridge)
Spanning the Delaware River at Fifth and Vine Streets, Philadelphia, PA

Ralph Modjeski, engineer
Paul Philippe Cret, architect, 1920–1926

Delaware River Port Authority
Telephone for public information: 856.968.2233
www.drpa.org

The Delaware River determined the location of Philadelphia and nurtured its growth as a major center of commerce and shipbuilding. But the Delaware was also a wide natural barrier, impeding the flow of land-based transport between New Jersey and Pennsylvania. Before the nineteenth century, residents of Philadelphia and Camden seem not to have contemplated bridging their river, and the proposals made during the nineteenth century came to nothing. Not until after World War I—when auto and truck production in the United States exceeded 500,000 vehicles a year and the busy little fleet of ferryboats plowing back and forth across the river could no longer keep pace with demand—was the Delaware River Bridge Joint Commission formed and a serious effort

to construct a bridge begun. The U.S. Congress authorized the bridge in 1921 and work commenced in 1922, with costs equally shared by Pennsylvania and New Jersey. When completed in 1926, the Delaware River Bridge was for a time the longest suspension bridge in the world.

One question early in the project was whether an architect or an engineer should design this great undertaking. Architect Warren Powers Laird (1861–1948), director of the architecture program at the University of Pennsylvania, initiated the debate by declaring in 1919 that the proposed bridge would be a work of architecture that could only be accomplished "by a master mind in architecture working in coordination with the best engineering skill." In response, the American Society of Civil Engineers declared that only "men qualified as civil engineers and not as architects" should be given responsibility for the bridge. Ultimately the Delaware River Bridge Joint Commission resolved the debate by appointing a team of engineers headed by Ralph Modjeski (1861–1940).

The Polish-born Modjeski came to America with his mother, an actress, in 1876. Inspired to study engineering by a visit to the Centennial Exhibition in Philadelphia, he was sent to Paris, where he eventually gained admission to the prestigious École Nationale des Ponts et Chaussées, graduating with distinction in 1885. Returning to America he secured work with a Midwestern bridge builder where he remained for seven years. After establishing his own office in 1893, Modjeski won commissions to design major steel bridges across the Mississippi and St. Lawrence Rivers. The American Society of Civil Engineers declared him American Engineer of the Year in 1903. Modjeski would eventually complete nearly 40 major bridges, earning him the title of America's greatest bridge builder. In addition to the Delaware River Bridge, he would serve as consulting engineer for the Tacony-Palmyra Bridge and the Henry Avenue Bridge spanning Wissahickon Creek, both with Paul Philippe Cret serving as architect.

Cret (1876–1945) was chosen to collaborate with Modjeski in 1920. Born in Lyon, France, and trained at the École des Beaux-Arts in Paris, Cret relocated to Philadelphia in 1903 as professor of design at the University of Pennsylvania, where he would help train an entire generation of Penn graduates in the Beaux-Arts style. Cret also enjoyed an independent practice, and in partnership with Albert Kelsey designed the Pan American Union building in Washington, D.C. During World War I Cret served in the French army, and following his discharge returned to Philadelphia in 1919 to resume both his teaching post and a thriving private practice. When appointed to the Delaware River Bridge project, Cret's office was small, he had never designed a major bridge, and his great projects of the 1920s were yet in the future. The appointment landed him directly into the

The Benjamin Franklin Bridge (1920–1926) spanning the Delaware River is the product of the successful collaboration of engineer Ralph Modjeski and architect Paul Philippe Cret. It is one of the iconic landmarks of Philadelphia.

CAMDEN

debate over what one historian of the bridge calls "the rationalism of the engineer and the aestheticism of the architect."

Fortunately both Modjeski and Cret realized how essential collaboration must be on such a project. As Cret wrote, if there is a divorce between architecture and engineering, "it is the work that suffers," and in 1927, shortly after the completion of the bridge, Modjeski wrote to Cret, "I want to express to you what great pleasure it has been to have you as collaborator in the great work of the bridge. I feel it is largely due to your art that we have succeeded in building a bridge of which we are all proud." The division of responsibility between engineer and architect relates to the basic components of a suspension bridge: the anchorages on each shore, the towers from which the cables are suspended, the cables themselves, and the deck that carries the roadbed. The deck and cables are purely an engineering problem that must be solved mathematically if a disaster such as the famous Tacoma Narrows Bridge collapse in 1940 is to be avoided. (It is hard to forget the newsreel footage of that bridge deck twisting in the wind.) The anchorages and towers, however, provide an opportunity for "art," as suggested by Modjkeski's letter quoted above. Cret also commented that the task of the architect, particularly in the instance of the anchorages, was "not to decorate, but to interpret—to clothe" their functionality, which had already been determined by the engineering requirements. In the instance of the 380-foot silicon steel towers, however, the team rejected a similar use of masonry. The towers, which flex in the wind, in Cret's words, "are not ashamed of being built of steel" and should not be concealed "under a masonry cloak." Each of these extraordinary, talented teams—engineers and architects—understood the role of the other. Ego never seems to have obstructed the creation of a bridge both functional and beautiful.

Writing in the *Architectural Record* for January 1927, Harold D. Eberlein commented, "The Delaware River Bridge is a very noteworthy addition to the bridge-building achievements of America and, indeed, of the world. That its construction was a signal triumph of engineering skill is quite generally recognized. That its design is a matter of no little architectural import and marks a new stage in the evolution of American civil architecture is a fact which the public at large has not as yet fully grasped." From the perspective of eighty years, the Delaware River Bridge, renamed for Benjamin Franklin in 1955, modified to carry a high speed rail line in the 1960s, and decoratively illuminated in 1988, remains one of the recognizable landmarks of Philadelphia. It is a credit to its engineer, its architect, and the cities it joins.

The heroic coats of arms of Pennsylvania, Philadelphia, New Jersey, and Camden that decorate Cret's anchorages and pylons are the work of French-born sculptor Leon Hermant (1866–1936), who came to America in 1904 to work on the French Pavilion at the Louisiana Purchase Exposition in St. Louis. He would later work with Cret on the Detroit Institute of Art (1927).

THIRTIETH STREET STATION

(Pennsylvania Railroad Station)
2901–2951 Market Street
Philadelphia, PA 19104

Graham, Anderson, Probst & White, architects, 1929–1933
National Register of Historic Places, 1978

Telephone for visitor information: 215.349.2270
www.30thstreetstation.com

As the United States plunged into the Great Depression following the stock market crash of 1929, the Pennsylvania Railroad was building what would prove to be its architectural last hurrah. The monumental Thirtieth Street Station for through passenger service would be the most visible component of a decades-long collaboration hammered out in the mid-1920s by the Pennsylvania Railroad and the City of Philadelphia to reconfigure the city's rail system.

The Pennsylvania Railroad Company had been created in 1846 to build a trunk line from Philadelphia to Pittsburgh in an effort to compete with New York's Erie Canal for western trade. It ultimately became the largest railroad in the United States in terms of assets and traffic with over 11,000 miles of track. In the 1920s no one could have imagined that fifty years hence this mighty corporation—whose rock-solid stock and bonds supported countless widows

➳ The Pennsylvania Railroad World War II Memorial (1952) was commissioned from sculptor and Pennsylvania Academy of the Fine Arts educator Walker Hancock (1901–1998). The base is inscribed: "In memory of the men and women of the Pennsylvania Railroad who laid down their lives for their country 1941–1945."

and orphans—would be forced into bankruptcy by a toxic mix of interstate highways, civilian airlines, and the decline of heavy manufacturing in the northeast and midwest.

The shining image of the early twentieth-century "City Beautiful" that had inspired the Benjamin Franklin Parkway (pages 268–272) was embarrassingly smudged by the sprawling presence of the Pennsylvania Railroad's Victorian-era Broad Street Station and its mammoth train shed. Erected next to City Hall in stages between 1880 and 1892, Broad Street Station was what railroaders call a "stub terminal"—a dead end—located in this case nearly a mile from the north/south main rail line. It handled 510 trains a day, of which 220 were through trains on their way to points north, south, or west. Stub terminals

➳ East façade of Thirtieth Street Station from the bank of the Schuylkill River. Rising up to the north is César Pelli's Cira Centre (2003–2005). To the left is one of four monumental eagles on the Market Street Bridge by German-born sculptor Adolph Alexander Weinman (1870–1952), originally executed for Pennsylvania Station in New York City (1910). When that station was unfortunately demolished in 1964, the pink granite eagles were given to the Fairmount Park Art Association.

The main concourse is 290 feet long, 135 feet wide, and 95 feet high. The coffered ceiling, decorated in red, gold, and cream, hangs from steel roof trusses supporting a heavy concrete slab designed to accommodate the weight of small airplanes landing on the roof.

create difficulty for through trains, requiring that they be reversed—a time-consuming and labor intensive activity that at Broad Street Station added half an hour to the schedule of every through train. In addition, tracks from West Philadelphia Station (at Thirty-Second and Market Streets) were carried to Broad Street on a massive masonry viaduct derisively known by Philadelphians as the "Chinese Wall" for its resemblance to the Great Wall of China. The viaduct, station, and train shed occupied many acres of valuable real estate; and its low underpasses impeded city traffic and depressed adjoining property values.

On June 11, 1923, a fire at the Broad Street Station destroyed engineer Joseph M. Wilson's 300-foot, single-span train shed, then the largest in the world (see Pennsylvania and Reading Railroad, pages 218–222). This catalyst set into motion a grand scheme of civic improvements that envisioned demolition of Broad Street Station and removal of the "Chinese Wall" to make way for redevelopment west of City Hall. A new gateway station for through trains would be constructed astride the north-south tracks on the west side of the Schuylkill River as the terminus of a new boulevard from City Hall, just as the Benjamin Franklin Parkway terminates at the Philadelphia Museum of Art. For its part the federal government agreed to construct a new post office (Rankin & Kellogg, 1931–1935) to the south of the new Thirtieth Street Station. Philadelphia would gain two more impressive architectural monuments.

But the Pennsylvania Railroad's retreat west to Thirtieth Street would strand the nearly 30,000 suburban commuters who daily were delivered to Broad Street Station in the heart of the city. To serve this constituency the railroad commissioned the Suburban Station building—in the 1600 block of what is now John F. Kennedy Boulevard. Ground was broken on July 28, 1927, and Suburban Station opened on September 28, 1930. The resulting twenty-story office building with handsome Art Deco flourishes was designed by Graham, Anderson, Probst & White. It rises above the actual station, which is located on a mezzanine floor below street level with the train platforms—connected by a tunnel from Thirtieth Street—located twenty feet below the mezzanine. The station in turn was connected to an underground pedestrian concourse leading

Austrian-born artist Karl Bitter (1867–1915) executed five sculptural reliefs for the Pennsylvania Railroad Broad Street Station (1895). One of these, an allegorical representation of the progress of transportation, was relocated to Thirtieth Street Station in 1935. It features the "Spirit of Transportation" borne through history on a chariot. To the left an oxen-drawn wagon represents historical modes of transport; to the right are a modern locomotive, steamship, and—prophetically—an airship.

to subway service, City Hall, and underground walkways to Locust Street to the south, Vine Street to the north, and Eleventh Street to the east.

Meanwhile work had begun on Thirtieth Street Station. More than a hundred submissions had been considered before the Pennsylvania Railroad settled on a proposal from the Chicago architectural firm founded in 1917 by Ernest Graham, William Anderson, Edward Probst and Howard White, successors to D. H. Burnham & Company, which had given Philadelphia the landmark John Wanamaker Department Store (pages 232–237). Noted for its "commercial classicism," this firm brought to the project extensive experience, including the recently designed Union Station in Chicago (1925) and Cleveland Union Terminal (1925–1929). According to Carroll L. V. Meeks, the leading historian of American railroad stations, Graham, Anderson, Probst & White, "doubly bolstered by their own Burnham Baroque tradition and the Pennsylvania Railroad's tendency to hugeness . . . , unhesitatingly built grandly in a wholly prewar spirit." The railroad would refer to its new headquarters as "Pennsylvania Station"; to the public it was and remains simply "Thirtieth Street."

Without question the scale of Thirtieth Street Station is colossal. The cruciform plan measures 639 feet north to south and 327 feet east to west. The steel and concrete structure is faced with Alabama limestone and the east and

↟ Original main floor plan of Thirtieth Street Station. Athenæum of Philadelphia Collection.

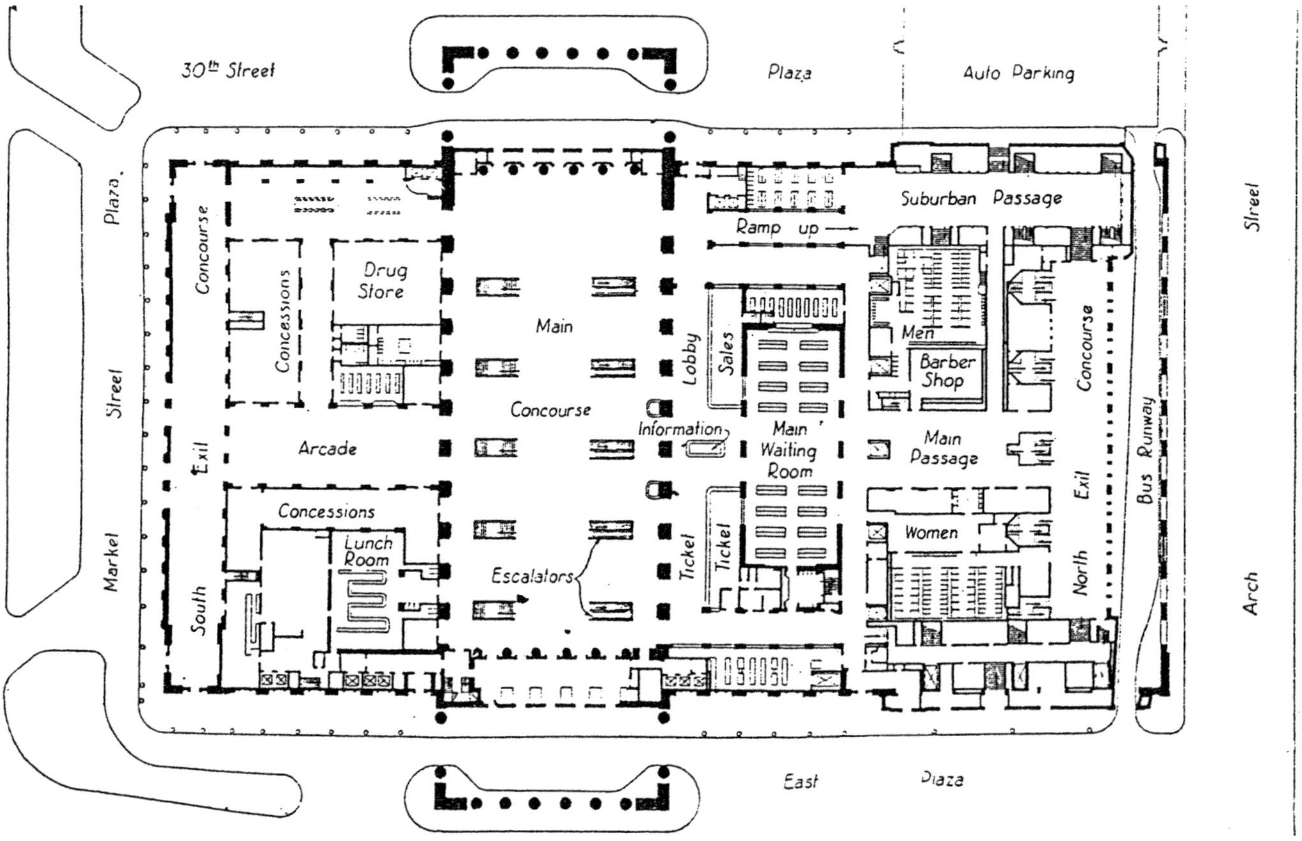

west façades are dominated by colonnaded porticos of giant order Corinthian columns (71 feet high, 11 feet in diameter) that lead to the Main Concourse floored in Tennessee marble with walls clad in Travertine. The doors, lighting fixtures, and other architectural fittings are cast bronze. The cynical observer might unfairly dismiss it as the wasteful extravagance of an overconfident corporation. But Thirtieth Street Station should not be viewed through the lens of twenty-first-century hindsight. It is a late product of the City Beautiful dream of impressive civic buildings modeled by the Beaux-Arts principles of classical symmetry and balance—the same vision that had given Philadelphia the Benjamin Franklin Parkway.

The new Pennsylvania Station at Thirtieth Street went into service on March 12, 1933, but the deepening depression followed by World War II delayed full implementation of the improvements envisioned in the 1920s. Broad Street Station continued to be used until 1952, delaying the removal of the Chinese Wall and the redevelopment of the area west of City Hall. As the fortunes of American railroads began to decline in the 1950s and 1960s, Thirtieth Street Station suffered along with America's other metropolitan gateway stations, although it fortunately did not share the fate of McKim, Mead and White's Pennsylvania Station in New York (1905–1910), which was demolished in 1964, or Daniel Burnham's Union Station in Washington, D.C. (1907), which was turned into an ill-fated National Visitors' Center for the Bicentennial and only renovated and reopened in 1998. Instead, as part of Amtrak's effort to upgrade Northeast Corridor service, Thirtieth Street Station underwent a major restoration and rehabilitation project (1989–1992), recapturing much of the original architectural grandeur. Today it is the second most active railway station in the United States.

UNITED STATES CUSTOM HOUSE

(U.S. Custom House and Appraisers' Stores)
200 Chestnut Street
Philadelphia, PA 19106

Ritter & Shay, architects, 1932–1934
National Register of Historic Places, 2004

Restricted access
http://w3gsa.gov

The United States Custom House by Ritter and Shay (1932–1934) rises over Independence National Historical Park and Society Hill. This view is taken from the south with the Merchants' Exchange in the foreground.

(*left*) The main entrance from Chestnut Street opens into a three-story rotunda with travertine walls and serpentine columns. Murals are by George Harding.

(*right*) This detail of the rotunda balcony illustrates the refined design of the Art Deco aluminum railings, bronze metalwork, and rich coloring of the ornamental plaster and murals.

Rising seventeen stories above Independence National Historical Park at Chestnut and Second Streets, the United States Custom House and Appraisers' Stores—to use its formal title—is something of an intrusion. It certainly is out of scale with the nearby Merchants' Exchange, First Bank of the United States, Second Bank, and Carpenters' Hall. Nonetheless, this massive limestone and red brick modern office building is an outstanding example of the federal government's architectural pretensions during the Great Depression of the 1930s. It also contains one of the most dramatic Art Deco interiors in Philadelphia.

There has been a customs service for the port of Philadelphia to collect tariffs and duties or to enforce trade regulations since the seventeenth century. After the American Revolution, officials of the newly fledged United States replaced the British collector of customs. Initially, customs officials appointed to Philadelphia operated out of rented space, first at Congress Hall (pages 32–37) and then at Carpenters' Hall (pages 42–47), where they remained until 1819 when the customs collector moved into a purpose-built building on Second Street below Dock Street. By 1844 this space was inadequate and the federal government purchased a larger building erected originally for the Second Bank of the United States on Chestnut Street (pages 80–85), where the collector of customs conducted business for the next century. (For that reason many illustrations of William Strickland's Second Bank are identified as the Custom House.)

In the early decades of the twentieth century—with shipping on the Delaware rapidly expanding—Philadelphia began to agitate for a modern facility to replace the Custom House in Strickland's building and the Appraisers' Stores warehouse on Second Street dating from 1868. Initially two structures were planned, one for offices in the business district and a warehouse for appraisals on the waterfront. The federal government opted for a single structure and acquired a site at Chestnut and Second Streets adjacent to the Victorian-era Appraisers' Stores warehouse. The Hoover administration awarded the contract to the Philadelphia architectural firm of Ritter and Shay in 1931, and construction proceeded as a Works Progress Administration project early in Franklin D. Roosevelt's first term. The building was dedicated on November 10, 1934.

The partnership of Verus T. Ritter (1883–1942) and Howell L. Shay (1884–1975) dates from 1920 and during the following decade they designed several major high-rise buildings that remain Center City landmarks: the Packard Building (1922–1924) at 1428 Chestnut Street with its massive Samuel Yellin iron gates; the Drake Apartment Hotel (1928–1929) at 1512 Spruce Street; and the Market Street National Bank (1929–1930) at 1219 Market Street with its ancient Mexican-inspired Art Deco terra cotta exterior by the O. W. Ketcham Terra Cotta Works.

EXIT

Because of its proposed location, the United States Custom House went through a complex design process. The new building would rise a city block from the intersection of Market and Second Streets, the epicenter of what had been colonial Philadelphia. The Sesquicentennial celebration had recently heightened awareness of the nearby shrines to the American Revolution, and on all sides of the site, low-rise red-brick-and-white-marble-trimmed structures offered silent witness to the historic character of the neighborhood. Some proposals intended to integrate the seventeen-story building are, in retrospect, amazing. Among the many conceptual drawings preserved in the Ritter and Shay Collection at The Athenæum of Philadelphia is one that contemplates the

↑ One of several rejected proposals for the Custom House by Ritter and Shay intended to integrate the new structure with the historic neighborhood near Independence Hall. Athenæum of Philadelphia Collection.

application to the Chestnut Street façade of a Late Georgian pediment supported by Ionic pilasters with an eagle in the tympanum. In the same design, the Custom House tower becomes Independence Hall on steroids, complete with pediment, Palladian window, and urns. Fortunately this silly proposal was rejected, although the urns (and several eagles) made it into the final design. According to the National Register nomination form, the final design for the lantern is based on "the archaeological scheme for the ancient lighthouse at Rhodes" that "symbolized the lighthouse guarding the port of Philadelphia."

The three-story limestone base of the Custom House has identical projecting pavilions on all fronts, and the Chestnut Street entrance consists of arched openings with keystones in the form of eagles. On either side of the entrance are aluminum lanterns. The arches hold pressed-aluminum panels of allegorical figures in the Art Deco mode, a modest hint of what is to come in the lobby, which opens into one of the finest Art Deco spaces in Philadelphia.

Upon entering, the visitor passes into a three-story rotunda ringed with eight fluted serpentine columns supporting a circular balcony reached by dramatically elegant circular stairs. The walls are covered in "book matched" Colorado travertine and the floors are terrazzo with serpentine borders matching the columns. A mural cycle by Brandywine School artist and illustrator George Harding (1882–1959) consists of allegorical images relating to the United States Customs Service such as Coast Guard cutters on ice patrol, lightships; various flag insignia; and navigating instruments.

The Custom House underwent a major upgrade in the 1990s, which included a new lighting scheme that has brought the building new prominence in the Independence National Historical Park neighborhood.

PHILADELPHIA SAVINGS FUND SOCIETY BUILDING

(Now Loews Philadelphia Hotel)
1200 Market Street
Philadelphia, PA 19107

Howe & Lescaze, architects, 1929–1932
National Historic Landmark, 1976

Telephone for visitor information: 215.627.1200
www.loewshotels.com

To understand the impact of the Philadelphia Savings Fund Society Building one need only turn back to its contemporary, the United States Custom House (pages 258–263). The difference could not be more dramatic. PSFS—the first International Style American skyscraper—is a sleek expression of early twentieth-century European modernism, a movement in architecture calling for buildings of simplified functional form, free of extraneous ornament, and erected of gleaming glass, steel, and concrete. By contrast, the massive limestone and brick Custom House, which its architects, Ritter and Shay, doubtless thought of as modern, is just the kind of derivative building encrusted with classical Georgian Revival balustrades, cartouches, eagles, and urns that Howe and Lescaze eschewed as "pseudo-aristocratic decoration." The difference between these buildings is all the more surprising in terms of their clients. No one expects a government agency to be architecturally adventuresome. But neither would it be in character for a venerable financial institution to be caught commissioning a trailblazing building—yet that is exactly what happened.

The Philadelphia Savings Fund Society had been founded in 1816 by reform-minded Quaker businessmen who expressed their desire to provide "mechanics and tradesmen" with a secure repository for their modest savings. Interest payments would be a "reward for saving" and offer "a profitable mode of investment to those workers who had no friends . . . or sufficient resources to assist them in the care and employment of their earnings." As a philanthropic institution, its deposits were invested in home mortgages, concentrated mainly in the working-class neighborhoods in which most of its customers lived. Gradually the bank shed its exclusively philanthropic mission; by 1929 it had become the third largest savings bank in the United States, housed in suitably conservative granite Italianate headquarters designed by Addison Hutton at Seventh and Walnut Streets.

James M. Willcox, president of PSFS from 1924 to 1934, appears to have made most of the important decisions with little contribution from his corporate building committee. Willcox wasn't particularly interested in modern architecture, but he wanted a monumental statement that would also appeal to commercial tenants who would occupy the ground floor and much of the office tower. In short, the building needed to be a sound real estate investment as well as a corporate flagship. At one point Willcox asked George Howe if, as he had been told, this "new style of architecture" would make obsolete all those preceding it. If true, Willcox is reported to have said, "it is highly important that I should know this and become thoroughly convinced of it." Willcox feared his architects might be venturing out to the point where style becomes ego. He trusted Howe, but wanted his word "as a gentleman" that the architects

⇝ The Philadelphia Savings Fund Society Building (Howe and Lescaze, 1929–1932) is widely considered the first "International style" skyscraper in the United States. In 2000 it was sensitively converted to a convention hotel.

were giving him a building that would serve the bank well and appeal to the tenants on whom economic viability depended. Thus reassured, construction proceeded. The building would be marketed—according to one real estate broker's brochure—as "Nothing More Modern."

George Howe (1886–1955) had come late to twentieth-century European modernism. (The term "International style" would not be coined until 1932.) Born in Worcester, Massachusetts, he attended Groton, Harvard, and the École des Beaux-Arts in Paris. After a brief period in the office of Frank Furness, he joined the highly successful firm of country house architects Mellor & Meigs, eventually becoming a partner. While with Walter Mellor (1880–1940) and Arthur I. Meigs (1882–1956), Howe had designed four branch offices for PSFS as well as an early submission for the Market Street site. When he left the firm and formed a partnership with William Lescaze, he took the PSFS account with him. Lescaze (1896–1969) was born in Switzerland and received his education

⇜ Detail of the curved, asymmetrical base of the PSFS Building at Twelfth and Market Streets with shop windows at the ground level, high banking room with its broad sweep of glass set in granite, and three floors of offices providing a transition to the tower with its cantilevers above.

in architecture at the École Polytechnique Fédérale in Zurich, graduating in 1919 and migrating to Cleveland, Ohio, where he worked for several years. He next moved to New York City, where he designed the Paris Modern interiors for the Macy's International Exposition of Art and Industry in 1928. While Howe was the lead partner, Lescaze—who was generally in charge of the drafting room—brought to the PSFS project greater familiarity with European forms and was responsible for the distinctive curving base and the cantilevers of the Market Street face of the tower.

The finished building rises thirty-six stories and, at 491 feet, was for many years the tallest office building in Philadelphia. The ground floor with its continuous band of show windows on both Market and Twelfth Streets was designed for retail tenants, while the tall clear-span banking room was located on the second floor; it was served by stairs and escalators accessed from an entrance asymmetrically placed at the western corner of the Market Street front. A tower of twenty-seven floors designed to provide the maximum uninterrupted rentable floor space is set back on three sides to provide natural light at all levels from the floor to ceiling windows. The exterior is finished in dark gray granite, sand-colored limestone, and gray and black brick; window frames and sash are aluminum, an early large-scale use of that material. The interior finishes are of the highest quality of marble, stainless steel, bronze and rare woods assembled with remarkable craftsmanship and attention to detail.

During construction it was determined that the building would be fully air conditioned—a major attraction to prospective tenants—and to obscure the cooling tower a large billboard with the legend "PSFS" in twenty-seven foot tall letters, illuminated by red neon at night, was installed on the roof. It could be seen for twenty miles.

In defending the design of the new building, George Howe wrote,

> the architects state it as their conviction that economic pressure will make the development of buildings of similar design inevitable in the immediate future . . . , all buildings not so designed will be obsolete before long. . . . Marble halls and fantastic domes have been overdone and no longer excite the public's interest. They have had their day. An era of sound and handsome but 100% practical building is at hand.

Of course not everyone agreed. Conservative ecclesiologist Elbert M. Conover (1885–1952) grumbled, "The day will come when even in America, we will become skillful enough to meet economic pressure without forcing upon the community such ugliness and such illogical designing." Howe coolly responded, "the buildings we erect will speak for themselves. Let the future be the judge of their merits." Hailed by the American Institute of Architects (Philadelphia Chapter) as the "Building of the Century," the PSFS building appears in every architectural textbook as an icon of early twentieth-century modernism.

Unfortunately the Philadelphia Savings Fund Society itself has not fared as well. Following the savings-and-loan crisis of the 1980s, the Meritor Savings Bank (the parent corporation of PSFS) was seized under controversial circumstances by the Federal Deposit Insurance Corporation in 1992 and its assets liquidated. The Loews Corporation purchased the building in 1997 and reopened it in 2000 as Loews Philadelphia Hotel. The iconic PSFS sign, however, as part of the original design, continues to shine.

BENJAMIN FRANKLIN PARKWAY

They called it the City Beautiful, an American vision of idealized classical architecture and city planning planted in the popular mind by the World's Columbian Exposition of 1893 in Chicago. Organized to celebrate the 400th anniversary of the discovery of the New World by Christopher Columbus, and designed largely by an architectural team headed by Daniel H. Burnham (pages 232–237), the fair covered 600 acres and attracted 27,000,000 visitors. Its centerpiece was the Court of Honor, a complex of white stucco classical buildings designed by a clutch of America's leading architects trained in the Beaux-Arts tradition, including Richard Morris Hunt, Charles McKim, and George Post. Fiske Kimball (1888–1955), first director of the new Philadelphia Museum of Art on the parkway, reflected on the impact of the Columbian Exposition in 1927.

> The cumulative impression of the classic phantasm was overwhelming. The throng of visitors, many of whom were seeing large buildings for the first time, was deeply stirred by the ordered magnificence and harmony of the Court of Honor. The example of unified effort and effect, associated with the classic forms in which it had been achieved, was stamped on the memory of the whole nation.

In Philadelphia this vision of "ordered magnificence and harmony" coalesced with a long-held desire to link Fairmount Park with Center City. A proposal dating from 1871 argued that if the park was truly to benefit the people of Philadelphia, "it must be brought within reach of all. It must be connected with Broad Street and with the centre of the city by as short a route as possible; and the avenues which lead to it must be made elegant and attractive." In 1884, Charles K. Landis (1835–1900), founder of Vineland, New Jersey, proposed a 130-foot-wide "grand avenue" beginning at the new City Hall on Penn Square and terminating at Fairmount Park. Shortly thereafter, proponents of such a boulevard succeeded temporarily in gaining political support for an 1892 refinement of the Landis scheme created by James H. Windrim, the City director of public works, whom we've already met as the youthful architect of the Masonic Temple (pages 172–179). Windrim's plan called for a 160-foot-wide boulevard boldly sundering the rigid grid of Philadelphia streets from City Hall, across Logan Square, and on to Fairmount Park. Then the scheme fell afoul of Philadelphia's notorious Republican political machine, which muckraking journalist Lincoln Steffens famously characterized as "corrupt and contented." The parkway project remained stalled for the next five years.

In 1900 Philadelphia architect Albert Kelsey (1870–1950) reenergized the parkway scheme by injecting visions of the "City Beautiful" into a speech at

← The Benjamin Franklin Parkway from Logan Circle looking northwest toward the Philadelphia Museum of Art.

the Drexel Institute entitled "A Rational Beauty for American Cities." A few days later he participated in the formation of the Art Federation of Philadelphia, composed of persons interested in urban reform. The Federation in turn appointed a boulevard committee, which eventually resulted in the founding of the Parkway Association of leading citizens who published a new plan for the parkway in 1902. Also lobbying for the parkway were the Fairmount Park Art Association (founded in 1871 to beautify the park) and the City Parks Association (founded in 1888 to create additional parks). In the face of such powerful forces, the City of Philadelphia finally approved the acquisition of the properties between City Hall and Fairmount. Demolition began in early 1907; ultimately 1,300 properties would be razed.

In the meantime, the Fairmount Park Art Association assembled a team of architects to oversee the parkway plan and its buildings. Included in this group

The Benjamin Franklin Parkway from the steps of the Philadelphia Museum of Art looking southeast toward City Hall.

The 1893 World's Columbian Exposition in Chicago introduced many Americans to the idealized vision of modern classical architecture and city planning and would profoundly influence Philadelphia in the first decades of the twentieth century. Athenæum of Philadelphia Collection.

were several men whose names will be encountered in the following pages: Paul Philippe Cret (1876–1945), Clarence C. Zantzinger (1872–1954), Charles L. Borie, Jr. (1870–1943), Milton B. Medary, Jr. (1874–1929), Horace Trumbauer (1868–1938), and Jacques Gréber (1882–1962). All were young, and several had European training. Cret, born in Lyon, France, had studied at the École des Beaux-Arts there and the École in Paris. In 1903 he was invited to Philadelphia to teach at the University of Pennsylvania and had been in the city less than four years when appointed to the committee. Like Cret, Clarence Zantzinger had studied at the École des Beaux-Arts in Paris. A native Philadelphian, he returned to the city after studies at Yale and the University of Pennsylvania and formed a partnership with Charles Borie, also a native Philadelphian who had studied civil engineering at the University of Pennsylvania. The firm of Zantzinger & Borie flourished from c. 1905; in 1910 Milton Medary became a partner and the firm name was changed to Zantzinger, Borie, and Medary. Medary was also a native Philadelphian who had studied at the University of Pennsylvania, although he did not graduate. (Penn later made up for this deficit by awarding him an honorary doctorate of fine arts.) The oldest of the group (by only a few years) was Philadelphian Horace Trumbauer, whom we've already met at the Union League and the Racquet Club (pages 169, 244). Trumbauer never attended university; rather he became an apprentice in the offices of G. W. and W. D. Hewitt before going out on his own. The youngest of this group of parkway contributors was Jacques Gréber, the son of the French sculptor Henri Gréber. He graduated from the École des Beaux-Arts in 1908 and first came to Philadelphia in

The future parkway route photographed from the tower of City Hall (1909) looking northwest toward Fairmount. Notice the tower of Broad Street Station in the center foreground and the dome of the Cathedral of Saints Peter and Paul at the top right. The parkway would sunder this grid of the nineteenth-century city by demolishing virtually everything in this view. City Archives of Philadelphia.

1913 to design the garden for the Wideners' Lynnewood Hall; he would later work with Trumbauer on several properties, designing French classical gardens, most notably for Edward T. Stotesbury's Whitemarsh Hall. During his long post-Philadelphia career, Gréber would design several urban plans around boulevards inspired by Georges Eugène Haussmann's transformation of Paris in the mid-nineteenth century.

A revised plan of the parkway was prepared for the Fairmount Park Art Association by Cret, Trumbauer, and Zantzinger in July 1907. In presenting the plan, Zantzinger remarked, "it is not an extension of Fairmount Park which is being created. It is an avenue in the city giving access to Fairmount Park." Zantzinger credited to his partner Charles Borie the vision of the parkway as the future location of educational and arts organizations clustered at the foot of Fairmount with a new museum for the city elevated on its acropolis as both terminus and focal point of the parkway.

While the politicians maneuvered, fund-raising and demolition continued in fits and starts over the next several years. In 1915 the Commonwealth of Pennsylvania granted cities the power to regulate construction within two hundred feet of publicly owned park land. In Philadelphia the Common and Select Councils promptly annexed the parkway to Fairmount Park, thus giving the semi-autonomous Fairmount Park Commission authority over the development of the parkway. The following year zoning guidelines were adopted and newly elected mayor Thomas B. Smith secured funding to complete the demolition and begin paving the new roadbed, a process that continued throughout the war

The Academy of Natural Sciences has been located on Logan Square since 1868. It was founded in 1812 "for the encouragement and cultivation of the sciences, and the advancement of useful learning." It renovated its building in anticipation of the Parkway construction. The additions were designed by James H. Windrim & Sons (1890–1892) and executed by Wilson Brothers & Company. The 1907–1909 modifications were by Wilson, Harris & Richards, successors of Wilson Brothers & Company.

years. At this point the Fairmount Park Commission engaged Jacques Gréber to reexamine the 1907 Cret-Zantzinger-Trumbauer plan. (Thirty-four-year-old Gréber was then designing the garden of Edward T. Stotesbury's Whitemarsh Hall. That Stotesbury was president of the Commission may have influenced the appointment.)

Over the next three years Gréber would prepare scores of drawings for the parkway landscape. According to David B. Brownlee, whose *Building the City Beautiful*—written to accompany an exhibition at the Philadelphia Museum of Art—is the most thorough account of the parkway, Gréber's greatest contribution was "converting the parkway from an urban boulevard into a green wedge of park, reaching inward toward the congested center of the city." Instead of a Haussmann-style Parisian boulevard lined with storied ranks of buildings, the architecture is "scattered through the landscape." Where Logan Square had been retained in the 1907 plan, it now became Logan Circle essentially as we know it today, with a pair of civic buildings inspired by the Place de la Concorde in Paris: the Free Library (pages 288–291) and the Municipal Court (now Family Court) building.

The Franklin Institute building at Twentieth Street and the Parkway was designed by John Torrey Windrim (1932–1934).

The completed parkway is itself a landmark of both national and international significance. Its campus penetrates the heart of the city and embraces a distinguished group of institutions housed in landmark-class buildings designed by Philadelphia's foremost early twentieth-century architects. Nonetheless, it falls short of the more expansive dreams of some supporters who envisioned a gathering of academic and medical institutions along with cultural societies, including Temple University, University of Pennsylvania School of Architecture, Medico-Chirurgical Hospital, and Philadelphia College of Pharmacy as candidates.

The monumental marble statue of Benjamin Franklin at the Franklin Institute by James Earl Fraser (1876–1953) was dedicated in 1938. Fraser had attended the École des Beaux-Arts and worked in the studio of Augustus Saint-Gaudens.

(Moore College of Art did make it to the parkway, see pages 144–147.) Proposed new buildings on the parkway for the Pennsylvania Academy of the Fine Arts (pages 186–191), the American Philosophical Society (pages 48–53), and a concert hall to replace the Academy of Music (pages 154–159) all failed to secure funding, in large part due to the Great Depression following the stock market collapse in 1929. Gréber's Episcopal Cathedral seems more a delineator's fantasy than a serious proposal.

The most important and successful building on the parkway was the Philadelphia Museum of Art (pages 278–283), but implicit in the thinking of parkway boosters was the assumption that Logan Circle would become an epicenter of Philadelphia arts and culture, drawing into its vortex diverse institutions previously scattered elsewhere in the city. The Roman Catholic Cathedral of Saints Peter and Paul (Napoleon Le Brun and John Notman, 1846–1864, see *Historic Sacred Places*, pages 152–57) and the Academy of Natural Sciences were already there. The Academy had outgrown its Broad and Sansom Streets home (John Notman, 1839–1840) and moved to a fashionable Gothic Revival building designed for it by James H. Windrim (1868) at Nineteenth and Race Streets, which in anticipation of the parkway was substantially rebuilt and expanded in the restrained Georgian Revival mode that Addison Hutton used at the Historical

↑ The Philadelphia Council, Boy Scouts of America building was designed by Charles Z. Klauder, 1929–1930. *The Ideal Scout* by the Philadelphia sculptor R. Tait McKenzie (1867–1938) stands in the diminutive courtyard. Originally executed in 1914, the sculpture appears in dozens of Boy Scout offices throughout the United States.

Society (pages 238–243). The Franklin Institute, founded in 1824 "for the promotion of the mechanical arts," had also outgrown its John Haviland building on South Seventh Street (pages 116–119) and was anxious to relocate. After several false starts, the Institute erected an imposing Indiana limestone Classical Revival building with a three-story pedimented Corinthian portico at Twentieth Street and the parkway designed by John Torrey Windrim (1866–1934). Behind the portico is Franklin Hall, based on the Pantheon in Rome, which contains James Earle Fraser's gigantic marble statue of a seated Benjamin Franklin.

Although the effort to relocate the Pennsylvania Academy of the Fine Arts on the parkway failed, the synergy of art museums clustered near the Philadelphia Museum of Art was, and remains, a compelling concept. Other early candidates for parkway sites were two small single-collector museums, one to house Jules Mastbaum's Rodin bronzes (pages 292–295) and the other, designed by Horace Trumbauer (1919) but never built, to house the art collection of John G. Johnson.

One of the largest civic structures erected on the parkway, certainly one of the tallest, was created for the administration offices of the sprawling Philadelphia public school system (pages 296–301). In contrast, the Philadelphia Council of the Boy Scouts of America commissioned a headquarters from Charles Z. Klauder (1872–1938) to be erected on the south side of the Parkway, next to the Board of Education Building and directly opposite the Rodin Museum (1929–1930). The resulting building in the Renaissance Revival mode is one of the most compelling Parkway structures and one that is too little known or appreciated by the general public. Two notable commercial buildings were also erected: the Insurance Company of North America building (Stewardson and Page, 1922–1925; pages 284–287) and the Fidelity Mutual Life Insurance Company building (Zantzinger, Borie, and Medary, 1925–1927; pages 301–305).

In 1937 the Philadelphia City Council officially named the parkway for Benjamin Franklin, and to many observers the great project that had consumed so much effort and treasure over the span of half a century seemed complete. In the years following World War II, however, the process of reshaping Philadelphia continued, and not all the changes were sympathetic to the original parkway plan. Some of the redevelopment at the City Hall terminus of the parkway was unfortunate. Other highly desirable civic improvements, such as linking the Schuylkill Expressway and Interstate 95 via the Vine Street Expressway, were probably unavoidable alterations to the parkway landscape. Architectural intrusions—the Youth Study Center (Carroll, Grisdale, and Van Alen, 1949–1950) for example—remain (at least temporarily) to remind Philadelphians of the dynamic forces for good and ill that continue to reshape their city.

PHILADELPHIA MUSEUM OF ART

Twenty-Sixth Street and Benjamin Franklin Parkway Philadelphia, PA 19130

Horace Trumbauer with Julian F. Abele, Zantzinger, Borie & Medary, architects, 1919–1928 National Register of Historic Places, 1971

Telephone for visitor information: 215.763.8100 www.philamuseum.org

It is difficult for most Philadelphians to imagine a time when their city did not have a handsomely housed, world class art museum dramatically positioned on the heights of Fairmount at the terminus of a grand boulevard linking the economic and political heart of their city to the largest urban park in the nation. As we have already seen, the Parkway did not come easily; neither did its art museum.

The origins of the institution that would become the Philadelphia Museum of Art can be traced to the Centennial Exhibition of 1876 and its grandest building, Memorial Hall, which served as the art gallery for that glorious enterprise (pages 200–205). With London's South Kensington Museum (now the Victoria

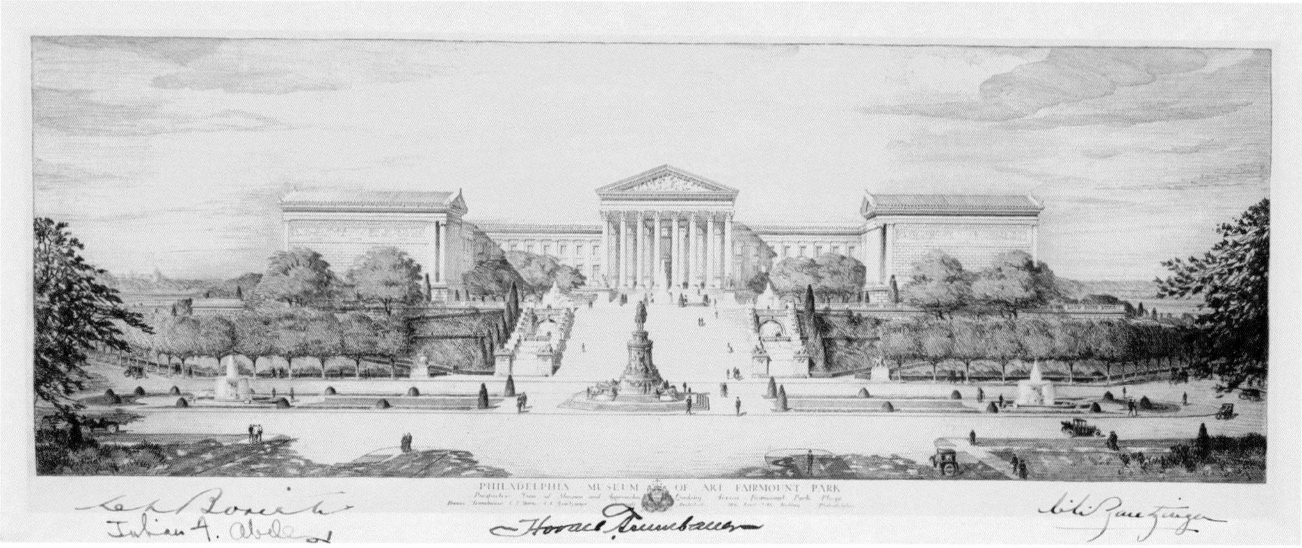

and Albert Museum) as a prototype, Memorial Hall would survive the Centennial as a museum of both art and industry, "for the improvement and enjoyment of the people of the Commonwealth." Chartered as the Pennsylvania Museum and School of Industrial Art, it was to provide "a Museum of Art, in all its branches and technical application, and with a special view to the development of the art and textile industries of the state." This bifurcated responsibility—art museum and school—ultimately led to the latter responsibilities being spun off as independent institutions (see University of the Arts, pages 92–95).

Memorial Hall quickly proved inadequate as an art museum, especially after the W. P. Wilstach collection together with a half-million-dollar endowment for additional acquisitions—a prodigious sum at the time—was received by the Fairmount Park Commission in 1893. Two of the commissioners, John G. Johnson and Peter A. B. Widener, both major collectors of art, served as advisors for the Wilstach Collection and began lobbying for a better building which might, they hinted, receive their collections in the future. Johnson, whose collection by a circuitous route ultimately made it to Fairmount, was quoted in the *Evening Bulletin* as remarking that Memorial Hall "is an architectural botch as a repository for good pictures."

By 1895, P. A. B. Widener was lobbying for a new museum building to be erected on the site of Lemon Hill, Henry Platt's Federal villa overlooking the Schuylkill (see *Historic Houses*, pages 90–93). The Fairmount Park Commission even conducted an architectural competition for the building, and a design by New York architect Henry Bacon (1866–1924) was selected by a distinguished panel of judges that included Daniel Burnham and Stanford White. But with plans for the parkway languishing, no action was taken on Bacon's design. Seven

Julian Abele's perspective of the proposed Philadelphia Museum of Art (c. 1917). Abele (1881–1950), the first African American to graduate from the University of Pennsylvania architecture program, was the chief designer for the firm of Horace Trumbauer & Associates. Fiske Kimball, first director of the new museum, called Abele "one of the most sensitive designers anywhere in America." Athenæum of Philadelphia Collection.

East front of the Philadelphia Museum of Art. In the foreground is the Washington Monument (1897) by sculptor Rudolf Siemering (1835–1905), which was moved to this location in 1928.

years later, however, conditions had changed; the parkway project was back on track. The city had also announced the closing of the Fairmount Water Works (pages 74–79), which meant that the abandoned reservoirs cut into the top of Fairmount would potentially be available as the site of a new museum. Widener promptly became an advocate for the Fairmount site. In 1907 he offered to pay for the new museum and give the city his collection on two conditions: the parkway would be aligned to the foot of Fairmount and the heights would be provided by the city as a building site. He also had a favorite architect, Horace Trumbauer, who had designed Lynnewood Hall for him in Elkins Park (pages 169, 244). At this point the Fairmount Park Art Association appointed the architectural team already discussed (pages 270–271) to develop a comprehensive plan for the parkway.

Matters continued to move at a glacial pace. Only in 1911 was a smaller team of architects (Zantzinger, Borie, and Trumbauer, soon to be joined by Medary) asked to prepare "a preliminary sketch for the art museum." At this point, a substantially completed building remained seventeen years in the future, a delay only partly attributable to wartime restrictions on building materials. For years the architectural team (the Trumbauer office versus Zantzinger, Borie and Medary) wrangled over the design and the Mayor and the City Councils over funding. By 1915 the frustrated Fairmount Park Commission issued an ultimatum: resolve the design conflict or the project would be turned over to others.

For what happened next we fortunately have the recollections of Howell Lewis Shay (pages 258–259), who was then working in the Trumbauer office. "I knew why [the two offices] hadn't been able to agree on a final design," he later wrote. "Mr. Trumbauer wanted one monumental building to be at the end of the Parkway. . . . . But Mr. Zantzinger and Mr. Borie wanted the Fairmount 'Acropolis' to be more like the Acropolis at Athens, with several 'temples' [positioned] around at random." Shay resolved the gridlock by proposing three Greek temple façades in the shape of an enormous letter E and connected by a series of galleries around a grand central courtyard. This basic concept, much refined, was approved by the Art Jury and accepted by the Fairmount Park Commission in 1917. At this point Julian Abele, chief designer in the Trumbauer office, prepared the often reproduced presentation drawings of the final design. Then the United States entered World War I, which further delayed the project.

Construction for the museum foundations finally began in 1919 but the progress was painfully slow and expensive; P. A. B. Widener had died in 1915 and with him the promise to pay for the museum. So straitened were the Fairmount Park Commission's finances that the commissioners risked the dangerous path of erecting the two end pavilions with the funds at hand, thereby hoping

At the top of the great stair in the east hall is the gilded copper version of Augustus Saint-Gaudens's idealized female nude from Stanford White's Madison Square Garden in New York (1893).

to embarrass the city to provide funds to finish the building and fill the gap. The strategy worked. The new museum was formally dedicated in 1928 with most of the interior still unfinished and only ten galleries and ten period rooms installed.

While references to the Greek Revival museum on its Acropolis are inescapable, the mammoth building differs in more than scale from anything ever erected in Periclean Greece or, for that matter, by eighteenth- and nineteenth-century neoclassical Anglo-American architects who thought they understood the ancient originals. Most obviously, the museum building is not white marble as might be expected; rather, it is five natural shades of golden buff dolomite limestone found only in southern Minnesota between the towns of Mankato and

The rear façade looms over the Fairmount Water Works complex. The museum occupies the former site of the original reservoirs, which held the river water before it was released into the mains under the city's streets.

Kasota. Even more surprising—although based on archaeological evidence first published by Leon V. Solon in 1918—is the lavish splash of primary polychromy that sets the museum apart from any major building erected in America before that time, while restoring to the ancient Greeks the architectural color that millennia of sun and rain have bleached from their buildings. Further inspiration from ancient Greek architecture resulted in the vibrantly colorful terra cotta detail in the capitals of the columns, entablature moldings, and antefixes on the eves. Here too were bronze acroteria on the pediments in the form of mythological beasts, one of which, the griffin—with the body of a lion and the head and wings of an eagle—was believed by the ancient Greeks to be the guardian of treasure. Appropriately the museum has adopted the griffin as its logo.

INSURANCE COMPANY OF NORTH AMERICA BUILDING

(Phoenix Condominium)
1600 Arch Street
Philadelphia, PA, 19103

Stewardson & Page, architects, 1922–1925
National Historic Landmark, 1978

Telephone for information:
215.854.1770
www.phillyphoenix.com

The only building associated with the Benjamin Franklin Parkway development that has been individually designated a National Historic Landmark is the Insurance Company of North America (INA) Building erected at the intersection of Sixteenth and Arch Streets.

Founded in 1792 to write marine insurance, INA was the oldest capital stock insurance company in the United States. It expanded into insuring buildings and their contents (a first among American fire insurance companies) in 1794 and is also credited with inventing the agency system of marketing insurance. It was the first company to issue policies nationwide. The company philosophy, according to, William Carr, author of the company history, was that "any risk can be underwritten for a price," earning INA the reputation as "the American Lloyd's of London."

Intending their INA Building to be the "Gateway to the Parkway," the architects created a frontispiece modeled on the ancient Roman triumphal Arch of Constantine.

The Insurance Company of North America building by Stewardson and Page (1922–1925) has been converted into a condominium called The Phoenix.

At the time the new building was commissioned as the INA home office, the company occupied a brownstone Victorian-era building at 232 Walnut Street (Cabot & Chandler, architects, 1880). Benjamin Rush, INA president from 1916 to 1939, had initiated a rapid expansion of his venerable company into all forms of insurance (except life); as part of the corporate image he wished to project, Rush envisioned a new building in the up and coming commercial heart of the city west of City Hall. He wrote,

The ground floor lobby was often used to display the extensive corporate collection of early fire equipment.

> While the building should be thoroughly modern, and up-to-date, the architect should be advised to try and preserve a colonial atmosphere, so as to take advantage of the past history of the Company, which [we] have found to be of considerable value in securing of business.

In the summer of 1922, the commission was awarded to the partnership of Emlyn L. Stewardson (1863–1936) and George B. Page (1870–1948), who would ultimately receive a gold metal for their INA building from the Philadelphia Chapter of the American Institute of Architects.

As instructed, the architects "preserved a colonial atmosphere" by adopting the vocabulary of Georgian architecture. But since no eighteenth-century Anglo-American architect or builder had ever designed a sixteen-story, steel-frame, brick and stone building, they admitted they were forced "to design the Building as it might have been designed in those days, had the opportunity been presented." Consequently Stewardson & Page settled for details drawn from "the Georgian period and particularly that phase of it as practiced by the Adam Brothers." The effect they sought was

> Gracefulness of proportion without over elaboration, in harmony with the purpose and dignity of [the] Company, and at the same time, with enough elaboration to justify its prominent position as the "Gateway to the Parkway" has been the thought that has suggested the design herewith presented.

The imagery of "Gateway to the Parkway" probably suggested the most distinctive feature of the INA building, its dramatic east façade frontispiece. Based on the Roman triumphal Arch of Constantine (315 C.E.), probably by way of Robert Adam's adaptation of the same feature for the south front of Kedleston Hall (Derbyshire, 1759–1765), the frontispiece projects on four Corinthian columns surmounted by nine-foot granite eagles perched on spheres—a company motif used throughout the building. The three openings between the columns are arched. The main entrance with cast bronze doors occupies the middle arch and above windows in the flanking arches are medallions (again echoing the ancient Roman prototype). From ground level a two-story pink Maine granite base supports a multistory brick shaft laid in Flemish bond topped by a four-story crown of white Indiana limestone. At the thirteenth- and fourteenth-floor levels a large cornice is supported by two pairs of Corinthian columns and flanking pilasters to create a three-bay loggia.

The original INA building interior is richly appointed with Kasota limestone walls, marble floors, Doric alcoves, and coffered ceilings. When the company occupied the building, the entrance lobby was often used to display an extensive corporate collection of early firefighting equipment, as can be seen in the accompanying photograph. Originally offices were in the main building shaft with the executive suite on the twelfth floor and above. The fifteenth floor contained employee and executive dining rooms and there was a large auditorium on the sixteenth floor.

In 1982 the Insurance Company of North America merged with Connecticut General Life Insurance Company to form CIGNA, a name based on the initials of the ancestral companies. In the late 1990s CIGNA began to narrow its focus and sold its property and casualty business. The corporate headquarters were moved to Two Liberty Place and the INA building was sold. After a $73-million renovation the building is now a luxury condominium called The Phoenix.

FREE LIBRARY OF PHILADELPHIA

1901 Vine Street
Philadelphia, PA 19103

Horace Trumbauer with Julian F. Abele, architects, 1923–1927
Philadelphia Register of Historic Places, 1971

Telephone for visitor information: 215.686.5322
www.library.phila.gov

Before the age of modern public libraries, open to all and supported by taxes, libraries were private affairs organized either as stock companies—in which the purchase of a share made one an owner—or as associations of dues-paying subscribers. The earliest such "subscription library" in Philadelphia was the Library Company founded by Benjamin Franklin and his friends in 1731 (pages 192–195) followed by the Union Library Company (1759), the Athenæum in 1814 (pages 132–137), the Apprentices' Library Company (1820), and the Mercantile Library (1821), to name only a few of the dozens that once flourished in the region. Most Philadelphia membership libraries either disappeared or were absorbed into the Free Library of Philadelphia after its founding in the late nineteenth century.

The Free Library of Philadelphia is today one of the largest and most highly regarded public libraries in the United States. It traces its history to the efforts of Dr. William Pepper (1843–1898), whom we have already encountered in his role as provost of the University of Pennsylvania (pages 214–217). In 1889 he convinced his uncle, George S. Pepper, to bequeath nearly a quarter million dollars to launch a free library for Philadelphia, which opened its first central branch at City Hall in 1894 under the motto Liber Libere Omnibus—Free Books for All. Within a decade the Free Library had expanded to fourteen branches. (Today the Free Library system includes fifty-four branches in all parts of the city.)

The space in City Hall quickly proved inadequate, as did the central library's second location at 1217 Chestnut Street, prompting a move in 1910 to the College of Physicians building at Thirteenth and Locust Streets. By that time planning for the parkway was underway, and Free Library officials requested that a new purpose-built central library building be situated there. On the Parkway Comprehensive Plan of 1911 the Free Library appears as one of a pair of monumental buildings on the north side of Logan Square; Free Library trustee

⚘ The Free Library of Philadelphia (left) by Horace Trumbauer with Julian F. Abele (1923–1927), and its companion, the Municipal Court (now Family Court) by John T. Windrim and W. R. Morton Keast (1938–1941), are based on twin *hôtels particuliers* on the Place de la Concorde, Paris, by architect Ange-Jacques Gabriel (1698–1782).

On the grand stair leading to the *piano nobile* reading rooms there is a bronze statue of a seated Dr. William Pepper by the Austrian-born sculptor Karl Bitter (1867–1915). The bust of John Milton is one of many portraits of literary figures that are scattered throughout the public spaces of the library.

P. A. B. Widener recommended that his favorite architect, Horace Trumbauer, be invited to design the new building.

Between the appointment of Trumbauer in 1911 and the actual excavation for the foundations in 1921, the Free Library project was bedeviled by site changes, funding delays, and several lawsuits that must have brought library officials to the brink of despair. Neither was the commission easy for its architects. The first design from the Trumbauer office for the Logan Square site alluded to Ange-Jacques Gabriel's mid-eighteenth-century twin *hôtels particuliers* from the Place de la Concorde, Paris (the Ministère de la Marine and Hôtel de Crillon), but without the prototype's ground level arcade and *piano nobile* open colonnade. This design was approved by the Art Jury. During the first long delay for lawsuits and funding, the site was altered as a consequence of Jacques Gréber's transformation of Logan Square into Logan Circle, requiring another Art Jury presentation in 1916. For this design, the chief designer in the Trumbauer office, Julian Abele, opened the *piano nobile* Corinthian colonnade, thereby heightening the similarity to Gabriel's Paris design. Then another round of lawsuits—none of which involved the design—delayed construction. Finally, in 1921, Trumbauer's

Call Desk

office submitted what would prove to be the final set of drawings for review by the Art Jury; these reflect even more similarities to the Paris original. This design was also approved, but with Paul Cret's grudging comment:

> The Place de la Concorde buildings being a master work, there is no doubt that the Philadelphia Library will be successful on the whole, as far as general proportions and detail are concerned. However, it will be a matter of regret to some that such an important building built by the city will not deserve more than the doubtful praise of being a copy of a good example.

At last work could proceed in earnest. The cornerstone was laid in 1923 and the library occupied its new building in 1927. Its companion on Logan Circle, the Municipal Court (now Family Court) Building, was designed by John T. Windrim and W. R. Morton Keast and finally erected in 1938–1941.

Julian F. Abele (1881–1950), the individual in the Trumbauer office believed to be most responsible for the Free Library design, was the first African American student to graduate from the Department of Architecture at the University of Pennsylvania. A native Philadelphian, he entered the Pennsylvania Museum and School of Industrial Art, where he earned a Certificate in Architectural Drawing in 1898. From the first, Abele was recognized as a gifted designer and renderer; he won several prizes and had designs exhibited at the Architectural League in New York, the Toronto Architectural Club, the Pittsburgh Architectural Club, and the T-Square Club in the pre-World War I period. He also traveled extensively in Europe, although there is no record that he attended the École des Beaux-Arts, as has occasionally been suggested. Returning to Philadelphia, Abele worked as an assistant to Trumbauer's chief designer, becoming chief designer in 1909, and retaining that position until Trumbauer's death in 1938. Well respected in the architectural community, Abele's work remained largely anonymous because of his race until late twentieth-century scholars began combing Trumbauer office records for traces of his work.

The Free Library design has several similarities with the New York Public Library (Carrère & Hastings, architects, 1897–1911), including a grand entrance hall and stairway leading to impressive reading rooms on the *piano nobile*. When the Philadelphia building opened, it was one of the largest and most technically advanced libraries in the world. But the subsequent three quarters of a century has taken its toll. The library announced in 2003 its plan to renovate and expand the central library, a responsibility entrusted to architects Moshe Safdie and Associates, who previously designed the Salt Lake City Public Library and the Vancouver Public Library.

The Main Reading Room remains essentially as it looked in 1927. Originally general illumination was provided by three-tier chandeliers and task lighting by table-top lamps.

RODIN MUSEUM

2201–2299 Benjamin Franklin Parkway
Philadelphia, PA 19101-7646

Paul Philippe Cret, architect, 1926–1929
Philadelphia Register of Historic Places, 1971

Telephone for visitor information: 215.763.8100
www.rodinmuseum.org

Philadelphia-born motion picture theater mogul Jules F. Mastbaum (1872–1926) was an obsessive collector of works by Auguste Rodin (1840–1917), the preeminent French sculptor of the late nineteenth century. Unfortunately for the collector, he didn't discover Rodin until the artist had died, leaving his estate to the French government, which established the Musée Rodin (1919) in the Hôtel Biron, which had been his Paris residence. Fortunately the museum was willing to sell bronze casts of works from the Rodin bequest; in this way Mastbaum secured such famous sculptures as *The Thinker*, *The Kiss*, and the incomparable *Burghers of Calais*. Mastbaum also agreed to underwrite the first

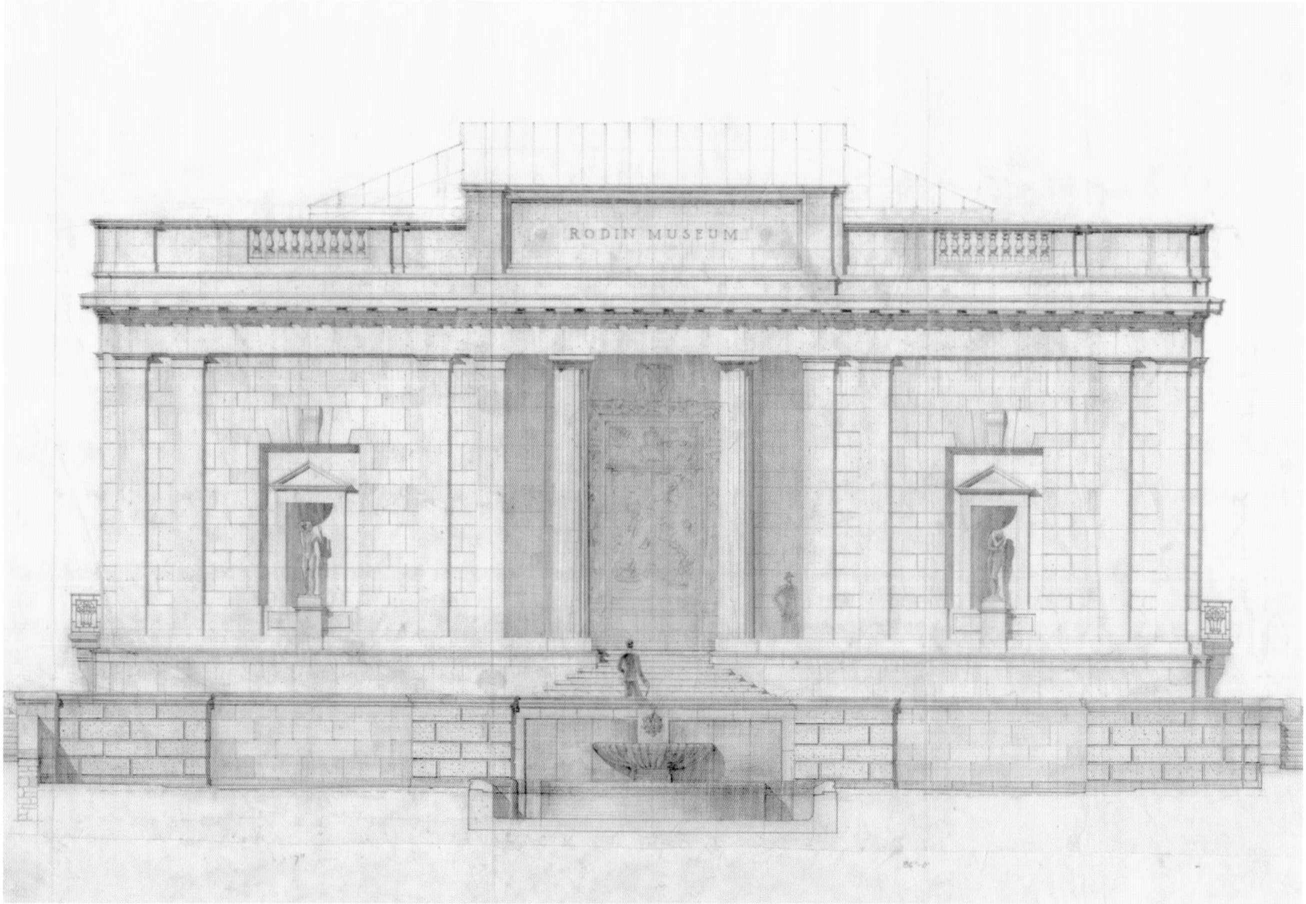

casting of the artist's masterpiece *The Gates of Hell*, which remained in plaster when the artist died.

With so many crates of art being dispatched to Philadelphia, Mastbaum determined to create a museum on the parkway to house the collection. He approached the Fairmount Park Commission with the idea and received preliminary approval. To design the gallery and its garden, he approached Jacques Gréber, who in turn invited Paul P. Cret—who had just completed the Barnes Foundation Gallery for Dr. Albert C. Barnes in Montgomery County (1922–1923)—to collaborate. The relationship between Gréber and Cret had not always been cordial, but now they happily pulled together. David B. Brownlee quotes a letter from Gréber to Cret written after a joint session on the Rodin design. "Let me tell you again," Gréber wrote, "that I am taking away from these several days passed in work at your side one of the most pleasant memories of my career. To see you study and direct the fine tuning of your projects is a real education that I hope not to lose."

Even when later reduced in scale by economic constraints, the resulting gallery is one of the most appealing parkway structures, distilling both antiquarian

Paul P. Cret and Jacques Gréber, Southwest Elevation of the Rodin Museum, July 22, 1927. Athenæum of Philadelphia, Cret Archives.

The forecourt gateway of the Rodin Museum on the Benjamin Franklin Parkway is a reproduction of a fragment of the Château d'Issy that Rodin had erected near his studio.

and classical elements that recognize the donor's desire for a traditional building yet executed in an unmistakably modern way. The entrance gateway, as Mastbaum requested, is a reproduction of fragments from the façade of the Château d'Issy that Rodin had salvaged and re-erected near his studio at Meudon. Through this screen, the visitor enters the garden with its reflecting pool, passes through the Doric columns of the recessed loggia, and steps directly into the main gallery. There are two smaller galleries for sculpture and a library intended to house Mastbaum's extensive collection of drawings, prints, and books related to Rodin's work. The entire impression—as at the Barnes Foundation Gallery—is one of residential rather than institutional scale. In the October 1931 issue of *Architecture*, John Junius summarized his reaction to the work. "The architecture

This view of the main gallery shows how smaller sculptures are arranged for display on marble shelves. Rodin's *The Burghers of Calais* (1889) occupies the central position.

of this museum is a fresh interpretation of the classic, with the careful attention to detail, and trained sense of proportion that distinguish the work of its designers."

Before the gallery could be constructed, however, Jules E. Mastbaum unexpectedly died at the age of fifty-four, leaving as executors his wife and attorney. Work was stopped and the promised operating endowment was withdrawn. Eventually the executors agreed to transfer the collection and complete the gallery at a reduced scale if the city agreed to be responsible for ongoing maintenance. Work recommenced in 1928 and was completed the following year.

BOARD OF EDUCATION ADMINISTRATION BUILDING

FIDELITY MUTUAL LIFE INSURANCE COMPANY BUILDING

Benjamin Franklin Parkway at North Twenty-First Street Philadelphia, PA 19130

Irwin Thornton Catharine, architect, 1929–1931 National Register of Historic Places, 1983 Converted to condominiums

(Reliance Standard Life Insurance Company; Ruth and Raymond G. Perelman Building, Philadelphia Museum of Art) 2501 Pennsylvania Avenue, Philadelphia, PA 19130

Zantzinger, Borie & Medary, architects, 1926–1927 National Register of Historic Places, 1973

Telephone for visitor information: 215.763.8100 www.philamuseum.org

Philadelphia's early twentieth-century Art Deco buildings have not achieved landmark status, although one of the best interiors, the Custom House by Ritter and Shay (1932–1934), has already been discussed (pages 258–263). Less celebrated examples that might easily have been mentioned in the context of this book are the N. W. Ayer Building (1927–1929) on Washington Square by Ralph Bencker (now a condominium) with its "jazz-modern" decoration, and the WCAU Building (1928) by Harry Sternfeld and Gabriel Roth at 1620 Chestnut Street (now part of the Art Institute of Philadelphia). Other candidates might include the shabby remaining interiors of the once grand motion picture palaces by Magaziner, Eberhard & Harris (the Uptown on North Broad Street) and Hoffman & Henon (the Boyd on Chestnut Street). Nor should the little appreciated United States Post Office at Thirtieth Street by Rankin & Kellogg (1932–1935) be overlooked. But for the purposes of this survey, the Board of Education Administration Building by a largely forgotten local architect, and the Fidelity Mutual Life Insurance Company Building by the celebrated architects of the Philadelphia Museum of Art have been selected to represent the Art Deco group of buildings; both stand on the Benjamin Franklin Parkway.

Early twentieth-century advocates of Art Deco embraced the machine and repudiated the traditional separation of the fine and industrial arts. The origins of the style are usually traced to the Paris exhibition of 1925, the Exposition

Internationale des Arts Décoratifs et Industriels Modernes, and the term is popularly used to describe the geometric decoration of art and architecture that spread throughout the world in the 1920s. Most critics argue there is no innate Art Deco form of architecture, only other styles—usually Classicist or Modernist—clothed with Art Deco ornamentation more broadly associated with the decorative arts. This is reflected in the National Register nomination of the Board of Education Administration Building, for example, where it is classified as "Neo-Classical" style, although the term "Modern Classical" might have been more appropriate, especially since some of the exterior forms—such as the oversized keystones and the bold rustication of the limestone—are exaggerated classical elements. The interior, however, is a virtual vocabulary of Art Deco decoration richly encrusted with abstract geometric decoration, in both floral and organic motifs, some derived from ancient Mexican, Egyptian, Moorish, and Far Eastern sources.

The architect of the Board of Education Administration Building was Irwin Thornton Catharine (1884–1944), son of Joseph W. Catharine, chair of the Philadelphia Board of Education. He received his certificate in architecture from the Drexel Institute in 1903, where he studied with Arthur Truscott. Shortly thereafter he was hired as an assistant draftsman for the Philadelphia Board of Education; by 1923 he had become an architect for the Board and in 1931 was

A stylized eagle on the roof parapet contemplates César Pelli's Cira Centre (2003–2005) near Thirtieth Street Station.

(*left*) The east entrance demonstrates the finely detailed exterior treatment.

(*right*) Art Deco motifs are applied to the walls, ceilings, and lighting fixtures of the public spaces of the interior.

(*left*) The "Modernized Classical" Board of Education Administration Building, designed by Irwin T. Catharine (1929–1931), faces the Benjamin Franklin Parkway. The interior is richly decorated in the Art Deco style.

This heating system grill is typical of the Art Deco detail lavished on the interior.

appointed superintendent of buildings. He held that position until 1937, when he retired. During his career Catharine designed many public schools, including the Moderne Central High School at West Olney and Ogontz Avenues.

The Board of Education Administration Building on the Benjamin Franklin Parkway at Twenty-First Street was dedicated on February 20, 1932. It is Catharine's best-known commission. It rises nine stories to a two-tiered tower. On the north front there are two three-story wings that project to create a courtyard closed by a masonry screen with four arched openings facing the Parkway. These arched openings are echoed by arched windows with lunettes holding bas reliefs by French sculptor Jules A. Melidon, who was on the faculty at the University of Pennsylvania. Around the main section with its tower are pilasters topped by sculptured heads of "World Leaders of Thought." These include Daniel Webster, Benjamin Franklin, Thaddeus Stevens, and William Shakespeare (on the north side); Alexander Graham Bell, Thomas Jefferson, Abraham Lincoln, and John Marshall (on the south side); Robert Fulton, Russell Conwell, Horace Mann, and William Penn (on the east side); and Isaac Newton, George Washington, Bayard Taylor, and Stephen Girard (on the west side).

The Board of Education Administration Building is one of the contributing structures of the Benjamin Franklin Parkway development, complementing the nearby Boy Scout headquarters, Franklin Institute, Free Library, Rodin Museum, and Philadelphia Museum of Art. It served for decades as the central administration building for the School District of Philadelphia until it was sold to private developers in 2003.

The Fidelity Mutual Life Insurance Company building was designed by the architects of the Philadelphia Museum of Art, Zantzinger, Borie & Medary

Main entrance of the Fidelity Mutual Life Insurance Building, now the Ruth and Raymond J. Perelman Building of the Philadelphia Museum of Art, was designed by Zantzinger, Borie & Medary, 1926–1927.

THE FIDELITY MUTUAL
IN THE HONOUR AND
IS FOUNDED THE
THE HOUSEHOLD IS
FIDELITAS

(pages 278–283), who faced the challenge of fitting their building onto a trapezoidal lot intersected by a street. The result is a three-story steel-frame, limestone-clad office building in what the architects called the "Modern Classic" style. The linear simplicity of the Fidelity building is interrupted by two blocky arched pavilions: the first of these opens to the city and serves as the primary entrance (referred to by one observer as the "gateway to the parkway"); the second pavilion spans Olive Street. These pavilions are richly ornamented with paired sculptural limestone figures by Lee Oscar Lawrie (1877–1963), who had studied with Augustus Saint-Gaudens and by the 1920s was nationally recognized as a designer of Art Deco architectural ornamentation. His many commissions included the New York Cathedral of Saint John the Divine, Rockefeller Center, Los Angeles Public Library, and Bertram Grosvenor Goodhue's (1869–1924) Nebraska State Capitol (1922–1932).

→ Detail of one limestone figure (*Fidelitas*) on the Fidelity Mutual Life Insurance Building by New York sculptor Lee O. Lawrie (1877–1963).

↓ One of Lawrie's faithful hounds guards the entrance to the Fidelity building.

♆ Along the flank elevations are bas reliefs by Jules A. Melidon representing the continents, in this case North America.

Just as the Board of Education Administration Building sculpture thematically expresses dedication to thought, the Fidelity building declares its owners' commitment to the "family as the basis of society and civilization." The monumental male and female figures carved from limestone represent the company's virtues of fidelity, friendship, frugality, and prudence; while at street level the recumbent canines reinforce the theme of fidelity. Above the entrance portal are gilded allegorical representations of various birds and animals referring to frugality, protection, wisdom, and charity.

Fiske Kimball looked down on the construction of the Fidelity Mutual building from the Art Museum site across the street. "The irregular site has been handled brilliantly to produce an unusual balanced composition," he wrote in *American Architecture* (1928). "The two immense arched portals contrast with long ranges of simple piers. Rich sculpture and color and gilding enhance the effect."

In 1972 Fidelity Life abandoned the building, which was eventually acquired by the Reliance Standard Life Insurance Company, which in turn relocated in 1999. The Philadelphia Museum of Art acquired the building in 2000 and engaged Gluckman Mayner Architects to sympathetically renovate and expand it to provide much needed museum education, exhibition, library, and conservation space. In recognition of their generous support of the acquisition, the building was reopened and dedicated to Ruth and Raymond G. Perelman in 2007.

Art Deco mail drop box from the Board of Education Administration Building.

BIBLIOGRAPHY AND SOURCES

This bibliography is separated into fifty groups, arranged alphabetically by landmark and listing the sources specific to each site. Quite a few of the items are reports and ephemeral publications, some of them known in only a few copies, especially those published in the nineteenth century. In many cases originals or photocopies of these are available at The Athenæum of Philadelphia, either catalogued in the book collection—which may be confirmed by consulting the Athenæum's On-Line Public Catalogue—or filed with the research notes for this book deposited at the Athenæum and arranged by the name of the landmark. The research files for *Historic Houses of Philadelphia* (Philadelphia: University of Pennsylvania Press, 1998) and *Historic Sacred Places of Philadelphia* (Philadelphia: University of Pennsylvania Press, 2005) have also been deposited with the Athenæum.

Philadelphia's built environment is the best documented in the nation. In the early 1980s, I conceived—and the National Endowment for the Humanities funded—a compilation of information on the architects and builders of Philadelphia, based largely on the rich collection of architectural drawings, manuscripts, and photographs in the care of The Athenæum of Philadelphia, where I was then Executive Director. The results of my research and that of my coauthor, Sandra L. Tatman, then curator of architecture at the Athenæum and now Executive Director, were published as the *Biographical Dictionary of Philadelphia Architects, 1700–1930* (Boston: G.K. Hall, 1985). From the beginning, Dr. Tatman and I knew the 900-page *Biographical Dictionary* was a preliminary step to what would ultimately be a larger project. (Like most G.K. Hall publications at the time, the text was a photo-offset of an unedited rough manuscript originally prepared for in-house use.) In 2000, however, the William Penn Foundation agreed to fund a project to establish an on-line database to be managed by the Athenæum offering biographical sketches and illustrated descriptions of buildings based on original documents preserved by approximately fifty institutions in the greater Philadelphia area. Where the *Biographical Dictionary* had contained biographical information on 1,200 architects and builders, by the time I retired from the Athenæum at the end of 2007, the Philadelphia Architects and Buildings database included biographies on 25,000 architects and builders and information on a quarter-million buildings and projects, supported by 125,000 images. Subsequently, the on-line database has become national in scope.

Perhaps most important, each architect, building, and image is supported by meticulously detailed sources and locations in regional institutions which have been surveyed by the PAB staff. *As a consequence, every landmark and architect mentioned in this book may be researched on the PAB Web site.* So complete and extensive is this resource that every individual site bibliography below could begin with an electronic citation to the PAB site.

ACADEMY OF MUSIC

The original competition drawings are preserved in the Academy of Music Archives, The Athenæum of Philadelphia, The Historical Society of Pennsylvania, and the University of Delaware.

Ardoin, John, ed. *The Philadelphia Orchestra: A Century of Music*. Philadelphia: Temple University Press, 1999.

Armstrong, W. G. *A Record of the Opera in Philadelphia*. Philadelphia: Porter & Coates, 1884.

Burgwyn, Diana. *The Kimmel Center for the Performing Arts: Home of the Philadelphia Orchestra*. Philadelphia: Regional Performing Arts Center, 2001.

Charter and Prospectus of the Opera House, or American Academy of Music. Philadelphia: Crissy & Markley, 1852.

Fisher, Sidney George. *A Philadelphia Perspective: The Diary of Sidney George Fisher Covering the Years 1834–1871*. Ed. Nicholas B. Wainwright. Philadelphia: Historical Society of Pennsylvania, 1967.

Kavanaugh, James Vincent. "Three American Opera Houses: The Boston Theatre, The New York Academy of Music, The Philadelphia American Academy of Music." M.A. thesis, University of Delaware, 1967. Copy at The Athenæum of Philadelphia.

Le Brun, Napoleon, and Gustav Runge. *Specification for the Construction of the American Academy of Music at*

Philadelphia. Philadelphia: Crissy & Markley, 1855.
Levinson, Nancy. "A Sudden Unusual Force: A Close Call in Philadelphia Raises Disturbing Questions." *Architectural Record* 178 (February 1990): 146–47, 174. Discusses failure of roof trusses.
Lewis, Michael. J. "The Architectural Competition for the Philadelphia Academy of Music, 1854–55." *Nineteenth Century* 17 (Spring 1997): 3–10. Best short account of the competition.
Marion, John Francis. *Within These Walls: A History of the Academy of Music in Philadelphia*. Philadelphia: The Academy of Music, 1984. Best general history.
Morrison, Craig. "The Academy of Music." *Marquee: The Journal of the Theatre Historical Society* 16, 4 (Fourth Quarter 1984): 5–9, 24.
Moss, Roger W. "Napoleon Le Brun," Tatman and Moss, 469–71.
———. "Gustav Runge," Tatman and Moss, 680.
Runge, Gustav. *Das Neue Opernhaus: Academy of Music in Philadelphia*. 2nd ed. Berlin: Von Ernst & Korn, 1882. Copy at The Athenæum of Philadelphia
Van Trump, James D. "The Philadelphia Academy of Music." *Charette* 46 (June 1966): 10–13.

ANNE AND JEROME FISHER FINE ARTS LIBRARY, UNIVERSITY OF PENNSYLVANIA

The Architectural Archives at the University of Pennsylvania houses 361 sheets of drawings catalogued under Furness, Evans & Company related to the library.

Bosley, Edward. *University of Pennsylvania Library: Frank Furness*. Photography by Mark Fiennes, drawings by Venturi, Scott Brown and Associates, John Hewitt. London: Phaidon, 1996.
Goldberger, Paul. "In Philadelphia, a Victorian Extravaganza Lives," *New York Times*, June 2, 1991.
Lewis, Michael J. *Frank Furness: Architecture and the Violent Mind*. New York: Norton, 2001.
Moos, Stanislaus von. *Venturi, Rauch, & Scott Brown Buildings and Projects*. New York: Rizzoli, 1987.
Thomas, George E. "'The Happy Employment of Means to Ends': Frank Furness's Library of the University of Pennsylvania and the Industrial Culture of Philadelphia." *PMHB* 126 (April 2002): 249–72.
Thomas, George E., and David B. Brownlee. *Building America's First University: An Historical and Architectural Guide to the University of Pennsylvania*. Philadelphia: University of Pennsylvania Press, 2000.
Thomas, George E., Jeffrey A. Cohen, and Michael J. Lewis. *Frank Furness: The Complete Works*. Rev. ed. New York: Princeton Architectural Press, 1996.
Venturi, Rauch, and Scott Brown. "A Master Plan for the Selective Restoration and Continued Use of the Furness Building." Prepared for the University of Pennsylvania. 4 vols. Philadelphia: Venturi, Rauch and Scott Brown, 1986. Copy available at Anne and Jerome Fisher Fine Arts Library, University of Pennsylvania.

ATHENÆUM OF PHILADELPHIA

The Athenæum of Philadelphia Minutes of the Board of Directors, 1814–2008, are preserved in the Athenæum Corporate Archives, as are the competition drawings by Notman, Walter, Strickland, Haviland, and others.

Dallett, Francis James. *An Architectural View of Washington Square*. Philadelphia: Privately printed, 1968.
Fisher, Sidney George. *A Philadelphia Perspective: The Diary of Sidney George Fisher Covering the years 1834–1871*. Ed. Nicholas B. Wainwright. Philadelphia: Historical Society of Pennsylvania, 1967.
Greiff, Constance M. *John Notman, Architect*. Philadelphia: The Athenæum of Philadelphia, 1979.
Moss, Roger W. "The Athenæum of Philadelphia." *Magazine Antiques* 114 (December 1978): 1264–79.
———. *Philadelphia Victorian: The Building of the Athenæum*. Philadelphia: The Athenæum of Philadelphia, 1998. Reproduces all the competition drawings of the 1840s.
Smith, Robert C. *John Notman and the Athenæum Building*. Annual Address. Philadelphia: The Athenæum, 1951.
Wendorf, Richard, ed. *America's Membership Libraries*, New Castle, Del.: Oak Knoll Press, 2007. Essay on the Athenæum appears on pp. 130–55.

ATWATER KENT MUSEUM

The University of Pennsylvania Rare Book Collection holds 26 volumes of Haviland's papers. His drawings are scattered among several institutions, including The Athenæum of Philadelphia and The Historical Society of Pennsylvania.

Baigell, Matthew Eli. "John Haviland." Ph.D. dissertation, University of Pennsylvania, 1965. Ann Arbor, Mich.: University Microfilms, 1981.
———. "John Haviland in Philadelphia, 1818–1826." *Journal of the Society of Architectural Historians* 25 (October 1966): 197–208.
Fairmount Park Art Association. *Independence Hall and Adjacent Historic Buildings: A Plan for Their Preservation and the Improvement of Their Surroundings*. Philadelphia: Fairmount Park Art Association, 1944.
Moss, Roger W. "John Haviland." Tatman and Moss, 343–47.
Sinclair, Bruce. *Philadelphia's Philosopher Mechanics: A History of the Franklin*

Institute, 1824–1865. Baltimore: Johns Hopkins University Press, 1974.

Webster, Richard J. *Philadelphia Preserved: Catalog of the Historic American Buildings Survey*. Philadelphia: Temple University Press, 1976. 57, 65, 74, 345.

THE BELLEVUE

The Philadelphia Historical Commission files contain correspondence, articles, and newspaper clippings, including building permits, sketches, plans, and material relating to the Legionnaires' disease crisis.

"Bellevue-Stratford Hotel, Philadelphia." *Architectural Review* 12 (June 1905): 138–40; plates 34–36.

"Bellevue-Stratford Hotel, Philadelphia." *Architectural Review* 19 (April 1913): 92.

"Bellevue-Stratford Hotel, Philadelphia." *T Square Club* (Philadelphia) (1913, 1914): 167, 186.

David, A. C. "Three New Hotels." *Architectural Record* 17 (March 1905): 167, 181–88.

Myers, Hyman. "The Restoration of the Fairmont Hotel, Philadelphia." *Technology & Conservation* (Winter 1979): 20–25.

Tatman, Sandra L. "Hewitt Brothers," Tatman and Moss, 367–77.

BENJAMIN FRANKLIN BRIDGE

The drawings for the Delaware River Bridge are part of the Paul P. Cret Archive at The Athenæum of Philadelphia and the Architectural Archives, The University of Pennsylvania.

Andariese, Walter S. *History of the Benjamin Franklin Bridge*. Camden: Delaware River Port Authority, 1981.

Chase, Clement E. "The Delaware River Bridge." *American Architect* 131 (March 1927): 329–35.

Cret, Paul P. "The Architect as Collaborator with the Engineer." *Architectural Forum* 49 (July 1928): 96–104.

Eberlein, Harold D. "The Delaware River Bridge Between Philadelphia and Camden." *Architectural Record* 61 (January 1927): 1–12.

Farnham, Jonathan E. "Staging the Tragedy of Time: Paul Cret and the Delaware River Bridge." *Journal of the Society of Architectural Historians* 57 (September 1998): 258–79. This essay is by far the best modern account of the bridge.

Izenour, George C., and Steve Izenour. "Animated Electric Light Enlivens Benjamin Franklin Bridge." *Architectural Lighting* 2 (January 1988): 22–29.

Tatman, Sandra L. "Paul Philippe Cret." Tatman and Moss, 172–75.

BOARD OF EDUCATION ADMINISTRATION BUILDING

"Administration Building for Education Board Will Adorn Parkway." *Real Estate Magazine*, Philadelphia, June 1929.

Bartley, Theodore T., Jr. Board of Education Building, National Register of Historic Places Inventory Form. U.S. Department of the Interior, Washington, D.C., 1983.

Benton, Charlotte, Tim Benton, and Ghislaine Wood, eds. *Art Deco 1910–1939*. Boston: Bulfinch Press, 2003.

Glazer, Irvin R. *Philadelphia Theaters: A Pictorial Architectural History*. Philadelphia: The Athenaeum of Philadelphia, 1994. Includes numerous images of Philadelphia Art Deco theater interiors.

Hillier, Bevis, and Stephen Escritt. *Art Deco Style*. London: Phaidon Press, 1997.

"Sculptured Groups at Board of Education's New Building Called 'Atrocities' by the Designer." *Philadelphia Evening Bulletin*, July 6, 1933.

"School District Sells 3 Phila Buildings." *Philadelphia Business Journal*, November 11, 2003.

Tatman, Sandra L. "Irwin Thornton Catharine." Tatman and Moss, 137–38.

BOATHOUSE ROW

Adams, William Taylor ("Oliver Optic"). *The Boat Club; or the Bunkers of Rippleton: A Tale for Boys*. 1855. Boston: Lee and Shepard, 1874.

Charleton, James H. "Boathouse Row." National Register of Historic Places Inventory Nomination Form. Washington, D.C.: National Park Service, 1985.

Dodd, Christopher. *The Story of World Rowing*. London: Stanley Paul, 1992.

Fairmount Park Commission. *Annual Reports*. Philadelphia, 1868–present.

———. *Laws Relating to Fairmount Park*. Philadelphia, 1933.

Heiland, Louis. *The Schuylkill Navy of Philadelphia, 1858–1937*. Philadelphia: Drake Press, 1938.

———. *The Undine Barge Club of Philadelphia, 1856–1924*. Philadelphia: Wm. F. Fell, 1925. See also the supplement, *The Undine Barge Club of Philadelphia, 1925–1955*. Philadelphia, 1956.

Moak, Jefferson M. "Boathouse Row." Philadelphia Register of Historic Places Nomination Form. Philadelphia Historical Commission, 1983. Copies in Commission files and at The Athenaeum of Philadelphia.

Pflaumer, Walter H., and George F. Joly, Jr. *One Hundred Years: History of the Bachelors Barge Club, 1853–1953*. Philadelphia: Offset Service Co., 1953.

Randall, Kathleen. "A Big Architecture Firm Picks Up Preservation." *Traditional Building* (March/April 1998): 9–12.

Thomas, George E., Michael J. Lewis, and Jeffrey A. Cohen. *Frank Furness: The Complete Works*. Rev. ed. New

York: Princeton Architectural Press, 1996.
Walker, Donald. *Walker's Manly Exercises: Containing Rowing, Sailing, Riding, Driving, Racing, Hunting, Shooting, and Other Manly Sports*. Philadelphia: John W. Moore, 1837.

CARPENTERS' HALL

Minute books of the Carpenters' Company of the City and County of Philadelphia are deposited with the library of The American Philosophical Society, Philadelphia.

Carpenters' Company of the City and County of Philadelphia. *Articles of the Carpenters Company of Philadelphia; and their Rules for Measuring and valuing house-carpenters work*. Philadelphia, 1786. The Articles have been reprinted several times. The most useful, with an introduction by the late Charles E. Peterson, dates from 2005 (Mendenhall, N.J.: Astragal Press).
Moss, Roger W. "Master Builders: A History of the Colonial Philadelphia Building Trades." Ph.D. dissertation, University of Delaware, 1972. Ann Arbor, Mich.: University Microfilms.
———. "The Origins of the Carpenters' Company of Philadelphia." In *Building Early America*, ed. Charles E. Peterson. Radnor, Pa.: Chilton, 1976.
Peterson, Charles E. "Carpenters' Hall." In *Historic Philadelphia from the Founding Until the Early Nineteenth Century: Papers Dealing with Its People and Buildings*, ed. Luther P. Eisenhart. Transactions of the American Philosophical Society 43, pt. 1. Philadelphia: American Philosophical Society, 1953. 96–123.
Peterson, Charles E. with Constance M. Greiff and Maria M. Thompson. *Robert Smith: Architect, Builder, Patriot, 1722–1777*. Philadelphia: The Athenæum of Philadelphia, 2000.

CONGRESS HALL

Anderson, Susan H. *The Most Splendid Carpet*. Philadelphia: National Park Service, U.S. Department of the Interior, 1978.
Blimm, Miriam. *Congress Hall: Independence National Historical Park*. Philadelphia: National Park Service, U.S. Department of the Interior, 1976.
Hartshorne, Penelope. Historic Structure Report Part II on Congress Hall, Independence National Historical Park, Architectural Data Section. National Park Service, U.S. Department of the Interior, Washington, D.C., 1960.
———. Congress Hall Historic Structures Report, Architectural Data Section, Part II. Philadelphia: Independence National Historic Park.
King, David. *The Complete Works of Robert and James Adam*. Oxford: Butterworth-Heinemann, 1990.
Kurjack, Dennis C. "Who Designed the 'President's House'?" *Journal of the Society of Architectural Historians* 12 (May 1953): 27–28.
Moss, Roger W. "William Williams." Tatman and Moss, 854–56.
Riley, M. Edward. "History of the Independence Hall Group." In *Historic Philadelphia from the Founding Until the Early Nineteenth Century: Papers Dealing with Its People and Buildings*, ed. Luther P. Eisenhart. Transactions of the American Philosophical Society 43, pt. 1. Philadelphia: American Philosophical Society, 1953. 7–41.
Weld, Isaac, Jr. *Travels Through the States of North America . . . during the years 1795, 1796, and 1797*. 3rd ed. London: Stockdale, 1800.

DORRANCE HAMILTON HALL, UNIVERSITY OF THE ARTS

An Account of the Origin and Progress of the Pennsylvania Institution for the Deaf and Dumb. Philadelphia: Pennsylvania Institution for the Deaf and Dumb, 1821.
Baigell, Matthew Eli. "John Haviland." Ph.D. dissertation, University of Pennsylvania, 1965. Ann Arbor, Mich.: University Microfilms, 1981.
———. "John Haviland in Philadelphia, 1818–1826." *Journal of the Society of Architectural Historians* 25 (October 1966): 197–208.
Lewis, Michael J. *Frank Furness: Architecture and the Violent Mind*. New York: W.W. Norton, 2001. See p. 116.
Thomas, George E., Michael J. Lewis, and Jeffrey A. Cohen. *Frank Furness: The Complete Works*. Rev. ed. New York: Princeton Architectural Press, 1996. See p. 188, cat. 57.
Toll, Jean B., and Mildred S. Gillam. "Pennsylvania School for the Deaf." In *Invisible Philadelphia: Community Through Voluntary Organizations*, ed. Toll and Gillam. Philadelphia: Atwater Kent Museum, 1995.
Van Allen, H. *A Brief History of the Pennsylvania Institution for the Deaf and Dumb. Illustrated with numerous engravings by W. R. Cullingworth*. Philadelphia: W.R. Cullingworth, 1893.

EASTERN STATE PENITENTIARY

Biancaniello, Jennifer. "Another Stone in the Wall: Building New Roles for a Historic Penitentiary in Philadelphia." Thesis, Temple University, 1997.
Bigell, Matthew Eli. "John Haviland." Ph.D. dissertation, University of Pennsylvania, 1965. Ann Arbor, Mich.: University Microfilms, 1981.
Cornelius, David Gregory. The Institutional Building Systems of John Haviland: A Study of Innovation and Influence: A Final Report Submitted to the Peterson Committee, Athenæum of Philadelphia, November 1999. Copy at The Athenæum of Philadelphia.
Haviland, John. Papers. 26 vols. Held by the Rare Book Collection, Van

Pelt Library, University of Pennsylvania.
Johnston, Norman. "American Notes: John Haviland, Jailor to the World." *Journal of the Society of Architectural Historians* 23, 2 (1964): 101–5.
———. "John Haviland, 1792–1852." In *Pioneers in Criminology*, ed. Hermann Mannheim. Publication 121: Patterson Smith Reprint Series in Criminology, Law Enforcement and Social Problems. Montclair, N.J.: Patterson Smith, 1972.
Johnston, Norman, with Kenneth Finkel and Jeffrey A. Cohen. *Eastern State Penitentiary: Crucible of Good Intentions*. Philadelphia: Philadelphia Museum of Art for Eastern State Penitentiary Task Force of the Preservation Coalition of Greater Philadelphia, 1994. The best secondary account for the general reader.
Kieran, Timberlake & Harris. Eastern State Penitentiary, Philadelphia, Pennsylvania. Conditions Report prepared for the City of Philadelphia. 6 vols. Typescript, 1989.
Lieber, Frances. *A Concise History of the Penitentiary of Pennsylvania together with a Detailed State of the Proceedings of the Committee Appointed by the Legislature, December 6th, 1834*. Philadelphia: Neall & Massey, 1835.
Moss, Roger W. "The Walnut Street Prison." In John L. Cotter, Roger W. Moss, Bruce C. Gill, and Jiyul Kim, *The Walnut Street Prison Workshop*. Philadelphia: The Athenæum of Philadelphia, 1988.
Teeters, Negley King. *They Were in Prison: A History of the Pennsylvania Prison Society, 1787–1937, Formerly the Philadelphia Society for Alleviating the Miseries of Public Prisons*. Philadelphia: John C. Winston, 1937.
Teeters, Negley King, and John D. Shearer. *The Prison at Philadelphia, Cherry Hill: The Separate System of Penal Discipline, 1829–1913*. New York: Columbia University Press for Temple University, 1957.
Thomas, Marianna, with Jeffery Cohen and others from the City of Philadelphia, the Philadelphia Historical Commission and the Eastern State Penitentiary Task Force of the Preservation Coalition of Great Philadelphia. Eastern State Penitentiary Historic Structure Report. 3 vols. Philadelphia, 1994. Includes an extensive bibliography of reports and other primary documents.
Vaux, Richard. *Brief Sketch of the Origin and History of the State Penitentiary for the Eastern District of Pennsylvania, at Philadelphia*. Philadelphia: McLaughlin Brothers, 1872.

FAIRMOUNT WATER WORKS

Fazio, Michael W., and Patrick A. Snadon. *The Domestic Architecture of Benjamin Henry Latrobe*. Baltimore: Johns Hopkins University Press, 2006.
Fisher, Sidney George. *A Philadelphia Perspective: The Diary of Sidney George Fisher Covering the Years 1834–1871*. Ed. Nicholas B. Wainwright. Philadelphia: The Historical Society of Pennsylvania, 1967. Fisher's comments on bathing are found on pp. 240–41.
"Frederick Graff and Frederick Graff, Jr." *Dictionary of American Biography*, ed. Dumas Malone. New York: Charles Scribner's Sons, 1931. 7: 466–68.
Gibson, Jane Mork. "The Fairmount Waterworks. Checklist of the Exhibition prepared by Robert Wolterstorff." *Philadelphia Museum of Art Bulletin* 84 (Summer 1988), nos. 360–61.
Hagner, Charles Valerius. *Early History of the Falls of Schuylkill: Manayunk, Schuylkill and Lehigh Navigation Companies, Fairmount Waterworks, etc.* Philadelphia, 1869.
Historic American Engineering Record. Rehabilitation: Fairmount Waterworks 1978. Conservation and Recreation in a National Historic Landmark. Report prepared by the U.S. Department of the Interior through the Heritage Conservation and Recreation Service and Historic American Engineering Record. Washington, D.C.: U.S. Department of the Interior, 1979. Copy at The Athenaeum of Philadelphia.
John Milner Associates, Inc., Architects. Adaptive Reuse Feasibility Study for the Historic Fairmount Waterworks, Philadelphia, Pennsylvania. Report prepared for the City of Philadelphia, Water Department. 2 vols. Typescript, West Chester, Pa., 1981. Copy at The Athenaeum of Philadelphia.
Powell, J. H. *Bring Out Your Dead: The Great Plague of Yellow Fever in Philadelphia in 1793*. 1949. Reprinted with a new introduction by Kenneth R. Foster, Mary F. Jenkins, and Anna Coxe Toogood. Philadelphia: University of Pennsylvania Press, 1993.
Sellers, Charles Coleman. "William Rush at Fairmount." In *Sculpture of a City: Philadelphia's Treasures in Bronze and Stone*. Philadelphia: Fairmount Park Art Association, 1974.

FIDELITY LIFE INSURANCE BUILDING

Alexander, Hartley Burr. "The Sculpture of Lee Lawrie." *Architectural Forum: Architectural Design* 54 (May 1931): 587–600.
Fidelity Mutual Life Insurance Company. *A Substantial New Building for a Substantial Old Company*. Philadelphia: Fidelity Mutual Life Insurance Company, 1927. Copy available at The Athenæum of Philadelphia.
Kimball, Fiske. *American Architecture*. Indianapolis: Bobbs-Merrell, 1928.
Philadelphia Museum of Art. *Developments* 16 (Spring/Summer 2007). Contains several articles on the dedication of the Perelman Building.
Solon, Leon V., and Harry Arthur Hopf. "Fidelity Mutual Life Insurance

Company Building, Philadelphia: Collaboration in Design." *Architectural Record* 63 (January 1928): 3–16, 73–76.

"Unveiling the Perelman." *Philadelphia Inquirer*, September 9, 2007. A special section about the Philadelphia Museum of Art expansion with several articles on the building, exhibitions, Richard Gluckman's design, and the donors.

Vrooman, W. Terry. *The First Hundred Years*. Philadelphia: Fidelity Mutual Life Insurance Company, 1978.

FIRST BANK OF THE UNITED STATES

NB: Samuel Blodget, Jr., spelled his name Blodget (not Blodgett) and Clodius LeGrand spelled his name Clodius (not Claudius).

Adams, Donald R. *Finance and Enterprise in Early America: A Study of Stephen Girard's Bank, 1812–1831*. Philadelphia: University of Pennsylvania Press, 1978.

Baigell, Matthew. "James Hoban and the First Bank of the United States." *Journal of the Society of Architectural Historians* 28 (May 1969): 135–36. Baigell first suggested the possible connections between Hoban, Blodget, and the Bank of the United States.

Blodget, Samuel, Jr. *Economica: A Statistical Manual for the United States of America*. Washington, D.C., 1806.

Craven, Wayne. "The Origins of Sculpture in America: Philadelphia, 1785–1830." *American Art Journal* 9 (November 1977): 4–33.

Holdsworth, John Thom and Davis R. Dewey. *The First and Second Banks of the United States*. National Monetary Commission, 61st Congress, 2nd Session, Document 571, Senate Documents, vol. 26. Washington, D.C.: Government Printing Office, 1910.

Kimball, Fiske. "James Hoban." In *Dictionary of American Biography*, ed. Dumas Malone. New York: Scribner's Sons, 1932. 9: 91–92.

Leach, Josiah Granville. *History of the Girard National Bank*. Philadelphia: J.B. Lippincott, 1902.

Moss, Roger W. "Samuel Blodget, Jr." and "Christopher Myers." Tatman and Moss, 76–77, 560–61.

Platt, John D. R., Penelope Hartshorne Batcheler, and Sarah M. Sweetser. Historic Structure Report, First Bank of the United States: Historical and Architectural Data, Independence National Historical Park, Pennsylvania. Denver Service Center, Historic Preservation Division, National Park Service, 1981.

Raley, Robert L. "Philadelphia's First Bank: A Reflection of Dublin's Royal Exchange." In *University Hospital Antiques Show* (1984): 70–74. Raley was the first to suggest that Christopher Myers, Jr., might have designed the First Bank of the United States.

Reiff, Daniel D. "James Hoban." In *Macmillan Encyclopedia of Architects*, ed. Adolf K. Placzek. New York: Free Press, 1982. 396–97.

Salisbury, Stephan. "Civil War Museum Finds a Home." *Philadelphia Inquirer*, August 8, 2007.

Tatman, Sandra L. "James Hamilton Windrim." Tatman and Moss, 871–73.

Wettereau, James O. "America's Oldest Bank Building." In *Historic Philadelphia from the Founding Until the Early Nineteenth Century: Papers Dealing with Its People and Buildings*, ed. Luther P. Eisenhart. Transactions of the American Philosophical Society 43, pt. 1. Philadelphia: American Philosophical Society, 1953. 70–79.

Wright, Robert E. *The First Wall Street: Chestnut Street, Philadelphia, and the Birth of American Finance*. Chicago: University of Chicago Press, 2005.

FORT MIFFLIN

Extensive files of photocopied primary material and finding aids relating to Fort Mifflin compiled by Jean K. Wolf are contained in the research files for his book, which have been deposited at The Athenæum of Philadelphia.

Bowling, Kenneth R. *Peter Charles L'Enfant: Vision, Honor, and Male Friendship in the Early Republic*. Washington, D.C.: Friends of George Washington University, 2002.

Brumbaugh, G. Edwin. *Fort Mifflin, on Historic Mud Island in the Delaware River*. Philadelphia: Greater Philadelphia Movement, 1959.

Dickey, John M. "Restoration of Fort Mifflin." Media, Pa.: Dickey, Weissman, Chandler, Holt, Architects, Planners, Engineers, 1971. Copy in the John Dickey Collection, The Athenæum of Philadelphia.

Dorwart, Jeffery M. *Fort Mifflin of Philadelphia: An Illustrated History*. Philadelphia: University of Pennsylvania Press, 1998. The best history of the fort based on recent research and primary documents.

Jackson, John W. *The Delaware Bay and River Defenses of Philadelphia, 1775–1777*. Philadelphia: Maritime Museum, 1977.

Martin, Joseph Plumb. *Private Yankee Doodle, Being a Narrative of Some of the Adventures, Dangers and Sufferings of a Revolutionary Soldier*. 1830. Ed. George E. Scheer. n.p.: Eastern Acorn Press, 1991.

Scull, G. D., ed. "The Montrésor Journals." In *Collections of the New-York Historical Society for the Year 1881*. New York: The Society, 1882.

Taylor, Frank H. *Philadelphia in the Civil War, 1861–1865*. Philadelphia: City of Philadelphia, 1913.

FOUNDER'S HALL, GIRARD COLLEGE

The primary sources for Founder's Hall are the Stephen Girard Papers on microfilm at The American Philosophical Society, the Thomas U. Walter

Collection at The Athenæum of Philadelphia, the Girard College Collection preserved at the college, and the Philadelphia City Archives.

Amundson, Jhennifer A. *Thomas U. Walter: The Lectures on Architecture, 1841–53*. Philadelphia: The Athenæum of Philadelphia, 2006.

Cutler, John B. "Girard College Architectural Competition." Ph.D. dissertation, Yale University, 1969. Ann Arbor, Mich.: University Microfilms, 1991.

Girard College Building Committee. *Final Report of the Building Committee of the Girard College for Orphans, . . . and an Account of the Final Transfer of the Buildings and Grounds to the Board of Directors. Annual Report, 1847*. Philadelphia: Lydia R. Bailey, 1848.

Laverty, Bruce, Michael J. Lewis, and Michele Taillon Taylor. *Monument to Philanthropy: The Design and Building of Girard College, 1832–1848*. Philadelphia: Girard College, 1998. The best and most comprehensive study of the competition and Walter's final design.

Peterson, Charles E., E. Newbold Cooper, and Agnes Addison Gilchrist. "The Girard College Architectural Competition, 1832." *Journal of the American Society of Architectural Historians* 16, 2 (May 1957): 20–27.

Schwarz, Robert D. *The Stephen Girard Collection: A Selective Catalog*. Philadelphia, Girard College, 1980.

Taylor, Michele Taillon. "Building for Democracy: Girard College Political, Educational and Architectural Ideology." Ph.D. dissertation, University of Pennsylvania. Ann Arbor, Mich.: University Microfilms, 1997.

Wildes, Harry Emerson. *Lonely Midas: The Story of Stephen Girard*. New York: Farrar & Rinehart, 1943.

Will of the Late Stephen Girard, Esq . . . with a short Biography of His Life. Philadelphia: Lydia R. Bailey, 1839.

FREE LIBRARY OF PHILADELPHIA

The Trumbauer office records are found in the architecture archives at The Athenæum of Philadelphia. The Free Library of Philadelphia has an extensive collection of the Trumbauer office drawings for its parkway building.

Brownlee, David B. *Making a Modern Classic: The Architecture of the Philadelphia Museum of Art*. Philadelphia: Philadelphia Museum of Art, 1997.

———. *Building the City Beautiful: The Benjamin Franklin Parkway and the Philadelphia Museum of Art*. Philadelphia: Distributed by University of Pennsylvania Press for the Philadelphia Museum of Art, 1989.

Free Library of Philadelphia. *Celebrating 75 Years on the Parkway: June 2, 1927–June 2, 2002*. Philadelphia: Free Library of Philadelphia, 2002.

———. *Free Library of Philadelphia, 1926: Horace Trumbauer, Architect*. Philadelphia: Free Library of Philadelphia, 1926 (?).

Platt, Frederick. "Horace Trumbauer: A Life." *PMHB* 125 (October 2001): 315–49.

Tatman, Sandra L. "Julian Francis Abele." Tatman and Moss, 1.

FREEDOM THEATRE

The extensive Edwin Forrest Home Records are housed at the Historical Society of Pennsylvania (Collection 3068). The archives of the Philadelphia School of Design for Women are preserved by the Moore College of Art and Design. Both may be consulted upon application.

Bryce, Mayo. "Moore College of Art and Design." In *Invisible Philadelphia: Community Through Voluntary Organizations*, ed. Jean Barth Toll and Mildred S. Gillam. Philadelphia: Atwater Kent Museum, 1995.

Moody, Richard. *Edwin Forrest*. New York: Knopf, 1960.

Moss, Roger W. "Stephen Decatur Button." Tatman and Moss, 122–25.

Rees, James. *The Life of Edwin Forrest*. Philadelphia: T.B. Peterson & Brothers, 1874.

Sinclair, Bruce. *Philadelphia's Philosopher Mechanics: A History of the Franklin Institute, 1824–1865*. Baltimore: Johns Hopkins University Press, 1974.

Tatman, Sandra L. "James Hamilton Windrim." Tatman and Moss, 871–73.

Walls, Nina de Angeli. "Art and Industry in Philadelphia: Origins of the Philadelphia School of Design for Women." *PMHB* 117 (July 1993): 177–99.

Webster, Richard J. *Philadelphia Preserved: Catalog of the Historic American Buildings Survey*. Philadelphia: Temple University Press, 1976. See the discussion of the Gaul-Forrest House, 296, 373 n. 31.

———. "Stephen D. Button: Italianate Stylist." M.A. thesis, University of Delaware, 1963.

HISTORICAL SOCIETY OF PENNSYLVANIA

Original drawings for the Historical Society building are in the Addison Hutton Collection at The Athenæum of Philadelphia and the archives of The Historical Society of Pennsylvania.

Carson, Hampton L. *A History of the Historical Society of Pennsylvania*. Philadelphia: Historical Society of Pennsylvania, 1940.

Griffith, Sally F. *Serving History in a Changing World: The Historical Society of Pennsylvania in the Twentieth Century*. Philadelphia: Historical Society of Pennsylvania/University of Pennsylvania Press, 2001.

Hawkins, B. Keven, Historical Survey of the Property on the Southwest Corner of Locust and Thirteenth Streets: Once the Site of the Mansion of John Hare Powel. Research report submitted to Roger W. Moss at The

University of Pennsylvania, 1985. Copy on file at The Athenæum of Philadelphia.
Tatman, Sandra L. "Addison Hutton." Tatman and Moss, 401–7.
Wainwright. Nicholas B. *One-Hundred Fifty Years of Collecting by the Historical Society of Pennsylvania, 1824–1974*. Philadelphia: Historical Society of Pennsylvania, 1974.
Whitehill, Walter Muir. *Independent Historical Societies: An Enquiry into Their Research and Publication Functions and Their Financial Future*. Boston: Boston Athenæum, 1962.
Yarnall, Elizabeth Biddle. *Addison Hutton: Quaker Architect, 1834–1916*. Philadelphia: Art Alliance Press, 1974.

INDEPENDENCE HALL

There are numerous Historic Structure Reports prepared by the staff of Independence National Historical Park, which may be consulted at the INHP Library. There are also copies of many of the reports at The Athenæum of Philadelphia. The most important of these are listed here.

Batcheler, Penelope Hartshorne. Independence Hall Historic Structures Report, Architectural Data Section: Part II Portion, the Central Hall and Tower Stairhall. Philadelphia: Independence National Historical Park, 1989.
———. Independence Hall Historic Structures Report, Architectural Data Section: Part II Portion, the Physical History of the Second Floor. Philadelphia: Independence National Historical Park, 1992.
———. Historic Structures Report, Part III on Independence Hall, Independence National Historical Park, Architectural Data Section: Repainting of Interior, Entrance Hall, and Tower Stairhall. Philadelphia: Penelope Hartshorne Batcheler, 1960.

The Independence Hall bibliography is vast. The most useful sources for this essay were the following.

Greiff, Constance M. *Independence: The Creation of a National Park*. Philadelphia: University of Pennsylvania Press, 1987.
Harris, Eileen and Nicholas Savage. *British Architectural Books and Writers, 1556–1785*. Cambridge: Cambridge University Press, 1990. Discusses the publications of William Halfpenny and other pattern book authors available to Philadelphia Master Builders.
Milley, John C., ed. *Treasures of Independence: Independence National Historic Park and Its Collections*. New York: Main Street Press, 1980.
Mires, Charlene. *Independence Hall in American Memory*. Philadelphia: University of Pennsylvania Press, 2000.
Moss, Roger W. "Edmund Woolley." Tatman and Moss, 882.
Nelson, Lee H. "Restoration in Independence Hall: A Continuum of Historic Preservation." *The Magazine Antiques* 90 (July 1966): 64–68.
Park, Helen. *A List of Architectural Books Available in America Before the Revolution*. Los Angeles: Hennessey & Ingalls, 1973. Discusses the history of Woolley's copy of Halfpenney.
Peterson, Charles E. "American Notes: Early Architects of Independence Hall." *Journal of the Society of Architectural Historians* 11 (October 1952): 23–26.
Riley, Edward M. "Historic Philadelphia from the Founding Until the Early 19th Century"; Riley, "History of the Independence Hall Group." In *Historic Philadelphia from the Founding Until the Early Nineteenth Century: Papers Dealing with Its People and Buildings*, ed. Luther P. Eisenhart. Transactions of the American Philosophical Society 43, pt. 1. Philadelphia: American Philosophical Society, 1953. 7–41.
Roach, Hannah Benner. "Thomas Nevel (1721–1797), Carpenter, Educator, Patriot." *Journal of the Society of Architectural Historians* 24 (December 1963): 153–64.

INSTITUTE OF THE PENNSYLVANIA HOSPITAL

Cooledge, Harold N. *Samuel Sloan, Architect of Philadelphia, 1815–1884*. Philadelphia: University of Pennsylvania Press, 1986.
———. "Samuel Sloan and the Philadelphia School of Hospital Design, 1850–1880." *Charette* 44 (June 1964): 6–7, 18.
Freeman, Jane. *The History of the Institute of Pennsylvania Hospital*. Philadelphia: Institute of the Pennsylvania Hospital, 1991.
Greiff, Constance M. *John Notman, Architect*. Philadelphia: The Athenæum of Philadelphia, 1979.
Kirkbride, Thomas S. *On the Construction, Organization and General Arrangements of Hospitals for the Insane*. Philadelphia: Lindsay & Blakiston, 1854.
"Sketch of the History, Buildings, and Organization of the Pennsylvania Hospital for the Insane." *American Journal of Insanity* (October 1845): 97–114.
Moss, Roger W. "Isaac Holden." Tatman and Moss, 391.
———. "Samuel Sloan." Tatman and Moss, 730–34.
Rothman, David J. *The Discovery of the Asylum: Social Order and Disorder in the New Republic*. New York: Aldine de Gruyter, 2002.
Tomes, Nancy. *A Generous Confidence: Thomas Story Kirkbride and the Art of Asylum-Keeping, 1840–1883*. New York: Cambridge University Press, 1984.
Yanni, Carla. "The Linear Plan for Insane Asylums in the United States Before 1866." *Journal of the Society of Architectural Historians* 62 (March 2003): 24–49.

INSURANCE COMPANY OF NORTH AMERICA BUILDING

Adams, George R. "Insurance Company of North America." National Register of Historic Places Inventory Nomination Form. Washington, D.C.: U.S. Department of the Interior, National Park Service, 1977.

Carr, William H. A. *Perils, Named and Unnamed: The Story of the Insurance Company of North America*. New York: McGraw-Hill, 1967.

Insurance Company of North America. *An Old Institution in a New Home*. Philadelphia: INA, 1926.

James, Marquis. *Biography of a Business, 1792–1942: Insurance Company of North America*. Indianapolis: Bobbs-Merrill, 1942.

"Luxury Phoenix in Center City Has Risen Out of Historic Company Headquarters." *Philadelphia Inquirer*, March 25, 2007.

McCosker, M. J. *The Historical Collection of Insurance Company of North America*. Philadelphia: INA, 1967.

Smart, James. *History of the Insurance Industry in Philadelphia*. Philadelphia: INA, 1976.

JOHN WANAMAKER DEPARTMENT STORE

The John Wanamaker Company archives have been deposited at the Historical Society of Pennsylvania. The Athenæum of Philadelphia holds several hundred Burnham and Francis H. Kimball competition drawings for the Wanamaker Store building.

Biswanger, Ray. *Music in the Marketplace: The Story of Philadelphia's Historic Wanamaker Organ from John Wanamaker to Lord and Taylor*. Bryn Mawr, Pa.: Friends of the Wanamaker Organ, 1999.

"A Modern Department Store: The Construction and Equipment of the Philadelphia Wanamaker Building," *Architectural Record* 24 (March 1911): 277–88.

Ewing, Cole, Cherry, Parsky. "Historic Structures Report: Restoration of John Wanamaker Philadelphia Department Store, 1300 Market Street, Philadelphia." Philadelphia, 1981. Copy available at The Athenæum of Philadelphia.

Ferry, John W. *A History of the Department Store*. New York: Macmillan, 1960.

Gibbons, Herbert Adams. *John Wanamaker*. New York: Harper & Brothers, 1926.

Moore, Charles. *Daniel H. Burnham, Architect, Planner of Cities*. Boston: Houghton Mifflin, 1921.

Sobel, Robert. *The Entrepreneurs: Explorations Within the American Business Tradition*. New York: Weybright and Talley, 1974.

Zulker, William Allen. *John Wanamaker: King of Merchants*. Wayne, Pa.: Eaglecrest Pess, 1993.

LAUREL HILL CEMETERY

Original drawings by Notman, Walter, and Strickland are preserved in the collections of The Athenæum of Philadelphia and The Library Company of Philadelphia. The Laurel Hill Cemetery Company archives remain in the care of the Company.

Curl, James Stevens. *The Victorian Celebration of Death*. Detroit: Partridge Press, 1972.

Dickey, John. Historic Structure Report, Laurel Hill Cemetery. 1979. John Dickey Collection, The Athenæum of Philadelphia. Includes blue line prints of gatehouse restoration, 1980.

Downing, Andrew Jackson. "Review of Laurel Hill." *The Horticulturist, and Journal of Rural Art and Rural Taste* (Albany, N.Y., July 1849): 9–12.

Greiff, Constance M. *John Notman, Architect*. Philadelphia: The Athenæum of Philadelphia, 1979.

Jackson, Kenneth T., and Camilo José Vergara. *Silent Cities: The Evolution of the American Cemetery*. New York: Princeton Architectural Press, 1989.

Laurel Hill Cemetery. *Regulations of the Laurel Hill Cemetery, on the River Schuylkill, near Philadelphia: the act of incorporation by the Legislature of Pennsylvania in 1837: and a catalogue of the proprietors of Lots to February 1, 1846*. Philadelphia: The Cemetery, 1846.

Magner, Blake A., ed. *At Peace with Honor: Civil War Burials of Laurel Hill Cemetery, Philadelphia, Pennsylvania*. Collingswood, N.J.: C.W. Historicals, 1997.

McDannell, Colleen. "The Religious Symbolism of Laurel Hill Cemetery." *PMHB* 111, 3 (July 1987): 275–303.

Meyer, Richard E., ed. *Cemeteries and Gravemarkers: Voices of American Cultures*. Ann Arbor, Mich.: UMI Research Press, 1989.

Schuyler, David. "The Evolution of the Anglo-American Rural Cemetery: Landscape Architecture as Social and Cultural History." *Journal of Garden History* 4, 3 (July–September 1984): 291–304.

Sloane, David C. *The Last Great Necessity: Cemeteries in American History*. Baltimore: Johns Hopkins University Press, 1991.

Smith, John Jay. *Guide to Laurel Hill Cemetery, Near Philadelphia*. Philadelphia: C. Sherman, 1844.

———. *Recollections of John Jay Smith*. Philadelphia: Lippincott, 1892.

Smith, R. A. *Smith's Illustrated Guide to and through Laurel Hill Cemetery, with a Glance at Celebrated Tombs and Burying Places, Ancient and Modern, an Historical Sketch of the Cemeteries of Philadelphia, an Essay on Monumental Architecture, and a Tour up the Schuylkill*. Philadelphia: W.P. Hazard, 1852.

Wunsch, Aaron V. "Laurel Hill Cemetery." National Historic Landmark

Nomination Form, U.S. Department of the Interior, Washington, D.C., 1998.
———. "Laurel Hill Cemetery." Historic American Buildings Survey. National Park Service, U.S. Department of Interior, Washington, D.C., 1999. HABS no. PA-1811. By far the most thorough and useful source on this important NHL site. Copy with original photographs at The Athenæum of Philadelphia.

MASONIC TEMPLE

The George Herzog Collection at The Athenæum of Philadelphia includes approximately 150 of his designs. The Masonic Temple designs are preserved at the Masonic Library and Museum, Philadelphia.

Art Association of the Masonic Temple, Philadelphia. *A Description of the Decorations of the Various Halls and Grand Banquet Room of the Temple, with Illustrations*. Philadelphia: Lippincott, 1904.
Barratt, Norris S., and Julius F. Sachse. *Freemasonry in Pennsylvania, 1727–1907*. Philadelphia: Grand Lodge Free and Accepted Masons of Pennsylvania, 1908.
Curl, James Stevens. *The Art and Architecture of Freemasonry: An Introductory Study*. Woodstock, N.Y.: Overlook Press, 2002.
Dedication Memorial of the New Masonic Temple, Philadelphia, September 26th, 29th, 30th, 1873. Philadelphia: Claxton Remsen & Haffelfinger, 1875. Copy at The Athenæum of Philadelphia.
Description of the New Masonic Temple, Broad Street, Philadelphia, Jas. H. Windrim, Architect, with an account of its Magnificent Gas Fixtures Furnished by Baker, Arnold & Co. Philadelphia: M'alla & Stavely, 1873. Copy at the Historical Society of Pennsylvania.
Huss, Wayne A. "Pennsylvania Freemasonry: An Intellectual and Social Analysis, 1727–1826. Ph.D. dissertation, Temple University, 1984.
Lewis, Michael J. *Frank Furness: Architecture and the Violent Mind*. New York: Norton, 2001.
Luellen, Mark C. "The Decorative Designs of George Herzog (1851–1920)." *Nineteenth Century* 12, 3–4 (1993): 18–26.
———. "The Decorative Work of George Herzog: 1851–1920." M.A. thesis, University of Pennsylvania, 1992. Copy available at The Athenæum of Philadelphia.
Masonic Temple Philadelphia, Pennsylvania. Philadelphia: Committee on Masonic Culture, 1993. Most recent edition of the official guidebook.
Poppeliers, John C. "The 1867 Philadelphia Masonic Temple Competition." *Journal of the Society of Architectural Historians* 26, 4 (December 1967: 278–84.
Tatman, Sandra L. "James Hamilton Windrim." Tatman and Moss, 871–73.

MERCHANTS' EXCHANGE

As with all buildings in Independence National Historical Park, the extensive Historic Structure Reports prepared by the National Park Service provide the best documentation. The Historic Building Report, Part I, Philadelphia Merchants' Exchange, Third and Walnut Streets, prepared by the Staff, Independence National Historical Park, Philadelphia, May 1958, includes the initial proposal to adapt the building for use as a visitors' center or regional offices, and on rebuilding Strickland's tower. It also includes copies of historic photos/prints/newspaper articles. The Historic Building Report, Part II, Supplement I, Architectural Data Section on Restoration and Reconstruction of Merchants' Exchange, INHP, was prepared by Joseph Petrak, Architect, November 1963. See also William D. Brookover, "Philadelphia Merchants' Exchange Conservation Strategy," Preservation Assistance Division, National Park Service, Washington, D.C., 1992, and Vitetta Group, "Rehabilitation of the Merchants' Exchange Building, Supplementary Historic Structures Report," Philadelphia, 1995. Copies of these reports are available from the Library and Archives of INHP.

Denison, John, ed. *Cyclopedia of Painters and Paintings*. New York: Scribner's, 1887.
Fairmount Park Art Association. *Sculpture of a City: Philadelphia's Treasures in Bronze and Stone*. New York: Walker, 1974.
Gilchrist, Agnes Addison. "The Philadelphia Exchange: William Strickland, Architect." In *Historic Philadelphia from the Founding Until the Early Nineteenth Century: Papers Dealing with Its People and Buildings*, ed. Luther P. Eisenhart. Transactions of the American Philosophical Society 43, pt. 1. Philadelphia: American Philosophical Society, 1953. 86–95. Although dated, this essay remains the best account of the construction history.
———. *William Strickland, Architect and Engineer, 1788–1854*. Philadelphia: University of Pennsylvania Press, 1950.
Hamlin, Talbot. *Greek Revival Architecture in America*. New York: Oxford University Press, 1944.
Moss, Roger W. "John Struthers." Tatman and Moss, 771.
Pierson, William H. *American Buildings and Their Architects*. Garden City, N.Y.: Anchor Doubleday, 1976.
Sutton, Robert Kent. *Americans Interpret the Parthenon*. Boulder: University of Colorado Press, 1992.
Tatman, Sandra L. "Louis C. Hickman." Tatman and Moss, 377.

Wainwright, Nicholas Biddle, ed. "The Diary of Samuel Breck, 1834–35." *PMBH* 103 (July 1979): 363–64.

Wolf, Zana C., and Charles Tonetti. Merchants' Exchange Building, National Historic Landmark Nomination Form. National Park Service, U.S. Department of the Interior, Washington, D.C., 2000.

MEMORIAL HALL

Giberti, Bruno. *Designing the Centennial: A History of the 1876 International Exhibition in Philadelphia*. Lexington: University Press of Kentucky, 2002.

Ingram, J. S. *Centennial Exposition: Described and Illustrated*. Philadelphia: Hubbard Bros., 1876.

Kise Straw & Kolodner. Existing Materials Conservation Schematic Submission for the Please Touch Museum at Memorial Hall, West Fairmount Park, Philadelphia, PA. KS&K, September 16, 2003.

Maass, John. *The Glorious Enterprise: The Centennial Exhibition of 1876 and H. J. Schwarzmann, Architect-in-Chief*. Watkins Glen, N.Y.: American Life Foundation, 1973. The best biography of Schwarzmann.

Magee's Illustrated Guide of Philadelphia and the Centennial Exhibition. Philadelphia: Magee, 1876; reprint New York: Nathan Cohen, 1975.

The Masterpieces of the Centennial International Exhibition Illustrated. Philadelphia: Gebbie & Barrie, 1876–1878.

Norton, Frank H., ed. *A Facsimile of Frank Leslie's Illustrated Historical Register of the Centennial Exposition, 1876*. 1876. Reprint New York: Paddington Press, 1974.

Obituary, Hermann J. Schwarzman [sic]. *Architecture and Building* 15, 4 (October 3, 1891): 163.

Sandhurst, Phillip T. *The Great Centennial Exhibition, Critically Described and Illustrated by Phillip T. Sandhurst and Others*. Philadelphia and Chicago: P.W. Ziegler, 1876.

NEW MARKET

The Philadelphia Historical Commission files include extensive material on the preservation and rehabilitation of the New Market, beginning in 1956, including the Head House Conservancy, restoration of the market shambles in 1962, Proposal for Redevelopment of the Market (1963) by Van Arkel & Moss & Ralph Heller, Developers. Also available at the Commission is the official volume of G. Edwin Brumbaugh's specifications for the restoration, May 21, 1962, and reports of archaeological excavations by Barbara Liggett, 1976.

Jackson, Joseph. *Encyclopedia of Philadelphia*. Harrisburg, Pa.: National Historical Association, 1932.

Liggett, Barbara. *Archaeology at New Market Exhibit Catalogue*. Philadelphia: The Athenæum of Philadelphia, 1978.

Tinkcom, Margaret B. "New Market in Second Street." *PMHB* 82 (October 1958): 379–96.

———. "Southwark, A River Community: Its Shape and Substance." *Proceedings of the American Philosophical Society* 114 (August 1970): 327–42.

Weart, William G. "Market Is Razed in Philadelphia." *New York Times*, March 16, 1956.

OLD CITY HALL

Independence National Historical Park. National Register of Historic Places Inventory. Nomination Form for Federal Properties, 1983.

Minutes of City Council, 1789–1793. City Archives.

Moss, Roger W. "David Evans (Sr.)." Tatman and Moss, 250.

Nelson, Lee H. Old City Hall, Historic Structure Report, Architectural Data Section. Philadelphia: Independence National Historical Park. National Park Service, U.S. Department of the Interior, 1970. Copy available at The Athenæum of Philadelphia.

Peterson, Charles E. "Library Hall: Home of the Library Company of Philadelphia, 1790–1880." In *Historic Philadelphia from the Founding Until the Early Nineteenth Century: Papers Dealing with Its People and Buildings*, ed. Luther P. Eisenhart. Transactions of the American Philosophical Society 43, pt. 1. Philadelphia: American Philosophical Society, 1953. 129–49.

Riley, Edward M. "Historic Philadelphia from the Founding Until the Early Nineteenth Century." In *Historic Philadelphia from the Founding Until the Early Nineteenth Century: Papers Dealing with Its People and Buildings*, ed. Luther P. Eisenhart. Transactions of the American Philosophical Society 43, pt. 1. Philadelphia: American Philosophical Society, 1953. 7–41.

PENNSYLVANIA ACADEMY OF THE FINE ARTS

Boyle, Richard J. "The Pennsylvania Academy of the Fine Arts, Its Founding and Early Years." *Magazine Antiques* (March 1982): 672–78.

Cohen, Jeffrey A. "John Dorsey." In James F. O'Gorman, Jeffrey A. Cohen, George Thomas, and G. Holmes Perkins, *Drawing Toward Building: Philadelphia Architectural Graphics, 1732–1986*. Philadelphia: University of Pennsylvania Press for the Pennsylvania Academy of the Fine Arts, 1986.

Day & Zimmermann Associates. *The Pennsylvania Academy of the Fine Arts: A Second Look, Building Restoration*. Philadelphia: Pennsylvania Academy of Fine Arts, 1977(?).

"First American Art Academy." *Lippincott's Magazine* 9, 16–17 (February–March 1872): 143–53, 309–21.

Lewis, Michael J. *Frank Furness: Architecture and the Violent Mind*. New York: Norton, 2001.

Morton, David. "Pennsylvania Academy Restoration: Furness Unfettered." *Progressive Architecture* 57, 11 (November 1976): 50-53.

Moss, Roger W. "John Dorsey." Tatman and Moss, 216–17.

Myers, Hyman. "The Three Buildings of the Pennsylvania Academy." *Magazine Antiques* (March 1982): 679–89.

O'Gorman, James F. *The Architecture of Frank Furness*. Philadelphia: Philadelphia Museum of Art, University of Pennsylvania Press, 1987.

Tatman, Sandra L. "Richard Arthington Gilpin." Tatman and Moss, 307–8.

Thomas, George E., Jeffrey A. Cohen, and Michael J. Lewis. *Frank Furness: The Complete Works*. Rev. ed. New York: Princeton Architectural Press, 1996.

PENNSYLVANIA HOSPITAL

The Board of Managers Minutes, Pennsylvania Hospital Archives, are preserved by the Hospital; microfilm copies are deposited at the American Philosophical Society Library.

Franklin, Benjamin. *Some Account of the Pennsylvania Hospital, From Its First Rise, to the Beginning of the Fifth Month, Called May, 1754*. Philadelphia: U.S. Gazette, 1817.

Morton, Thomas G., assisted by Frank Woodbury. *The History of the Pennsylvania Hospital, 1751–1895*. Philadelphia: Times Printing House, 1895.

Moss, Roger W. "David Evans and David Evans, Jr." Tatman and Moss, 250.

———. "Joseph Fox." Tatman and Moss, 278–79.

———. "Samuel Rhoads." Tatman and Moss, 656–58.

Johnson, Allen. "Thomas Bond." In *Dictionary of American Biography*, ed. Johnson. New York: Scribner's, 1929. 2: 433–34.

Packard, Francis R. *Some Account of the Pennsylvania Hospital: From Its First Rise to the Beginning of the Year 1938*. 2nd printing with a continuation to the year 1956 by Florence M. Greim. Philadelphia: Lea & Febiger, 1957.

Peterson, Charles E., with Constance M. Greiff and Maria M. Thompson. *Robert Smith: Architect, Builder, Patriot, 1722–1777*. Philadelphia: The Athenæum of Philadelphia, 2000.

Shryock, Richard H. *Medicine and Society in America, 1660–1860*. 1960. Ithaca, N.Y.: Cornell University Press, 1962.

Tomes, Nancy. *The Art of Asylum-Keeping: Thomas Story Kirkbride and the Origins of American Psychiatry*. Philadelphia: University of Pennsylvania Press, 1994.

Williams, William H. *America's First Hospital: The Pennsylvania Hospital, 1751–1841*. Wayne, Pa.: Haverford House, 1976.

PHILADELPHIA AND READING RAILROAD TERMINAL HEAD HOUSE AND SHED

An extensive collection of original Reading Railroad Terminal Head House and Shed drawings is available at The Athenæum of Philadelphia.

Harwood, Herbert H. "Philadelphia's Victorian Suburban Stations." *Railway History Monograph* 4 (July 1975): 1–47.

Highsmith, Carol M. *Reading Terminal and Market: Philadelphia's Historic Gateway and Grand Convention Center*. Washington, D.C.: Chelsea, 1994.

Meeks, Carroll L. V. *The Railroad Station: An Architectural History*. 2nd ed. New Haven, Conn.: Yale University Press, 1964.

Stover, John F. *The Life and Decline of the American Railroad*. New York: Oxford University Press, 1970.

Wilson, Joseph M. "The Philadelphia and Reading Terminal Railroad and Station in Philadelphia." *American Society of Civil Engineers Transactions* 33 (August 1895): 115–84.

PHILADELPHIA CITY HALL

McArthur's original drawings survive in the care of the Philadelphia City Archives. The Philadelphia Historical Commission has extensive files on the building, as well as a complete copy of the 3-volume *Master Plan for the Restoration, Modernization and Rehabilitation of the Philadelphia City Hall* (Vitetta Group, Kelly/Maiello, and John Milner Architects, Inc., October 27, 1995). It contains the most detailed bibliography ever assembled relating to the building. The following items were useful for the preparation of this essay.

Calder, Alexander Milne, and John McArthur, Jr. *Sculptures and Ornamental Details in Bronze & Iron of the New City Hall*. 5 vols. Philadelphia, 1883.

Faust, Frederick. *The City Hall, Philadelphia: Architecture, Sculpture & History*. Philadelphia: F. Faust, 1897.

Gillette, Howard, Jr. "Philadelphia's City Hall: Monument to a New Political Machine." *PMHB* 97 (April 1973): 233–49.

Gurney, George. "The Sculpture of City Hall." In *Sculpture of a City: Philadelphia's Treasures in Bronze and Stone*. Fairmount Park Art Association. New York: Walker, 1974.

Lewis, Michael J. "'Silent, Weird, Beautiful': Philadelphia City Hall." *Nineteenth Century* 11, 3–4 (1992): 13–21.

Maass, John. "Philadelphia City Hall." *Charette* 44 (January 1964): 23–26.

———. "Philadelphia City Hall: Monster or Masterpiece?" *AIA Journal* 43 (February 1965): 23–30.

The New City Hall, Philadelphia: Directory of Offices Occupied; or Allotted and in Process of Completion, with Diagrams of the Various Floors and Other Miscellaneous Information Appertaining to the Building. Issued by George G. Pierie, Chief of Bureau of City Property. Philadelphia: Printed for the Commissioners, 1900.

Wodehouse, Lawrence. "John McArthur, Jr. (1832–1890)." *Journal of the Society of Architectural Historians* 28 (December 1969): 271–83.

PHILADELPHIA CLUB

Bell, Malcolm, Jr. *Major Butler's Legacy: Five Generations of a Slaveholding Family*. Athens: University of Georgia Press, 1987.

Burt, Nathaniel. *The Perennial Philadelphians: The Anatomy of an American Aristocracy*. 1963. Foreword by Roger W. Moss. Philadelphia: University of Pennsylvania Press, 1999.

Rivinus, F. Markoe. "Philadelphia Club." In Jean Barth Toll and Mildred S. Gillam, *Invisible Philadelphia: Community Through Voluntary Organizatons*. Philadelphia: Atwater Kent Museum, 1995.

Rules and Regulations for the Government of the Philadelphia Club. Philadelphia: John Clark, 1834.

Thomas, George E., Michael J. Lewis, and Jeffrey A. Cohen. *Frank Furness: The Complete Works*. New York: Princeton Architectural Press, 1991.

Thurlow, Matthew A. "The Philadelphia Club at the Thomas Butler House, 1850–1870: A Furnishings Plan for the Billiard Room and Second Floor Dining Room." Paper for Brock Jobe, University of Delaware, 2004. Copy on file at The Athenæum of Philadelphia.

Wister, Owen. *The Philadelphia Club, 1834–1934, Being a Brief History of the Club for the First Hundred Years of Its Existence, Together with Its Roll of Officers and Members to 1934*. Philadelphia: Philadelphia Club, 1934.

PHILADELPHIA CONTRIBUTIONSHIP FOR THE INSURANCE OF HOUSES FROM LOSS BY FIRE

The Philadelphia Historical Commission Philadelphia Contributionship File includes copies of insurance policies and various Contributionship reports. The Athenæum of Philadelphia Collection contains the diary, letters, and account books of Thomas Ustick Walter.

Adams, George R. "National Register of Historic Places Inventory—Nomination Form." National Park Service, U.S. Department of the Interior, 1977.

Bainbridge, John. *Biography of an Idea: The Story of Mutual Fire and Casualty Insurance*. Garden City, N.Y.: Doubleday, 1952.

Moss, Roger W. "Joseph Fox." Tatman and Moss, 278–79.

———. "Samuel Rhoads." Tatman and Moss, 656–58.

———. "Thomas Ustick Walter." Tatman and Moss, 821–29.

Philadelphia Contributionship for the Insurance of Houses from Loss by Fire. *Fire-Marks: Their Origin and Use*. Philadelphia: The Contributionship, 1914.

———. *A Short History of the Oldest American Fire Insurance Company*. Philadelphia: The Contributionship, 1925.

Schweitzer, Jane K. "Collins & Autenrieth, Architects in Victorian Philadelphia." M.A. thesis, University of Delaware, 1981.

Tatman, Sandra L. "Collins & Autenrieth." Tatman and Moss, 156–59, 17–18.

Wainwright, Nicholas B. *A Philadelphia Story: The Philadelphia Contributionship for the Insurance of Houses from Loss by Fire*. Philadelphia: William Fell, 1952.

Wojtowicz, Carol. "The Story of a Building: The Philadelphia Contributionship, 212 South Fourth Street, 1836 to the Present." *Annual Report for the Year Ended December 31, 1976*. Philadelphia: The Philadelphia Contributionship, 1977.

PHILADELPHIA HIGH SCHOOL FOR CREATIVE AND PERFORMING ARTS

A portfolio of Addison Hutton's drawings for the Ridgway Library is preserved by the Library Company of Philadelphia.

Durden, Charles. "Ridgway Library: A Temple in Decay." *Philadelphia Inquirer Magazine*, June 8, 1969, cover and 8–12, 14, 16, 18, 20.

Library Company of Philadelphia. *Why the Library Company Should Move*. Philadelphia: The Library Company, 1960.

James F. O'Gorman, Jeffrey A. Cohen, George Thomas, and G. Holmes Perkins, *Drawing Toward Building: Philadelphia Architectural Graphics, 1732–1986*. Philadelphia: University of Pennsylvania Press for the Pennsylvania Academy of the Fine Arts, 1986. The Library Company building competition in 1879 is discussed by George E. Thomas on pp. 145–47.

Thomas, George E., Jeffrey A. Cohen. and Michael J. Lewis. *Frank Furness: The Complete Works*. Rev. ed. New York: Princeton Architectural Press, 1996.

Urban Partners and Kise Franks & Straw. *South Broad Street: Economic and Cultural Development Plan: Executive Summary*. Philadelphia: Central Philadelphia Development Corporation, 1992.

Wilson, Robert H. "New Home for an Old Institution." *Philadelphia Sunday Bulletin Magazine*, February 9, 1964.

Wolf, Edwin. *At the Instance of Benjamin Franklin: A Brief History of the Library Company of Philadelphia*. Philadelphia: The Library Company, 1976.

Yarnall, Elizabeth Biddle. *Addison Hutton, Quaker Architect, 1834–1916*. Philadelphia: Art Alliance Press, 1974. See introduction by George Tatum.

PHILADELPHIA MUSEUM OF ART AND THE PARKWAY

Brownlee, David B. *Building the City Beautiful: The Benjamin Franklin Parkway and the Philadelphia Museum of Art*.

Philadelphia: University of Pennsylvania Press, 1989. This is the best account of the convoluted history of the Art Museum design process.
———. *Making a Modern Classic: The Architecture of the Philadelphia Museum of Art*. Philadelphia: Philadelphia Museum of Art, 1997.
Kathrens, Michael C. *American Splendor: The Residential Architecture of Horace Trumbauer.* New York: Acanthus Press, 2002.
Patterson, Doris. "The Invisible Man Behind the Art Museum." Typescript in the Ritter and Shay Collection, The Athenæum of Philadelphia.
Patton, George E. *Philadelphia Museum of Art, Historic Landscape Report & Management Plan*. Philadelphia: George E. Patton, 1982.
Philadelphia Museum of Art. *The New Museum and Its Service to Philadelphia.* Philadelphia: Pennsylvania Museum and School of Industrial Art, 1922.
Platt, Frederick. "Horace Trumbauer: A Life in Architecture." *PMHB* 125 (October 2001): 315–49.
Roberts, George, and Mary Roberts. *Triumph on Fairmount: Fiske Kimball and the Philadelphia Museum of Art.* Philadelphia: Lippincott, 1959.
Solon, Leon V. "The Philadelphia Museum of Art, Fairmount Park, Philadelphia: A Revival of Polychrome Architecture and Sculpture." *Architectural Record* 60 (August 1926): 97–111.
———. "Principles of Polychrome in Sculpture Based on Greek Practice." *Architectural Record* 43 (June 1918): 526–33.

PHILADELPHIA SAVINGS FUND SOCIETY

A vast body of literature exists for this building. The following items are a selection of the best articles and books.

"A New Shelter for Savings: George Howe and William Lescaze, Architects"; "Planning Engineering, Equipment: The Philadelphia Savings Fund Society Building." *Architectural Forum* 57 (December 1932): 483–98, 543–50. This is the earliest and most readily accessible documentation on the design and construction.
Jordy, William, "PSFS, Its Development and Its Significance in Modern Architecture." *Journal of the Society of Architectural Historians* 21 (May 1962): 47–83. A seminal article much used by later authors.
"The PSFS Building: Philadelphia, Pennsylvania, 1929–1932." *Perspecta 25, Yale Architectural Journal* (New York: Rizzoli, 1989): 78–141.
Flanagan, Barbara. "PSFS to Loews: Spell It Out" *Metropolis* 20 (November 2000): 152–55.
Stephens, Suzanne. "Project Diary: The Landmark PSFS building by Bower Lewis Thrower Architects and Daroff Design Is Reincarnated as a Loews Hotel." *Architectural Record* 188 (October 2000): 137–47.
Stern, Robert A. M. "PSFS: Beaux-Arts Theory and Rational Expressionism." *Journal of the Society of Architectural Historians* 21 (May 1962): 84–102. A seminal article much used by later authors.
Tatman, Sandra L. "George Howe." Tatman and Moss, 394–96.
Wolf, Jean K., and Charles Evers for Tony Atkin & Associates, "PSFS Sign: A Study of the Design and Significance." Report prepared for Mellon Bank, 1994. Copy on file at The Athenæum of Philadelphia.

PHILADELPHIA ZOOLOGICAL GARDENS GATEHOUSES

Architectural drawings of some buildings on the grounds of the Zoo are deposited on long-term loan at The Athenæum of Philadelphia, including those by George W. and William D. Hewitt, Walter Mellor and Arthur I. Meigs, Paul P. Cret, Horace T. Fleisher, Stephen M. Ford, Bolton, Martin & White, and others. They may be consulted upon request.

Cadwalader, William Biddle. *Bears, Owls, Tigers, and Others: Philadelphia's Zoo, 1874–1949*. New York: Newcomen Society in North America, 1949.
Hulfish, Edwin E. *Illustrated Guide and Handbook of the Zoological Garden, Philadelphia*. Compiled according to the present arrangement of the garden by Edwin E. Hulfish. Philadelphia: Allen, Lane, & Scott, 1875.
Lewis, Michael J. *Frank Furness: Architecture and the Violent Mind*. New York: Norton, 2001.
O'Gorman, James. *The Architecture of Frank Furness.* Philadelphia: Philadelphia Museum of Art, 1973. 2nd ed. with revised check list 1987.
Philadelphia Zoological Society. *Art and Architecture at the Philadelphia Zoo.* Rev. ed. Philadelphia: Philadelphia Zoological Society, 1988.
Thomas, George E., Jeffery A. Cohen, and Michael J. Lewis. *Frank Furness, The Complete Works*. Rev. ed. New York: Princeton Architectural Press, 1996.

PHILOSOPHICAL HALL

Carter, Edward C., II. *"One Grand Pursuit": A Brief History of the American Philosophical Society's First 250 Years, 1743–1993*. Philadelphia: American Philosophical Society, 1993.
Hindle, Brooke. *The Pursuit of Science in Revolutionary America, 1735–1789*. 1956. Reprint New York: Norton, 1974.
Jones, Arthur W. "Philosophical Hall, 1785–1890." Report prepared for the American Philosophical Society, 1999. Copy on file at The Athenæum of Philadelphia.
Lingelbach, William E. "Philosophical Hall, the Home of the American Philosophical Society." In *Historic*

Philadelphia from the Founding Until the Early Nineteenth Century: Papers Dealing with Its People and Buildings, ed. Luther P. Eisenhart. Transactions of the American Philosophical Society 43, pt. 1. Philadelphia: American Philosophical Society, 1953. 43–69.

Moss, Roger W. *Philadelphia Victorian: The Building of the Athenæum*. Philadelphia: The Athenæum of Philadelphia, 1998.

Riley, M. Edward. "The Independence Hall Group." In *Historic Philadelphia from the Founding Until the Early Nineteenth Century: Papers Dealing with Its People and Buildings*, ed. Luther P. Eisenhart. Transactions of the American Philosophical Society 43, pt. 1. Philadelphia: American Philosophical Society, 1953. 7–41.

RACQUET CLUB OF PHILADELPHIA

The original Horace Trumbauer drawings for the Racquet Club are part of the Trumbauer Collection, The Athenæum of Philadelphia.

Baltzell, E. Digby. *An American Business Aristocracy*. New York: Macmillan, 1958.

Burt, Nathaniel. *The Perennial Philadelphians: The Anatomy of an American Aristocracy*. 1963. Paperback edition with a foreword by Roger W. Moss. Philadelphia: University of Pennsylvania Press, 1999.

Lejeune, Anthony. *The Gentlemen's Clubs of London*. New York: Mayflower Books, 1979.

McFadden, John J. W. F. *The Racquet Club of Philadelphia*. Devon, Pa.: Cooke Publishing Company, 1989.

Philadelphia Evening Bulletin. October 7, 1907.

Philadelphia Record. October 6, 1907.

Platt, Frederick. "Horace Trumbauer: A Life in Architecture." *PMHB* 125 (October 2001): 315–49.

Tatman, Sandra L. "Horace Trumbauer." Tatman and Moss, 799–807.

Thomas, George E., Michael J. Lewis, and Jeffrey A. Cohen. *Frank Furness: The Complete Works*. Rev. ed. New York: Princeton Architectural Press, 1996.

Toll, Jean Barth and Mildred S. Gillam, eds. *Invisible Philadelphia: Community Through Voluntary Organizations*. Philadelphia: Atwater Kent Museum, 1995. A brief history of the Racquet Club appears on 1177–81.

Webster, Richard J. "Philadelphia Racquet Club." National Register of Historic Places Inventory Nomination Form, 1979.

RODIN MUSEUM

Seventy of the Paul P. Cret drawings for the Rodin Museum are contained in the Cret Collection at The Athenæum of Philadelphia. Correspondence between Cret, Jacques Gréber, and Homer Rosenberger relating to the Benjamin Franklin Parkway and the Rodin Museum may be consulted at the Rare Books and Manuscripts Collection, University of Pennsylvania.

Brownlee, David B. *Building the City Beautiful: The Benjamin Franklin Parkway and the Philadelphia Museum of Art*. Philadelphia: Philadelphia Museum of Art, distributed by University of Pennsylvania Press, 1989.

Grossman, Elizabeth Greenwell. *The Civic Architecture of Paul Cret*. New York: Cambridge University Press, 1996.

Junius, John. "The Rodin Museum, Philadelphia." *Architecture* 64 (October 1931): 189–95.

Obituaries of Jules E. Mastbaum. *Philadelphia Inquirer*, *New York Times*, December 8, 1926.

Tancock, John L. *Rodin Museum Handbook*. Philadelphia: Philadelphia Museum of Art, 1969, 2004.

Tatman, Sandra L. "Philadelphia and the Rhetoric of Modernism: Prelude to PSFS." Ph.D. dissertation, University of Delaware, 1994.

SECOND BANK OF THE UNITED STATES

The most important documents for the history of the Second Bank of the United States are contained in the Historic Structure Report prepared by the professional staff and consultants for the Independence National Historical Park over several decades. A full set of these is available in the library and archives of INHP upon application, and photocopies of the key sections are a part of the research files for this book deposited at The Athenæum of Philadelphia.

Gilchrist, Agnes Addison. *William Strickland, Architect and Engineer, 1788–1854*. Philadelphia: University of Pennsylvania Press, 1950.

Govan, Thomas P. "Fundamental Issues of the Bank War." *PMHB* 83 (July 1958): 305–15.

Hammond, Bray. *Banks and Politics in America*. Princeton, N.J.: Princeton University Press, 1957.

———. "Jackson, Biddle, and the Bank of the United States." *Journal of Economic History* 7 (1947): 1–23.

———. "The Second Bank of the United States." In *Historic Philadelphia from the Founding Until the Early Nineteenth Century: Papers Dealing with Its People and Buildings*, ed. Luther P. Eisenhart. Transactions of the American Philosophical Society 43, pt. 1. Philadelphia: American Philosophical Society, 1953.

Holdsworth, John Thom, and Davis R. Dewey. *The First and Second Banks of the United States*. National Monetary Commission, 61st Congress, 2nd Session, Document 571, Senate Documents, vol. 26. Washington, D.C.: Government Printing Office, 1910. This is a succinct and clear presentation of the history of both banks in the context of banking history in the United States.

Huxtable, Ada Louise. "Peale Appeal: Portraits of the Nation's Founders

Go Back on View." *Wall Street Journal*, February 22, 2005.
Moss, Roger W. *Philadelphia Victorian: The Building of the Athenæum*. Philadelphia: The Athenæum of Philadelphia, 1998. Includes discussion of Strickland's designs for the Athenæum and the grand scheme to combine several like organizations in a building on Walnut Street between Fifth and Sixth Streets.
———. "William Strickland." Tatman and Moss, 767–71.
Salisbury, Stephan. "Bank with Rich Past Reframes Its Mission." *Philadelphia Inquirer*, December 1, 2004.
Stuart, James and Nicholas Revett. *The Antiquities of Athens*. 4 vols. London, 1762–1816. William Strickland's copy of the first edition is at The Athenæum of Philadelphia.
Wainwright, Nicholas Biddle, ed. "The Diary of Samuel Breck, 1827–1833." *PMHB* 103 (April 1979): 233–34.
Wilburn, Jean Alexander. *Biddle's Bank: The Crucial Years*. New York: Columbia University Press, 1967.

THIRTIETH STREET STATION

Burgess, George H., and Miles K. C. Kennedy. *Centennial History of the Pennsylvania Railroad Company, 1846–1946*. Philadelphia: Pennsylvania Railroad Company, 1949.
Chappell, Sally Anderson. *Architecture and Planning of Graham, Anderson, Probst, and White, 1912–1936: Transforming Tradition*. Chicago: University of Chicago Press, 1992.
Dunson, Edward. "West Philadelphia Station, Pennsylvania Railroad Station, Pennsylvania Station 30th Street, Penn Central Station, Penn Central 30th Street Station." National Register of Historic Places Inventory—Nomination Form. Washington, D.C.: U.S. Department of the Interior, National Park Service, 1978.
Graham, Anderson, Probst, White. *The Architectural Work of Graham, Anderson, Probst & White, Chicago, and Their Predecessors, D. H. Burnham & Company, and Graham Burnham & Company*. London: Batsford, 1933.
Howard, Neal D. "Philadelphia Improvements of the Pennsylvania Near Completion." *Railway Age* (July 28, 1934).
"Large Suburban Terminal Opened in Philadelphia." *Railway Age* (November 15, 1930).
Meeks, Carroll L. V. *The Railroad Station: An Architectural History*. 2nd ed. New Haven, Conn.: Yale University Press, 1964.
Underkofler, Allen P. *The Philadelphia Improvements*. Bryn Mawr, Pa.: Philadelphia Chapter, Pennsylvania Railroad Technical & Historical Society, May 1979, September 1980.

UNION LEAGUE OF PHILADELPHIA

Baltzell, E. Digby. *Philadelphia Gentlemen: The Making of a National Upper Class*. 1958. Philadelphia: University of Pennsylvania Press, 1979.
Heller, Karen. "A More Perfect Union League." *Philadelphia Inquirer Magazine*, June 8, 2003.
Lathrop, George Parsons. *History of the Union League of Philadelphia, from Its Origin and Foundation to the Year 1882*. Philadelphia: Lippincott, 1884.
Mendte, J. Robert. *The Union League of Philadelphia Celebrates 125 Years, 1862–1987*. Devon, Pa.: William T. Cooke, 1987.
Nolan, Thomas. "Recent Philadelphia Architecture." *Architectural Record* 29 (March 1911): 214–64.
Tatman, Sandra L. "John Fraser." Tatman and Moss, 281–82.
Torchia, Robert Wilson. *Portraits of the Presidents of the United States*. Philadelphia: The Abraham Lincoln Foundation of the Union League of Philadelphia, 2005.
Whiteman, Maxwell. *Gentlemen in Crisis: The First Century of the Union League of Philadelphia, 1682–1962*. Philadelphia: The Union League of Philadelphia, 1975.
———. *Paintings and Sculpture at the Union League of Philadelphia*. Philadelphia: The Union League of Philadelphia, 1978.
———. "Union League of Philadelphia." In Jean Barth Toll and Mildred S. Gillam, *Invisible Philadelphia: Community Through Voluntary Organizatons*. Philadelphia: Atwater Kent Museum, 1995.

UNITED STATES CUSTOM HOUSE

Two manuscript collections are important for the history of the Custom House. General Correspondence, Record Group 121, National Record Center, Washington, D.C.; and Ritter and Shay Collection, The Athenæum of Philadelphia.

Craig, Louis. *The Federal Presence: Architecture, Politics, and Symbols in United States Government Building*. Cambridge, Mass.: MIT Press, 1977.
Hood, Walter Kelly. "Words, Wars and Walls: The Art Life of George Matthews Harding." Ph.D. dissertation, Northwestern University, 1966.
United States Custom House National Register of Historic Places Registration Form. National Park Service, U.S. Department of the Interior, Washington, D.C., 2004.
Pitz, Henry C. *The Brandywine Tradition*. Boston: Houghton Mifflin, 1969.
Strong, Ann, and George E. Thomas. "A Group Enthusiasm." *The Book of the School: 100 Years, The Graduate School of Fine Arts of the University of Pennsylvania*. Philadelphia: Graduate School of Fine Arts, University of Pennsylvania, 1990.
Thomas, George E. "Howell Lewis Shay" and "Ritter and Shay." In *Philadelphia: Three Centuries of American*

Art: Bicentennial Exhibition, April 11–October 10, 1976. Philadelphia: Philadelphia Museum of Art, 1976.
Tatman, Sandra L. "Ritter and Shay," Tatman and Moss, 664–66, 713–14.

UNITED STATES NAVAL HOME

The official records of the U.S. Naval Home are in the custody of the National Archives—Mid-Atlantic Region, Philadelphia, in four record groups beginning in 1838. The Historical Commission of Philadelphia files document the decades-long debate over the conversion of the Naval Home complex into a luxury home development by Toll Brothers Inc.

Baumert, Frederick C., Suzanne M. Pentz, and David G. Cornelius. United States Naval Home: Report of the Conditional Assessment and Restoration Recommendations. Prepared for Robert D. Solvibile, Sr. by Keast & Hood, Co. Philadelphia: Keast & Hood, 2003. Copy available at The Athenæum of Philadelphia.
De Conde, Alexander. *The Quasi-War: The Politics and Diplomacy of the Undeclared War with France, 1797–1801*. New York: Scribner's, 1966.
Gilchrist, Agnes Addison. *William Strickland, Architect and Engineer, 1788–1854*. Philadelphia: University of Pennsylvania Press, 1950.
Gleaves, Albert. "The United States Naval Home, Philadelphia. *United States Naval Institute Proceedings* 57, 4 (April 1931): 473–76.
Hamlin, Talbot. *Greek Revival Architecture in America*. New York: Oxford University Press, 1944.
Maynard, W. Barksdale. *Architecture in the United States, 1800–1850*. New Haven, Conn.: Yale University Press, 2002.
Salisbury, Stephan. "New Life for Old Naval Home Site." *Philadelphia Inquirer*, July 15, 2005.
Shippen, Edward. "Some Account of the Origin of the Naval Asylum at Philadelphia." *PMHB* 7 (1883): 117–42. The basis for most later accounts of the early history of the Naval Asylum, often without credit.
Smith, J. B. *The United States Naval Home and Its Governors*. Philadelphia: Naval Home, 1964. Copy available at The Athenæum of Philadelphia.
"United States Naval Asylum." *Atkinson's Casket or Gems of Literature, Wit and Sentiment* 12 (December 1832): 552–54. Contains Strickland's description of the building which is widely copied without credit, including his misspelling of "Illyssus."
Wallace, Roberts and Todd. U.S. Naval Home Reuse Study, Philadelphia. Prepared by Wallace, Roberts and Todd, Day and Zimmermann Associates, [and] Hammer, Siler, George Associates. Philadelphia: Wallace Roberts and Todd, 1982.

VICTORY BUILDING

The Philadelphia Historical Commission maintains extensive correspondence and clipping files on the effort to preserve the Victory Building while owned by real estate speculator Samuel Rappaport.

Buley, R. Carlyle. *The American Life Convention, 1906–1952: A Study in the History of Life Insurance*. New York: Appleton-Century-Crofts, 1953.
Merkel, Phillip L. "Going National: The Life Insurance Industry's Campaign for Federal Regulation After the Civil War." *Business History Review* 65 (Autumn 1991): 528–53.
Official Office Building Directory and Architectural Handbook of Philadelphia. Philadelphia: Commercial Publishing and Directory, 1899.
Philadelphia Public Ledger. August 24, 1875.
Shahriari, Sara. "The Victory Building Reborn as Luxury Condos." *Philadelphia Inquirer*, June 17, 2005.
Webster, Richard J. "New York Mutual Life Insurance Company Building." National Register of Historic Places Inventory—Nomination Form. Washington, D.C.: U.S. Department of the Interior, 1979.
———. *Philadelphia Preserved: Catalog of the American Historic Buildings Survey*. Philadelphia: Temple University Press, 1976.

WAGNER FREE INSTITUTE OF SCIENCE OF PHILADELPHIA

The Wagner Free Institute of Science preserves the papers of William Wagner and the construction and renovation records of the building.

Announcement of the Wagner Free Institute of Science for the Collegiate Year 1858–59. Philadelphia: King & Baird, 1858.
Bruce, Robert V. *The Launching of Modern American Science, 1846–1876*. Ithaca, N.Y.: Cornell University Press, 1987.
Cremin, Lawrence A. *American Education: The National Experience, 1783–1876*. New York: Harper & Row, 1980.
First Annual Announcement of the Wagner Free Institute of Science for the Collegiate Year 1855–56. Philadelphia: Henry B. Ashmead, 1855.
Glassman, Susan, and Eugene Bolt. "Wagner Free Institute of Science." National Register of Historic Places Form [National Historic Landmark] U.S. Department of the Interior, National Park Service, Washington, D.C., 1989. Best summary of the current status of the subject.
Historic American Buildings Survey. HABS no. PA 6667. Contains drawings and black and white photographs of the building. Can be accessed via http://memory.loc.gov/pnp/habshaer/pa.

Moss, Roger W. "John McArthur, Jr." Tatman and Moss, 510–12.
Tatman, Sandra L. "Collins & Autenrieth." Tatman and Moss, 136–59, 17–18.
"Wagner, William." *Dictionary of American Biography*. New York: Scribner's, 1936. 19: 313–14.
Warren, Leonard. *Joseph Leidy: The Last Man Who Knew Everything*. New Haven, Conn.: Yale University Press, 1998.

WALNUT STREET THEATRE

Baigell, Matthew Eli. "John Haviland." Ph.D. dissertation, University of Pennsylvania, 1965. Ann Arbor, Mich.: University Microfilms, 1981.
———. "John Haviland in Philadelphia, 1818–1826." *Journal of the Society of Architectural Historians* 25 (October 1966): 197–208.
Glazer, Irvin R. *Philadelphia Theatres, A–Z: A Comprehensive, Descriptive Record of 813 Theatres Constructed Since 1724*. Westport, Conn.: Greenwood Press, 1986.
Hornblow, Arthur. *A History of the Theatre in America: From Its Beginnings to the Present Time*. 2 vols. Philadelphia: J.B. Lippincott, 1919.
Kean, Manuel. *The Walnut Street Theater: Philadelphia's New Center for the Performing Arts*. Philadelphia: Kean Archives, 1971.
Pollock, Thomas Clark. *The Philadelphia Theater in the Eighteenth Century*. Philadelphia: University of Pennsylvania Press, 1933.
Quinn, Arthur Hobson. "The Theater and the Drama." In *Historic Philadelphia from the Founding Until the Early Nineteenth Century: Papers Dealing with Its People and Buildings*, ed. Luther P. Eisenhart. Transactions of the American Philosophical Society 43, pt. 1. Philadelphia: American Philosophical Society, 1953. 313–17.
Weil, Martin Eli. "The Exterior Restoration of the Walnut Street Theatre in Philadelphia." *Monumentum* 14 (1976): 51–65.
Young, William C. *Documents of American Theater History*. Vol. 1, *Famous American Playhouses, 1716–1899*. Chicago: American Library Association, 1973.

Exterior stair detail by Frank Furness, Anne and Jerome Fisher Fine Arts Library, University of Pennsylvania.

INDEX

Page references in *italics* refer to photographs and the information in photograph captions.

↞ The justly famous "Eagle" in the grand court of the John Wanamaker Department Store is by August Gaul (1869–1921) and dates from 1904.